Y

After Suicide: A Ray of Hope

A guide for the bereaved, the professional
caregiver, and anyone whose life has been touched
by suicide, loss or grief.

Eleanora "Betsy" Ross

Turn Your Grief Experience into a Growth Process

Lynn Publications
Iowa City, Iowa

D1222791

After Suicide: A Ray of Hope

AFTER SUICIDE: A RAY OF HOPE
Copyright, 1990, Eleanora "Betsy" Ross

Lynn Publications, A Division of Ray of Hope, inc.
P.O. Box 2323, Iowa City, Iowa 52244

Photo by Joan Liffring-Zug.
Cover design by Esther Feske.

The author gratefully acknowledges the following for permission to reprint previously published material:

Harvard College Library, for a portion of "Final Harvest" by Emily Dickinson.

Houghton Mifflin Company, for a line from "Too Young to Die" by Francine Klagsbrun, © 1976 by Francine Klagsbrun.

Health Communications, Inc., for a portion from "Bradshaw On: The Family" by John Bradshaw, © 1988.

Thomas Moore Press, for a paragraph from "Living Through Personal Crisis" by Ann Kaiser Stearns, © 1984 by Ann Kaiser Stearns.

Springer Publishing Company, Inc., for a portion from "Family Therapy for Suicidal People," by Joseph Richman, © 1986.

Charles C. Thomas, Publisher, for a portion from "Survivors of Suicide" by Albert C. Cain, © 1972.

Billy Graham Evangelistic Association, from "Decision" Magazine, Jan., 1988, for a portion from the article "Don't Let Them Die" by Rich Van Pelt, © 1987 by BGEA.

Aitkin & Stone, for a portion from "The Savage God" by A. Alvarez, originally published by Weidenfeld and Nicolson, London, © 1971 by A. Alvarez.

The Westminster Press, for a portion from "After Suicide" by John H. Hewett, ©1980 the Westminster Press.

McCall's Magazine, © October 1988, by WWT Partnership.

Reader's Digest, for a portion from an editorial review of Allan Bloom's book, "The Closing of the American Mind" by Ralph Kinney Bennett, © Oct. 1989.

Simon & Schuster, Inc., for a portion from "The Closing of the American Mind" by Allan Bloom © 1987, as reviewed in Reader's Digest, 1989.

Revision and expansion of booklet *After Suicide: A Unique Grief Process*, Ray of Hope, inc., 1979, 1982, 1985.

Second edition; first edition published by Ray of Hope, inc., 1986.

Library of Congress Catalog Card Number 88-90533
ISBN 0-940179-01-6

10 9 8 7 6 5 4

Printed in the United States of America.

Dedication

To my children
Daryl, Becky and David Anderson

And

In Loving Memory of

William W. Ross—from Eleanora "Betsy" Ross.

John Douglas Stewart—from Ann Elizabeth Stewart.

Darlene Eckert Sayer—from Edwin Eckert (brother) and
Verabeth Eckert Bricker (sister).

Dr. Jerome Tanous—from Pam (wife) and children.

Danny, we miss you—from Mom, Dad, sisters and brother.

Steven J. Meeker—from Orville and Lovey Meeker (parents).

Joyce Marie Joseph—from Bob and Lori Forsyth (parents).

Donald Blaesi—from Roberta (wife) and sons.

Aaron Johnson—from Bill and Marcelyn Johnson (parents).

Robert L. Godwin III—from Catherine and Bob Godwin (parents).

Douglas Karr Gorrell—from Ann (mother) and Steven Sulnes
(brother).

Russell G. Harris—who only saw one set of footprints. Hopefully,
he's found the other set.

Paul Trider—from your friend.

Don R. Davis—from B. Jane (wife); J. Doug and Donna (children);
Linda (daughter-in-law); and Lizzie, Sara, Tim, Katie and
Willie (grandchildren).

Acknowledgments

It is my pleasure to acknowledge those who have helped me in writing this book. Far more people than I can mention have influenced this work and I am deeply grateful to them all.

So, thank you. . .

. . .to the support group members, clients, and countless others who opened their hearts to share their stories and thoughts.

. . .to Dr. Joseph Richman for his counsel and belief in my ability.

. . .to my children, Daryl, Becky and David Anderson, for their patience and love.

. . .to my parents who made my existance and destiny possible.

. . .to Hannelore Bozeman for her spiritual guidance, her faith in this ministry, and for her editing of both editions. Without her, the first edition would never have been written.

. . .to Joyce (Woodring) Strabala who shared in the vision and creation of Ray of Hope and for her Christian friendship.

. . .to Matthew Johnson for his insights, advice and editing.

. . .to Verabeth Bricker for her grand enthusiasm and inspiration.

. . .to my dear friends, Pastor Paul and Haven Hasel, Walt and Mary Blankenship, and all the Bible study group members who prayed this project through innumerable obstacles and delays.

. . .to Janet Sommerfeld, my housemate, for her pleasant sense of humor and her help with Ray of Hope files and correspondence.

. . .to my physicians, especially Dr. Stewart.

. . .to the Omaha-Council Bluffs Ray of Hope support group; especially Mike Millea, Pam Tanous, Rev. George Barger, Jim Kennedy and Roberta Blasesi.

. . .to all those who critiqued this manuscript. Especially Prof. Albert Cain, Joe Thigpen, Ruth Loewinsohn, Rev. David Vigen, Joan Liffring-Zug, John Zug, and Michelle Nagle Spencer.

. . .to Norman Sage, JoAnn Peiffer, Faye Teeple, Warren and Connie Lewis, Lfd., Prof. Kenneth Kuntz, Rabbi J. Holstein, Prof. Frederick Wenz, Dr. John Donaldson, Hope Dunn, Margaret Reaney, Jim Sangster, Bradley L. Lee, Barbra Loren, Richard Wilder, G. Gilmore, and librarians at the Coralville Public Library, Iowa City Public Library and University of Iowa Library.

And finally, to everyone for their encouragement and support.

Contents

Part I: Voices of Survivors

Part II: Growing Through Grief

A Minister's View of Suicide

Part III: About Suicide

Part IV: Appendices

Foreword

Joseph Richman, Ph. D.

I am absolutely delighted that this book by Eleanora "Betsy" Ross is available. It fills a long delayed need and it is therefore a welcome task for me to offer this testimonial.

This book should be in the hands of the family and friends of all those who have suffered a loss through suicide. It outlines not only the dilemma of the survivors—their guilt, shame, sense of stigma and turmoil of conflicting emotions; their tendency to withdraw while dwelling on the trauma—but also the procedures and attitudes needed for recovery and a return to normal life.

Through her own grief experience, Ms. Ross has earned the right to be a model to others. Her mature understanding and empathy have helped many people, perhaps more than she herself realizes, and her message should reach many others.

Wise beyond her years, the author has much to offer, both to survivors and to professionals at all levels. Her knowledge and experience has contributed significantly to my forty years of work as a clinical psychologist and psychotherapist. I have learned much from her. Her slogan, "Turn a Grief Experience into a Growth Process," can be adopted by all those concerned with helping others deal with grief. It has become a major goal in my own work.

Ms. Ross' faith in people, and her stubborn refusal to give up on those in the depth of despair are important and impressive aspects of her overall character. With sensitivity, empathy, and compassion, she addresses survivors directly and honestly, cutting through defenses and opening the floodgates of pent-up feelings and emotions. By encouraging true grief and mourning, her book helps initiate the healing process.

Her recommendations on how to work through grief to a positive, self-actualizing outcome apply not only to the survivors of suicide but to all those who are mourning over lost loves. Since loss is an inevitable part of life, we can all benefit from this book. We are all survivors.

Dr. Joseph Richman is a Professor Emeritus at the Albert Einstein College of Medicine in New York City, a senior Psychologist at the Bronx Municipal Hospital Center, a faculty member of the New York Center for Psychoanalytic Training, has a private practice and conducts workshops and seminars. He has published the book Family Therapy for Suicidal People, *as well as more than sixty articles and book chapters.*

Preface

On August 20, 1975, my husband, Bill Ross, shot and killed himself. In the moment following that gunshot, I became a member of a select group of over one million Americans—a suicide survivor-victim. Some experts estimate as many as 30,000 to 50,000 suicides occur annually and figure at least six to ten persons are directly affected by every completed act. They believe that over 3,000,000 suicide survivors presently exist. Suicidologists recognize these people have much in common. For example:

Terminology: Suicide is the only form of death which is stigmatized by terminology. We say that people commit suicide, commit crimes and are committed to institutions. We do not say they commit heart attacks or cancer. We say they died by a heart attack or cancer—why not say they died by suicide? (Some terms coming into use are: completed suicide or suicided.)

Deliberate: It is the only form of death in which the deceased die on purpose—deliberately—and we question "why?" Not just why did they die, but why did they *die on purpose?*

Investigation: Suicide is investigated as if a crime may have occurred. Family members may feel as if they are under suspicion. As a result, spontaneous grief, which must be held in check during investigation, can lead to unresolved or incomplete grief.

Focus: With suicide the primary focus is almost always on the act of suicide itself rather than on the survivors' welfare.

Silence and Confusion: Lukas and Seiden, *Silent Grief,* emphasize that only death by suicide is surrounded by a conspiracy of silence—a cover-up versus truth. We question what to tell children, sick or elderly family members, the community, and the media.

Insurance: Only when death is ruled a suicide are the survivors deprived of insurance benefits. Even when payment is made, the family often undergoes rigorous questioning beforehand. Regardless of how practical or necessary the insurance company's reasons might be, many survivors feel they are being victimized economically and financially because of the suicide.

Judgment: Suicide is the only mode of death in which we form opinions concerning the right or wrong of it, and make moral judgments about both the deceased and the survivors, as indeed, do the survivors themselves. Because of that, shame and embar-

2

rassment about the method of death often overshadow the survivors' love and pride for the suicide victim.

Self-blame: It is a form of death where people judge their own actions, attitudes and responsibility in relation to the cause of death. That's different than regretting something one did or didn't do. Survivors replay the events preceding the suicide over and over in their mind's eye and fantasize how it might have been different "if only I'd done this or that."

Involvement: Survivors may carry lasting scars because they are involved in a more personal and violent way than are survivors of non-suicide deaths. For instance, most deaths in America today occur in hospitals or nursing homes. We are, for the most part, relatively uninvolved in those deaths. But the majority of suicides occur in the home between 3 P.M. and midnight. These are violent deaths, and survivors are involved from the moment they witness the act or find the body. And guess who those witnesses are!

The American Medical Association reports that almost half of all of suicides are witnessed, either visibly or audibly, by the spouse. The next largest category of witnesses is children. When we include percentages of parents and siblings as witnesses, we have a nearly 65% of immediate family members involved with the death in an extremely traumatic manner.

Memories: Some survivors are haunted by the memory of finding the body or witnessing the death. The shock and violence associated with self-inflicted death is quite different than that of natural death. They ponder the mysterious aspects of suicide. Unanswered questions may complicate or delay grief resolution. Rather than healing in time, this grief often feeds on itself through shame, guilt, humiliation, and anger.

Multiple Losses: Survivors must deal with multiple losses and issues. They must deal with the tragedy of death and the trauma of suicide which are two separate, yet related, issues. Survivors grieve not only over the loss of someone by death but over all the losses generated by stigma and shame; not only the loss of position in the community (which changes with any death of a family member) but of reputation and social good-will; not only the loss of friends, but the loss of face and of self-confidence when they know or suspect that they are the object of gossip, curiosity and speculation.

Embarrassment: The lengthy searching for an answer to "why" is also an effort to save face for the victim and survivors with a

3

justifiable explanation for the act. Survivors feel betrayed, embarrassed and psychologically exposed. They struggle to restore the family's reputation, to reorganize their place in society, and to rebuild their individual sense of self-worth. That's a lot of work.

Self-worth: It's not unusual for death, an accident, or any kind of loss to invoke unresolved or delayed grief regarding earlier losses. But when death is by suicide, the resulting shock and searching process can trigger a different kind of unresolved grieving—the kind related to some past trauma which affected our sense of self-worth, self-image, self-confidence or well-being—the kind of loss we don't consciously take the time to grieve about, such as childhood experiences which have produced feelings of confusion, shame, isolation and rejection. The pain of these experiences may be repressed and unresolved simply because of the helplessness and vulnerability of being a child.

Relationships: Left unresolved, the psychological aftermath of a death by suicide may continue to undermine the lives of survivors for months or even years, resulting in family dissension and/or alienation. The blow to one's self-image and the length of time involved in working through this grief often causes survivors to feel that relationships with others have been permanently affected.

Legacy: Suicidologists agree that many of today's survivors will become tomorrow's victims. Survivors inherit a legacy of suicide which includes everything from social stigma to self-rejection. Only death by suicide "causes those left behind to turn so fiercely against others and themselves."[1] Studies show that survivors are subject to early death from other causes. They are more prone to accidents, multiple operations, alcoholism, illness, emotional disturbances, physical problems, malnutrition, and a variety of conditions related to extended depression and unresolved grief. In addition, survivors are at an increased risk to suicide themselves, especially during the first year of bereavement.[2]

Support: There seem to be no "right things" to say to comfort survivors of suicide in their greatest pain. The usual comments, such as, "Well, you did your best for him/her," or, "He/she lived a good life," seem inappropriate. Often, it is easier to say nothing or stay away from the bereaved altogether. So what can we do to help?

The best way to help survivors is with the development of *postvention* programs. Postvention, a term coined by Edwin Shneidman, refers to all aspects of research and education which

4

provide understanding and care for these survivors.

Suicide prevention refers to education about the indicators of suicide. Printed material, films and workshops are examples.

Suicide intervention is action which prevents a suicide from being completed, such as is the function of crisis lines and emergency services. (Counseling and family therapy, however, clearly can be any part of all three aspects.)

Suicide postvention programs teach survivors about the grief process, and how to help themselves, the family, and others. In support groups, for example, the bereaved may express themselves in an empathetic, non-threatening atmosphere. Through sharing with others, such persons can examine family behavior patterns that might contribute to self-destructive behavior. They can discover family strengths which lead to a new level of wholeness. Postvention care may actually serve to prevent suicide, not just during or after the crisis, but a month, a year, or a generation later.

An extra value of the self-help survivors movement is the message it might have for those who are not yet survivors. Survivors possess knowledge and wisdom to help others at risk, or those who have relatives or someone who shows signs of suicide.

This book is not meant to be a scholarly work. There are, however, ideas and observations which could be used for in-depth studies of survivor grief, such as:

(1) Some forms of attention and curiosity concerning suicide as a natural (or unnatural) substitute for personal involvement with death and dying.

(2) Death and suicide as separate crises; the event of death followed by a normal grieving process, verses the act of suicide complicated by post-traumatic stress syndrome.

(3) The value of the searching process in rebuilding or restoring the self-image or reputation of both victim and survivors.

(4) The problems with rejection and abandonment associated with after suicide grief as a trigger for tapping into unresolved grief from childhood abuse or other early life trauma as a significant factor in relation to the degree and duration of survivor grief.

Although this book cannot present perfect solutions, it offers many ideas and insights which have been helpful to me personally and as a grief counselor for suicide survivors. People have asked me to write about what I think. That's what I have done, no claim to anything more. I am not a psychiatrist or psychologist. But I am a survivor who has worked closely with survivors for fifteen years, and this book presents my observations. Other suggestions and recommendations come from the experience of professionals who are working with suicide survivors, and from survivors themselves who have attended Ray of Hope support groups.

The book is organized so the reader can turn to the subject of interest rather than to start at the beginning and read through. The book is written for you, the survivor, and also for those of you who want to help. Although our stories are different, our loss is similar, and we share the same pain. Whatever the differences, your life and mine are forever changed; we share the same legacy.

Bill's suicide turned my life completely around. When I finally stopped spinning, I discovered his death was not meaningless, and my grief was not a waste of time. Eventually, the experience provided me with the key to get in touch with myself, with God, and with others in a new and exciting way.

If this book leans to the Christian perspective of healing, it's because that's how I am. My message is a ministry. This ministry was a gift—a healing for myself and others—so I give tribute and recognition to the giver. I realize, however, that not all people share this view—nor is this ministry only for those who share my view. Take what you can from the message and blend it with your beliefs and experience so you can grow and heal as is best for you.

This book is my way of taking you by the hand and saying, "Look, what has happened to you is fact, not fantasy. You hurt. Your spirit hurts. You're in such pain that the ends of your hair hurt. And you want to quit hurting." Before that can happen, you need to know what you can expect to experience or feel, and what you can do about it. This book offers you help in getting through this dark, murky period in your life without falling in. The journey, though tiring and tormenting at times, can be interesting. If you want to, you can come through this a better or different person, rather than just another suicide survivor-victim.

This journey is not a preoccupation with death. It is a celebration of life.[3] You can turn your grief experience into a growth process. That is the reason for this book.

Part I
Voices of Survivors

Note: Unless a story is signed with the contributor's full name, all names and facts that could lead to the identification of the survivors have been changed in order to protect their privacy.

Hope is a thing with feathers
That perches in the soul
And sings the tune without the words
And never stops at all.

Emily Dickinson

A Ray of Hope
(my story)

Note: As I stated in the preface, suicide causes survivors to question death and themselves in a unique way. First, we examine the event, then circumstances leading up to the event. Next, we examine the personality of the deceased; then ponder our relationship with that person which leads to an examination of our own character and its development until a sort of Freudian-self-and-family psychological analysis has taken place. The search goes beyond just looking for an answer to "why suicide?" My story illustrates that process in greater detail than the other personal stories. It was my need and willingness for self and family analysis that brought about a personal healing which was, for me, much more than just solace from grief and an answer to the "why?"

"Just keep telling me you love me," my husband said on the phone. "I want that to be the last thing I hear." As I did, he quietly hung up the receiver, walked out of the phone booth, took a rifle from the trunk of his car, placed it behind his right ear and blew off the back of his head. Bill's months of despair and depression had ended; my years of grief and agony were just beginning.

Bill's alcoholism had caused many problems during his life and our stormy four-year marriage. It brought out such ugly things in this otherwise kind and interesting person. I had lived with both love and terror during those years and that was the reason for our present separation of nearly a year. Before meeting Bill, I'd had no experience with alcoholism and did not know what to expect or how to handle it. I soon learned. At first I made all the usual mistakes of trying to control things or to reason with him.

Charming, witty and affectionate while sober, Bill went through a complete personality change when drinking. Every day, I'd wonder, "What's his mood today? What will he do? Should I hide, or what?" To Bill, booze meant fighting, and if I were nearby, I became the target. I was 4'11" tall and he was 5'11". I weighed 95 pounds and he weighed 195. Only once did I try to hit him back and I gave him a black eye. Afterwards Bill thought it was funny. He would point to his eye and then hold my hand up for people to see. "Look at that little fist," he'd say. "Sharp as a pool cue. Almost put my eye out." But, most of the time the odds were not in my favor. I had been thrown through a door and down some steps.

I learned to anticipate his drinking bouts and lived "perpetually packed and ready to flee." That's true. I kept a small suitcase near the door with everything I might need. I even left it partially unzipped in case I needed to slip something into it at the last minute. I had extra sets of car keys within reach in every room and outside where I could find them in an instant and get away before being hurt. I'd return in the morning when I knew he'd be sober.

One time I miscalculated. Bill met me at the door, still drunk and swinging. A slap caught me off guard, knocking me down. Terrified, I lay as still as I could with my arms over my head. He watched me a minute, then nudged me with his foot until I rolled onto the grass. "And don't clutter up the sidewalk," he said before going back inside. After a while I got up and followed him inside. He had passed out. Later, he was contrite and apologetic, explaining to me that he drank too much and got upset because he loved me so much. "I'm so afraid I'm going to lose you and that if you don't love me back I'll have to beat you until you do," he said, thinking that was a pretty good joke. It wasn't.

I loved Bill and wanted this marriage to work but was also afraid of him and didn't know what to do about it. Then one day, I saw a sign on the library door that said, "If someone you love drinks too much, call AL-ANON ----." I did, and an hour later met with a woman who listened to my story, told me about alcoholism and gave me some pamphlets. For the first time I learned our situation was not unique and that I had alternatives other than to just run away and hide a night at a time. Incredible as it seems, I had not known that. I had truly believed to leave our marriage would mark me as a coward or failure. After all, I already had one divorce. I believed I needed to prove I could make a marriage work—that it was all up to me—and all my fault if it didn't.

I began to attend Al-Anon meetings and learned about women who stay with men who abuse them. I learned Bill's alcohol addiction was controlling both of us—everything we both said and did. Booze—not Bill—was the enemy. I was told I'd have to make a decision about alcohol—live with it or leave it. I listened at those meetings, I learned, but a part of me didn't quite accept the extremes of "love it or leave it" as the only possible solutions.

So, I tried a different tactic. I told Bill I'd seen a divorce lawyer and would go through with it if he didn't stop drinking. He replied, "If that's all that is wrong, I just won't drink when we were together.

10

I'll wait and drink only when you are back in Iowa."

I thought this just might work because Bill and I lived a unique life-style. Most of the time, he travelled from one construction job to another in a large motor-home. I alternated between spending weekends with him at his job sites and weekdays in Iowa, where my ten-year-old son, David, attended school. I kept the trailer, which was David's and my home before I married Bill, parked on my folks' farm. Usually David stayed with friends or my parents when I was with Bill. This plan would keep David away from Bill. If Bill kept his promise I'd be safe and I'd save the marriage. I thought I was pretty clever.

To show his good intentions, Bill volunteered—with a great show of "Look-what-I'm-doing-for-the-little-woman" to attend an AA meeting. Throughout the meeting I pretended to be too entranced by the speakers to notice Bill's meaningful side-long glances. We were no sooner out the door he snorted, "Did you see those people? They're a bunch of drunks! And they even admit it! We don't need AA. We're better than that!" "We?" I mouthed.

To prove his good intentions and ability to control his drinking Bill rented a beautiful furnished home near his job so we (David included) could spend the summer together. Then he took us both on a two-week vacation to Yellowstone Park, the Rockies, and a working dude ranch owned by one of his old rodeo buddies. It was a fabulous place. The ranch bunk house (remodeled for visitors) was situated so that we slept at night with our feet in Colorado and our heads in Wyoming—a rather unique distinction, I was assured.

On our return from the West, Bill bought me a new car and outfitted David with a custom-made snappy little red go-cart, complete with driver's suit and helmet to match. I figured we had these things coming to us.

However, this is something women should ask themselves about if they consistently object to attending Al-Anon or leaving abusive alcoholic men. Gifts and material possessions can be a pretty good payoff, as can attention and sympathy from being the "long-suffering-black-and-blue martyr." Both actions are an attempt to control as was Bill's extravagance and my own conditional ultimatum to him.

Some women try to control the guy's drinking by meeting him at the bar right after work, and either drinking with him or exchanging information with the other wives. Information such as, how to divert his attention so she can rescue some of the just cashed paycheck, and later convince him that he lost it, spent it, or the bartender swiped it.

There's a wealth of information to be shared on how to shame an alcoholic and gain favors, or get revenge. It's not intentional deceit on the wife or family's part—it's pure "gut survival." That's why alcoholism is called a family disease. It makes people feel, think and act in ways they wouldn't if they felt safe and secure. It alters one's mental, emotional and physical health.

Within days of settling into the rented house in Michigan, Bill began to complain of nervousness and headaches. "If I drink just a little bit I'll feel better," he said. "After all, I stayed stone sober for over three weeks and that ought to prove to you that I can control it. No bar hopping—just a little wine at home in the evenings."

The following Friday, when Bill was only three minutes late for supper, I knew the dry spell was over. Before Bill arrived home two hours later, David and I had grabbed food, Ace (his black kitten), ran for David's bedroom and shoved the dresser in front of the closed door. For two days Bill shouted and raged, pounded on the door, threatened to kill us both, broke dishes, harassed the neighbors and occasionally passed out. During those lulls David and I replenished supplies. Although Bill was a violent drunk, he was not a sloppy one. He always walked straight—straight into whatever was in front of him. He would stop, blink, re-aim himself, and walk straight again—into another wall, person or object. The house looked as if he'd walked straight into everything.

I knew I could never expose David to this again and made the decision to leave. I couldn't let Bill know our plans or he would have forcibly stopped us and I was afraid he might harm one or both of us (even though he was quite proud of David while sober).

We stayed in David's room until Bill left for work Monday morning. That evening, Bill was sober—but defensive rather than apologetic. "Can't a man even make a little mistake?" he'd ask, trying to play on my guilt. I didn't answer him.

"Sometimes you make me so mad that if I was a snake I'd bite myself," he said, trying to joke. I carefully smiled, agreed, but did not offer a response. David just stayed out of sight. "If you and your kid don't lighten up, I'll have to get drunk again," he warned.

Bill must have suspected our plans to leave, however. As I later learned, I had withdrawn our savings from a branch bank just

12

minutes before he tried to close the account at the main bank.

Quietly and slowly, over the next two days, we packed things in my car and made other preparations. I went to a doctor and asked for a prescription of antibuse (pretending it was for myself). I ground it up and put on Bill's sandwiches the day we left, hoping he'd feel too sick to follow us.

After leaving the bank I rented a small U-Haul trailer to move my electric organ and David's go-cart. But when I opened the trailer door back at the house the smell of horse poured out at us. That meant another flying trip to the dealer and home again where my landlord and his wife gladly helped us pack up and get on our way. Just outside of town David's kitten got frightened and carsick so I went back to find a vet and some medication. It was getting late and I just hoped Bill had eaten his sandwiches.

On the second trip out of town the trailer tire went flat and I had to go back to get it fixed. The third time I left town a thick fog rolled in off the lake and I missed a turnoff and drove east instead of west. I ended up in downtown Toledo near midnight, but refused to stop. I turned around and continued the long trip back to Iowa despite another low tire, a cranky kid, a recovered frisky kitten, an unprotected turtle, and another wrong turn which took us through downtown Chicago at 7:30 a.m.

When we pulled up to my trailer four hours later, Bill was snoozing on the front steps, hat over his face. (I had never given him a key to my trailer, either before or after we were married.) "Howdy." He waved at us. "What took you so long?" David clutched the dash board, I clung to the steering wheel and we just looked at each other.

Bill refused to leave my trailer and return to his job, claiming, "I'm not drunk now." He wasn't, but I called the sheriff anyway. The sheriff arrived a few minutes later and tried to arrest Bill. (Trespassing was all I could think of.) Bill shoved his hands in his pockets, planted his feet, looked up at the officer and said, "I ain't goin." They argued for a while and finally the officer said, "Well, I can't beat him up and I won't shoot him, but if he promises to leave quietly after you've talked a few minutes, I'll wait. Is that okay?"

What could I do but agree. I tried to persuade Bill our marriage was over—that I refused to live with alcohol as a part of my life. Finally he left, convinced I would change my mind.

I didn't, despite the following weeks filled with phone calls from Bill, crying, pleading, begging and bargaining. Soon afterwards he began to threaten to harm my family and me. When that didn't work, he began threatening to kill himself.

On Christmas Eve, Bill called me from his company's office on the East Coast and begged to come home for Christmas. I missed him terribly, but had to say no because I could tell he was already drinking. "You're dead," he said, and hung up.

The following morning I received a phone call from a young woman who asked, "Are you married to Bill Ross?" I said yes and she said, "Well, I think you ought to know he nearly killed my mother last night." While in a drunken stupor Bill had taken a woman to a motel and beaten her senseless. I later learned she was tiny, red-haired and wore glasses. It could have been me if I had let him come home.

An initial charge of attempted murder was changed to aggravated battery. Released on bail, Bill signed into a substance abuse recovery program. A few days later, he called me from there. "I understand how you feel about me," he said, "and I don't blame you if you hang up on me. But, something important has happened and no one will understand better than you. Please listen." I hung up.

Every few days, he'd call. Sometimes I hung up. Sometimes I screamed accusations till I lost my voice. He simply listened and would say, "I know how much you need to say those things. You're right, and I don't blame you. I say them to myself too."

At last, after three months of this, I listened. Bill told me that while he was sitting in jail a priest came to see a young man who had wrecked his car (while drinking) and whose wife had been killed. The young man sobbed and asked the priest for help who replied that in spite of his actions, God still loved him and wanted to heal his pain if he repented and asked for forgiveness.

"That priest could have been talking to me," Bill said. "In a flash I realized what I'd done to _____, to you, to so many others, and to myself. I am so ashamed. I want that healing and forgiveness too. I don't even remember hurting_____. I have only a vague memory of trying to fight off demons or monsters that I thought were attacking me. I always thought my drinking was either a big joke or other people's problem. Now, it's hard to believe I've hurt someone this bad. I want to try to do something to make up for all that. At least, I can tell people what alcohol has cost me. If you ever let me come home again, I want it to be right."

I agreed to talk with Bill on the phone during the months ahead while he waited for his hearing. He had to look for another employer since the assault had cost him his job with a prominent construction company, and he faced a lawsuit by the injured party.

During those eight months, Bill was haunted by guilt, even though he tried to make amends with the people he had wronged over the years. The prospect of prison frightened him. "I'll go crazy if I'm locked up. I'd rather die by my own hand than lose my mind in prison," he'd tell me.

Often, I'd answer the phone in the early morning hours to hear Bill crying in desperation and fear. "I had to call someone. The desire to kill myself is so strong, it's as if something is pushing me, and I'm afraid I can't stop it." Later, he would say, "It seems as if suicide is the only solution. I've hurt myself, you, and so many other people, and I can't seem to fix things. I love life. I want to live but I deserve to die. I'm ashamed, and I don't know what else to do but kill myself. I don't know if I can hold on until the hearing. I've never been afraid of anything before in my life."

Reluctantly I agreed to meet Bill on weekends and see him through this troubled time. We sought advice from a number of professionals. Most ministers encouraged Bill to have faith but he didn't seem to understand how to do that. One clergyman flatly stated, "You'll go to hell, you know," and refused to talk with us any longer. As we sat in the church parking lot, Bill asked, "Does God doom a man to hell just because he has problems have driven him to a despair he can't handle? I just can't believe He does. I think I know God and I can't believe He's that unjust. Won't God understand if I kill myself it's not because I want to die, but because I don't know what else to do?" I had no answer to that.

"We've only started to look for help," I said evasively. "We have an appointment with a psychiatrist this afternoon. Let's hear what he says." That psychiatrist said to me, "Ignore him. He won't kill himself. He's just trying to keep you involved. Don't let him dwell on his problems. Change the subject." He actually advised me to call Bill's bluff and dare him to carry out his threat. I knew better than that and refused to try it.

I tried to help, listen, and reason with Bill as much as I could but at times I felt as hopeless and helpless as he did. Finally, I took the advice of the psychiatrist. I turned to Bill and said, "I'm sick of this. I don't want to hear it anymore."

Startled, Bill gazed at me. I had the sinking feeling I had said

15

something wrong and started to retract my statement but he stopped me. "Forget it, honey," he said. "I understand. I don't blame you." He sat quietly for a moment, then added, "There's no point in seeing anyone else. They just don't believe me."

"Maybe they don't know how to help you," I answered, although silently I had to agree with him. It puzzled me that so many knowledgeable people rejected Bill's pleas for help. On the one hand, I sensed Bill's problem was a threat to them, but I could not understand why. I just knew something was dreadfully wrong, other than Bill's threats of suicide. I knew part of the problem was Bill's own attitude. He was difficult to counsel because he wanted instant answers and instant relief.

No one seemed to take Bill's threats seriously. Most people did try to point out alternatives or to encourage him to be patient, but it wasn't enough somehow. Now I realize the professionals we saw (picked at random for the most part) were not right for Bill's problem. We needed to see someone who was knowledgeable about alcoholism *and* suicide *and* depression. He also needed a counselor who would have listened more and then encouraged a definite course of action, working along with him. The community in which we lived at that time in 1975 did not have a resource or referral service.

On the other hand, I could understand why no one took him seriously. Bill's appearance and reputation contradicted his present depression. He was an aggressive, colorful character who radiated a zestful, adventuresome spirit. A captivating story teller with a folksy sense of humor, he often referred to himself as a wild-Irish-Indian cowboy because of his heritage and rodeo background.

In addition, Bill had previously threatened or attempted suicide when he had been drinking. Some of those attempts —or gestures—had been quite melodramatic.

One time he became angry because I refused to join him at a job site near Canada. I knew he'd been drinking and wouldn't go near him, although he was sure it was because I had a new boyfriend. As soon as he was drunk enough, he rented a small plane, flew it out over the lake on half a tank of gas, and dunked the plane in the water when the tank was empty (or so he said). Of course, this happened within sight of a tanker so he was rescued. And, of course, he just happened to be wearing his new custom-made suit and best boots. He was hospitalized with two broken ribs, but insisted on getting out of bed to call me and tell me what he'd done.

"I nearly died," he yelled over the phone. "And if I had, you'd be a rich woman with plenty of money to have any man you want!"

I listened and then said, "You woke me at 5:00 a.m. to tell me that? I don't need your insurance money to find another man. I already have what I need for that," and hung up. They tell me he screamed, "Bitch!" at the phone, then hung up, turned to the group of silent wide-eyed nurses, shrugged, grinned and said, "Oh hell, guess I'll get some breakfast at a fancy restaurant before I go back to work. Who wants to come with me?"

Another time, during a separation, he rented a small plane and flew to a friend's ranch in Texas. Apparently, his plan was to saddle up a horse, ride into the desert at night and sit under a mesquite tree until he could "will himself to die as the old unwanted Indian chiefs used to do." Before riding away from the ranch he called to tell me about his plan. I wasn't worried. I knew he would be back in time for breakfast. (He was.) "O.K.," I said sleepily, "have a good time," and snored into the phone. "You'll see," he shrieked, "you'll be sorry," and banged down the receiver. Before he hung up I could hear masculine snickering and joking in the background. Like many others, I believed Bill was "all talk."

During the time of his treatment, my emotions were mixed. Our marriage had been tender and violent, safe and frightening, happy and sad. I had been in a perpetual state of shock myself as I had tried to adjust to continual separations and reconciliations.

Before treatment, his suicidal threats and gestures had been either a nuisance or entertaining, and obviously manipulative. But now, there was a new tone; a mixture of sadness and desperation. I wanted to be free of all this stress and anxiety of never knowing what would happen next. I felt as if I were suffering from battle fatigue. To my horror, I sometimes found myself imagining how much better things would be if he would carry out his threat.

Despite his voice of doom and discouragement, and my concerns, I still had hope for his improvement and, possibly, our future together. During those months of rehabilitation, he looked for work continuously by calling the many construction companies he had worked for in the past. The typical answer was, "Sorry, Bill, we have nothing open now but we'll call you as soon as we do." Bill was sure the refusals were personal. "They've heard about what I've done and where I live now," he'd say, "and they don't want me."

Whenever someone would remind him that construction activity was at an all-time low, Bill always responded, "I can't wait. I need work now. I'm too old to learn anything else."

While looking for work, he became increasingly active in AA. Gradually, I saw him accept the fact he was an alcoholic and I began to see a new maturity and wisdom in him. I believed he had reached the turning point many alcoholics apparently have to go through before recovery begins.

I'd heard and believed the myth that people who talk about suicide don't do it. I talked myself into believing I had talked him out of it. "After his court hearing," I told myself, "things will be better." I also believed the aura of sadness I glimpsed from time to time would soon vanish. It did—but only with his death.

Only one hour after last talking with Bill, on that Wednesday I received another phone call informing me he was dead. I stared into the space of my living room, the receiver dangling from my hand. My mind raced with memories and questions, trying to settle somewhere. "Bill killed himself," I screamed silently. "He really did it." With a horrible sinking feeling, I realized I had known Bill would kill himself but I hadn't believed he would. And I had not been with him to stop him.

Immobilized, I sat by the phone and remembered our last weekend together, just three days earlier. We were sitting in the restaurant where we always met when he told me the hearing date had been set for the following Wednesday. Bill had dreaded this moment more than anything and had talked about it constantly. On those weekends when we were together, I often awoke at night to find him staring out the window. I always asked, "What's wrong?" He always answered, "You know." I always said, "Tell me again." And he would.

But that Saturday morning something about him had been different. He appeared relaxed, no longer worried and anxious. When I questioned him about this new attitude, he said, "Let's not talk about it. I've been Gloomy Gus long enough. Let's just enjoy the weekend." He grinned at me and told the waitress, "She doesn't really want the coffee. She just likes to hold the cup." I smiled at his kidding and thought to myself, "Now this is the old Bill."

What a pleasant change to see him smiling quietly at me while I bubbled with optimism for the future. He decided to live with his married son while we remained separated for the time being. We agreed it would take time to put the marriage back together. "I don't like it," he said. "But I'll do it for you."

Later that evening, it was Bill who reassured me by saying, "No matter what the judge says or what happens, you'll be fine. You're smart, you're pretty, and you're a good person." He was quiet for a moment, then chuckled. "I feel like I've been turned upside down, spun around and not pointed in any direction. I guess that will change in a few days." I had snuggled closer, pleased that he was joking and happy at last.

"Here, I want you to have this—keep it safe for me," said Bill the following morning. I looked up from my packing to see him holding out his most prized possession, a silver buckle that said, "Champion Bulldogger of the Year. Kalispell, Montana, 1941."

"Oh, no, you keep that." I pushed his hand away. "Anyway, if you are sentenced I'll get it when I'm here for the hearing."

"No, honey—no," he protested. "I don't want you here. If I see you in the courtroom and I'm sentenced to prison, I won't be able to stand it. I'll fall apart and I don't want to do that in public. Anyway, I want to know you're safe at home with your family and people who care for you when you get the news, whatever it is."

I argued with him but he remained firm and I finally gave in. I took the buckle. "I'll see you as soon afterward as possible," I assured him. I was satisfied at last that he was going to face the hearing and its outcome.

With the phone still in my hand, I thought about Bill's call just an hour earlier. He had been about to leave for his hearing and asked me, "If I promise not to kill myself, and if I don't go to prison, will you agree to let me come home right away?" I sensed a trap in his question and I wasn't ready to say yes. After the physical and verbal abuse that had periodically marked Bill's alcoholism, I had to be sure he'd stay sober once he was on his own again. I couldn't take any chances. I still loved him, still wanted our marriage to work, but I needed more time. Although he knew how I felt, I explained it to him again. "We've already discussed this," I said.

"Yes, I know—I understand," Bill replied, and paused. "Well," he said slowly, "just keep telling me you love me. . ."

Still sitting by the phone, I thought to myself, "If only I'd been there with him, he would still be alive. If only I had realized he had actually been serious." Stunned and confused, I questioned my self-worth, my capacity to love, and even my motives for not wanting Bill to come home right away. I sensed a growing need to understand the "why" of his death, along with a dreadful fear I would find no answer. Bill had robbed us of any chance to put our lives back together. He had the last word—the upsmanship on power and control. I was as helpless as he had been, but with no way to reply or retaliate.

Suddenly, my brain did this fast shuffle and everything fell into place: his refusal to talk about the future, his unusual calm, not wanting me with him today, giving me the buckle—all were clues of his intentions. He knew he would do it! Damn him! *He knew!* I felt as if someone had poured a pan full of hot hatred over me. How dare he do this to me! Then, shocked at my own reaction, I asked aloud, "But how can I hate him when he hurt so much?"

At that moment I heard someone reply, "Well, it's for the best. I always knew there was something wrong with him." Startled, I looked around the room. When had all these relatives come in? I must have called someone. Vaguely, I realized hours had passed and I was still sitting there. How long had people been there, visiting while I sat isolated with my whirling thoughts? I didn't remember calling anyone but I obviously had.

I stared at my aunt, my mind echoing her words. For the best? My God, I thought, *Bill is dead!* The reality of it hit me and I fled to my bedroom and locked the door. My mother followed me, knocking on my door, wanting in. "Please wait," I pleaded. "Give me some time alone. I'll be out soon."

Like Jesus, who withdrew into solitude away from the crowd, I needed, at the time, to be alone with God. I sank to my knees, pounded the floor with clenched fists and cried, "Please God, make a miracle! Make him back alive!" Then, whispering the scream so no one would hear, "Bill, you S.O.B., why couldn't you wait?" and "Oh, Bill, I am so sorry," and "Oh, God, help me."

From the living room I could hear my mother complaining. "She won't let me in there with her. How can she be so mean? We come to be with her and she runs to her room. We might as well go home and leave her alone."

I pulled myself to my feet, choked back the sobs and walked into my living room. I realized I'd made a mistake for wanting a few minutes alone to cry and pray—for not letting her with me when I broke down. I knew she had a way of making others seem so much worse or different than they really are, but I was just too distraught to have to deal with it then. With all my being I wanted someone to say, "We understand and we care. You grieve however you need to. We'll all be here for you." But no one did and I didn't ask. I stood as tall as I could and said, "Thank you for coming. I'll be all right." And, oh, how I did try to be.

One week later, I began my second year of undergraduate study at the University of Iowa. I drove over seventy miles a day round trip to classes, maintained a 3.6 grade point average, paid my own way with scholarships and loans, and worked part-time to make enough for trailer payments. David, in his early teens, was busy with a job after school and on weekends. I spent hours shooting and developing a series of photographs entitled, "My Dad's Hands", (which won several local awards) and joined a volunteer Christian witness mission group. This hectic schedule was a curse because it kept me too busy to grieve; a blessing because it kept me too busy to die.

But no matter where I was or what I did, Bill was always on my mind. Nothing made sense. I understood why he had killed himself, and I did not understand. I felt responsible but I knew I was not. I could believe he was dead; I could not believe he had killed himself. I wanted to be alone; yet needed to be with people. I wondered what others were thinking. Often confused, forgetful, and unable to concentrate, I feared for my sanity. I worried because I wanted to sleep so much.

I spent endless hours reliving those last days together and his last phone call. I replayed conversations and events, going over and over what actually happened, then creating different circumstances in my mind's eye—circumstances where Bill did not die. Sometimes the fantasies were so strong I could almost believe I had willed them to be true. Then, I'd go through shock all over again after realizing it was only a fantasy. I think I would have gone crazy if it hadn't been for David and Daryl.

Both boys helped as much as they could. David knew how much I hurt and was so gentle with me. One Sunday morning, I awoke sobbing and couldn't stop. For nearly an hour, I heard Dave clattering around in the kitchen. Suddenly, he appeared in my room with a tray: brittle bacon, burnt toast, weak coffee, pretty-good scrambled eggs, and a plastic flower in a juice glass. It was the loveliest breakfast I ever had. I gobbled it all.

Daryl, in his mid-twenties, spent hours drinking coffee and

listening to me talk. Patient and sensitive, he would often call and say, "I just had a feeling you were not O.K. and needed to talk." He was always right. But all this was too much burden for my sons and I was thankful that my daughter, Becky, had family, friends, and a good job in Florida.

David had suffered from Bill's drinking as well as from the earlier divorce between his father and myself. I worried about him and felt guilty because I was not doing my best as a mother. Sometimes, I lost my temper for reasons he couldn't understand and I couldn't have explained either. I tried to spend time with David, often taking my homework along while he and a friend bowled or attended a movie. But we didn't communicate. Talking took so much energy, my mind wandered, and I had no real interest in life. I simply went through the motions. David needed both his parents but his father was physically absent (with a new wife and family) and I was emotionally absent with my thoughts and pain.

In his way, David felt as rejected, betrayed and abandoned as I did. Even in the worst of times, children try to protect their parents. David was angry at Bill because he had left me which had put David into the role of my protector, and angry with me because he still needed me to be his protector. Our roles had been altered, and unable to understand, he naturally resented it.

My mind groped for order, needing to settle on one belief, one feeling, but every belief or feeling raised more questions. Bill had been bright, talented and healthy. Why couldn't he have waited for the court decision? Why didn't he give us more time? Why didn't I pick up on his clues? Why wasn't I with him that day? Had I hoped he would kill himself? Why didn't anyone else stop him? Who was to blame? Every question brought conflicting answers. With no answers, I had no sense of direction. "If only I knew *something* for sure," I'd yell at the air.

I wanted to blame someone other than Bill and myself. I walked around imagining confrontations between myself and others whom I perceived as letting both of us down. In my imagination, I scolded the lawyer who had said, "Don't talk to me about Bill's suicidal feelings. I'm not his baby-sitter." And I shamed Bill's relatives who had known Bill's gun was in his car but had not removed it even when they could have. I saw myself returning to the psychiatrist's and clergymen's offices and yelling, "See! See what you did!? You think you know so much, but you let my husband die! What do you

22

think of yourselves now?" I wanted people to ask me how Bill died so I could retort, "He killed himself because we all wanted him to. So there and so what! Make something of it!"

I yearned to talk about Bill, our love, our motor home, the fun we had together. But whenever I mentioned his name, family members would walk away or change the subject. Some people only wanted to know the grisly details. I longed for someone to ask how I felt or what I needed. Sometimes I found myself explaining or justifying Bill's act, our relationship, or even myself to people. It seemed as if there was something wrong with me because my husband had killed himself or because I was grieving.

I wanted another chance to help Bill. I was afraid to go on alone—afraid I couldn't—knew I had to. I wasn't ready to let him go—to say good-bye—we hadn't had enough hello's yet.

It was difficult to believe Bill was dead because I had not seen him dead. He died three hundred miles away and I had been unable to attend his funeral. Now I realized this was interfering with my ability to accept his death. At times my mind suspected this was all a cruel trick. Once I phoned the company he had worked for and asked to speak to him. It helped to hear someone say, "I'm sorry. Mr. Ross died some time ago."

I missed Bill's funeral because there had been no one to accompany me on the trip and I had been too shocked and confused to drive myself. "Let his son arrange things," my family said. "Anyway, he was an alcoholic, you were separated, and he killed himself. Why do you even want to be there?" No one from my family sent flowers and I received no cards. Later, some women at church apologized, saying, "We wanted to offer you comfort, but didn't know what to do. Your parents said not to contact you so that's why we never called or visited you." It was as though his life and our love were shameful, worthless, or hadn't existed.

My family's hostility toward Bill was understandable because his drinking had caused them a lot of embarrassment and stress. Much of that embarrassment was due to Bill's drunken phone calls, which were gleefully enjoyed by neighbors on the party line. He harassed my family with threats of dropping a bomb on my trailer. (I didn't worry if there was distance between us because he would pass out, but there was some cause for alarm if he were nearby.) Once he stuffed crushed flowers in my mailbox; another time he put a hangman's noose outside my door. Both times he was drunk. My

23

family had reason to fear and resent him.

But I did not understand their hostility toward me. I needed their support and understanding (not punishment) while going through this painful transition. They had been very supportive of me during the divorce from my first husband and I couldn't see how this was different. I tried to explain to my parents how rejected, lonely and hurt I felt.

"I wish you'd forget him," my father said angrily, "and as long as you are going to be depressed and difficult don't come around bothering the rest of us. Especially your mother. Ever since you were born I've had to listen to her go on and on about how much you hated her even when you were a baby. You were born with a mean streak and your mother and I think all the family should know it. We can make sure no one ever believes you. No one, not even your children, should have anything to do with you." I must have looked strange because he paused, then added in a softer tone, "That's the only way I know to keep your mother from getting upset and from upsetting me and everyone else when you are around."

Too stunned to reply, I did as I was told. I returned to my mobile home next door, closed my door, and withdrew from everyone. The sense of betrayal and the feeling that I couldn't trust anyone stayed with me for a long time. I developed an overwhelming fear of loss and people which began to affect all my relationships. Bill had lost his life; I was losing my right to grieve, and my right to live a normal life.

I gave in to my feelings only during the forty-minute drive home from campus. Missing Bill's presence or his arms around me was so painfully consuming that my entire body hurt at times. This pain would return, as if the same arm were cut off over and over. At those times, I wished Bill had been buried rather than cremated so I could stomp on his grave. Sometimes that was funny because I could almost hear Bill say, "That's my little red-head. Even-tempered. Mad all the time." Other times my body shook with the deep sobs I had held in all day. Pounding the steering wheel, I would scream, "Damn you. I could kill you for doing this to me!" or, "Come back, I miss you." When I turned into my driveway, I'd turn off all the tears.

It's ironic that as much as I wanted empathy and to talk about Bill, I sometimes couldn't handle it when it was offered. My Aunt Genevieve and Uncle Harry had enjoyed Bill's company; had compared motor home stories and traded jokes. Weeks after Bill's death we met on the street and I told them Bill was dead. When my aunt tried to express sympathy I was so overcome I could not respond. I cut her off. She had lost a son a few years earlier and could have related to my grief, but I did not know how to respond to her expression of concern. I had learned to grieve alone, but it was killing me.

Sorrow seemed to be an entity of its own. It hovered around the corners of my days, waiting to drop over me and take my breath away. I feared these attacks. More and more, I thought I knew what Bill must have been thinking before he shot himself. I'd lose myself in imagining every thought and movement up to the moment he pulled the trigger, as if I could think his thoughts and feel his feelings. Sometimes, I'd jump because I thought I could actually hear the shot. I wondered if suicide would be a release for me as well and thought about death. Death would be an easy escape from silence and loneliness, but I couldn't inflict this hurt onto my children.

I was so tired. Not sleepy tired or physically tired—but wasted tired. I had to have relief.

I felt incredibly alone and discouraged. One day I drove into my driveway to find my parents working in the yard near my trailer. One of them glanced up and asked me how I was. Touched by this unexpected expression of concern and interest, I impulsively decided to confide, and said, "I'm so tired, lonely and discouraged that sometimes I think I just want to go inside my trailer, turn on the gas and end it all."

"Well," said my mother quietly, "if that's the way you really feel, why don't you?" They were both eyeing me sideways. As usual, in these situations, I reacted as I had been trained to while still a small child. It was as if I could hear an old tape still playing, "Don't you dare talk back, young lady. Don't you dare say a word." My heart lurched, and I froze in mid-step for a long moment, unable to believe what I'd heard, but with the words "Why don't you?" swirling around my head.

In a trance, I went inside my trailer and attempted to do just that. Looking back, I don't remember my actions but I do remember *watching myself* lock the doors, stuff rugs and towels around them, turn on the gas furnace and sit down beside it. Then the phone rang, and you know how it is with phones—they are the boss—even when you're in the middle of trying to die. It was within arm's reach so I managed to answer it. It was David, wanting to know if he could bring a friend home that evening and if I'd make tacos. The call was a Godsend because it knocked me back into rationality, but to my horror, after hanging up, I could not get my legs to move from the floor toward the gas handle. I reached for the phone again and managed to call Connie and Warren Lewis who ran the local ambulance service and funeral home.

"Help me," I cried to Connie, "I can't make myself move," and told her what had happened. In just a few minutes I could hear their siren screaming its way down the road, and a state patrol car pulled up from the other direction. Together, Connie and the officer tore the trailer door off its hinges, turned off the gas and carried me to the ambulance. Connie took me home with her, tucked me in a chair with a blanket, gave me something to help me stop shaking and sat down beside me. By the time she drove me back home, she had convinced me to seek help.

I had one special friend, Joyce Woodring, that I did talk with from time to time but I had tried to be careful not to bother her too much, and had held in many of my really deep feelings. But, this was a crisis and I had to have help. I called her and she responded by offering to come over and stay with me until I had talked it out. That was what I needed. It was the first turning point for me.

I talked about the good times and the bad times with Bill. Joyce and I laughed together over the rodeo stories he used to tell. One of Bill's six brothers, Gene, had been the world's champion bulldogger three times in the late 1930s and early 1940s. Bill was full of stories about Roy Rogers, Tim Holt, Jim Shoulders and other rodeo stars of those times. "You'll have to meet these people someday," he'd say. "That Roy Rogers is a little fella but a hell of a nice guy. Howard and I carried him all over New York one time. He wanted to learn about cowboys but fell asleep early in the evening. Howard would just hoist him over his shoulder and off we'd go. Roy spent the whole evening like that—draped over Howard's shoulder." Another time, Roy wrote a song about Howard—a parody to "Pistol Packing Mama." "I'd like to meet them," I said. "But when?"

"Oh there's time," Bill would answer. "Those old cowboys never die. They just sit around and lie to each other." I had taped the stories as Bill told them and now Joyce and I listened together.

I told Joyce all about the time we were driving the motor home at night through South Carolina to Florida, when Bill pulled off and parked suddenly along the beach. I thought he was finally going to sleep. "I've got something to show you," he said. "Come along."

I helped him build a fire near a sand dune and then he settled me in the sand with a blanket and disappeared into the motor-home. He re-emerged with a bottle of wine and commenced to dance—Indian style—around the bonfire, waving the bottle and singing a song about how "Old Cowboy Pete Roped the Devil." Bill was dressed in nothing but his white undershorts, cowboy boots, ten gallon hat, and a Mexican serapé over his shoulders. "I'll never forget that sight," I told Joyce.

I recalled how the thick silvery hair on his chest curled around my fingers and how I loved to trace his facial features in the moonlight. Before Bill died, I had written a poem about him called "Tracing a Memory" and I shared it with Joyce.

"Tell me how you met Bill," she said. We smiled at each other. She'd heard the story before but knew how much I loved to tell it.

I was going through a divorce when I met Bill. "I have just the person for you to meet, " a friend told me. "He'll perk up your spirits." She invited me to a party that evening.

"Is that your little dog?" asked the tall, good-looking man in a western dress suit to whom I'd just been introduced. He smiled and looked down beside me. Puzzled, I looked around, and the man chuckled. "There's no little dog," he said. "I just wanted your full attention." (The "invisible little dog" would later become a bond between us and we named him Spook.)

He already had my attention because I'd been staring at him. "I've got a face like the coast line of Ireland, don't I? Rugged."

"You have an accent," I said, side-stepping the question. "Where are you from?"

"There's your opportunity, Willie," laughed the fellow beside him. "Tell her the story. Tell her where you came from."

"It's a long story. Sure you want to hear it?" I did.

"Well, I was born on a ranch in southwestern Oklahoma. The youngest of a pack of twelve. My mother was home alone that day—my dad and brothers were all out tending cattle or off rodeoing—when she heard some yelling. She hurried to look out the window and saw this band of Indians coming. Well, she ran out to the barn and got on this little mare and started riding as hard as she could for the breaks—that's what we call a patch of bad country

27

out there—near where my dad was. The mare was about to foal and danged if all the excitement didn't cause them both to go into labor. So she stopped under this mesquite bush where I was born and the mare dropped her foal at the same time. My mother put me astride the colt, she hopped back on the mare and we outdistanced the Indians."

He chuckled, smiling down at me again when I shook my head and laughed. "I knew that was going to be a big lie the minute you started talking," I told him. "But I think, somehow, I almost believe it." "I've got flannel mouth," he said, still smiling, "It flaps like the seat of a pair of red long johns hanging on the clothesline on a windy day. That means I talk a lot." He was right.

Something had been puzzling me about the way he smiled down at me. Now I knew what it was. He didn't smile with his mouth but with his eyes. He'd tip his head a little, crinkle the corners of his eyes and as the warmth of the smile filled his face, it flooded over on me.

"I think I'm going to call you Betsy," he commented a bit later. "It goes so well with Ross." Before I could answer he chuckled and said, "Don't you know? You're going to marry me."

I think I had known.

Bill explained that his background and life style were far different from mine. "I've rodeoed hard, worked hard, fought hard, and played hard," he said. "And when we Rosses get to drinking we're apt to take offense right quick and talk to a man by hand. Think you're up to riding the river with a man like that?"

"Anytime you get out of line, you just lean over so I can reach you and I'll talk back by hand," I told him.

A strong arm folded me close to his chest and he lay his chin in my hair. "I believe my little redhead has a taste for excitement," he said. "When do you want to get married?"

"If you'll choose the month," I answered, "I'll choose the day."

"Next month."

"The first."

"The little dog is a witness to all this," he chuckled. "You can't go back on your word, now." (As things worked out, it was over a year before we were married.)

I talked to Joyce about our favorite motor home adventures; how Bill would stand in the motor-home door, wait until I walked away some distance, then drop a lasso over my shoulders and pull me back to him with the rope for a kiss (we always got applause if there was an audience); and about the time the motor home rolled into a ditch when Bill had pulled off the road in order to use the bathroom at the back—how he tumbled out and rolled down the aisle, trousers around his knees; and about the time I got my arm stuck in the magazine rack and could do nothing but giggle until Bill came and lifted me up so I could get loose.

As I confided in Joyce, she laughed in the right places and cried in the right places. She never interrupted, never reminded me how others have grieved, never implied my grief was unimportant and never tried to prove "she had suffered more."

The most important gift Joyce gave me was to let me grieve in my own way. I expected her to tell me I shouldn't feel guilty, but she didn't. She would merely say, "Tell me how that feels," or, "Maybe you're right." With that response I could at last explore my feelings, including questions about God. I told her how I was mad at God because I had turned everything over to Him, expecting it to be healed, but instead Bill had died and my pain continued.

At one time, our minister, Pastor Paul, had asked me if I was praying for Bill's drinking problem to be healed because it would make things better for me, or because that's what God wanted for him. I had to admit, the idea of his sobriety for my own convenience was uppermost in my mind. That's not to say my prayer was wrong, but rather, that sometimes some seemingly very good prayers may not be answered if the motive is primarily a selfish one. I asked to be forgiven for that and released both Bill and my attitude to God, saying, "You do whatever is your will with Bill regardless of how it affects our future." Three months later, Bill killed himself.

Could that have been God's will? No, I don't think so. No senseless tragedy is part of God's divine will, but maybe some things are within his permissive will. Some of those tragedies may be accidents, some may be mistakes, some are due to human frailty, some may be sin, and some, we'll never understand.

Isn't it interesting how we give ourselves the credit when something goes the way we want it to but hold God responsible when it doesn't, with comments like, "Well, it was (or wasn't) God's will." I think of that when I hear something of nature described as "an act of God." Just how do you know what's an act of God?

I have a warranty for my decorator phone that says it is not protected against damage from lightning and other "acts of God."

Does that mean it *is* protected from acts of the devil? And if so, how does one know if lightning is not an act of the devil?

Sometimes I wonder if God feels as if he can never do anything right—if he ever shakes his head and says, "Come on, folks, give me a break." We either see him as a "nice-good-God" or a "big-bad-God." At this time, in my kitchen with Joyce, that's how I felt.

I recalled how Bill had been moved by his experience in jail and wanted to be baptized. During this time, my mother put us in touch with Ralph Peterson, a Baptist minister in southern Illinois, who was also a recovering alcoholic. He counseled us and offered to baptize Bill, who agreed to it only if I would join him. I had already been baptized by sprinkling when I was a baby. This time, in February, 1973, had marked the beginning of a special new phase of my relationship with God. But now, talking with Joyce, I wondered if Bill were being punished for suicide, and why didn't I feel comforted by God?

Joyce offered her family as an "extended family" for David and me and suggested we stay in touch daily. We did. She even installed a longer phone cord so she could move around her house while we talked. Taking advantage of her listening ear, I told her my story over and over. Her quiet, gentle patience and acceptance allowed me to begin working toward an understanding of what had happened to Bill and what was happening to me. Joyce both helped and allowed me to probe all the implications in Bill's death, our relationship and my present struggle with grief. We discussed the spiritual aspects, searching to discern something of value in all this. As I strove to regain my faith and put it to work, my grief process gradually became a growing experience. Joyce was a gift from a compassionate and concerned God, for with the talking and sharing, healing began to seep into my wounded spirit.

Joyce urged me to rejoin our Bible study group and to talk to our minister. I did. "We don't know what sort of spiritual contact, if any, took place in that split-second between the time Bill pulled the trigger and the time death was final," Pastor Paul said, "But what we do know is God understands better than we do the illness of alcohol and depression. His love, mercy and healing are greater than any human can offer. An example is that of the prodigal son where the father (God) comes running to the son, not the sinful son to the father. Forgiveness, love and healing are the emphasis rather than 'sin-guilt.'" He encouraged me to search the Scriptures for answers. As I did, I discovered verses which comforted me concerning Bill's salvation and others which gave me permission to grieve. I also learned that early Christians prayed for the salvation of souls of departed Christians—whether their deaths were by assassination or self-inflicted.

With these revelations and with the support I received from friends and my children, I began to experience a renewal of faith. For the first time since Bill's death, I saw a ray of hope. I was beginning to get the rattle out of my mind. Maybe there was growth in the midst of turmoil—order from the chaos—after all.

It was two years after Bill's death before I could carry out his request to bury his ashes in a special place of our own. Sitting in the warm sunshine beside the tiny grave I had dug, I thanked God that Bill had been part of my life. We had shared the same spirit of adventure, and I'd always miss his special sense of humor. I smiled when I remembered how he would stand in the bathroom door watching me primp and say, "Someday, honey, I'm going to build you a bathroom with a house around it." Life with Bill had been filled with excitement and laughter but my preoccupation with our relationship was the cause of much of my pain now. I realized I had been grieving on more than one level—not just that of missing Bill, but about what had happened to me. I was beginning to want to do other things but grief still dominated my life.

It was time to release him in order to free myself. I opened the canister and let his ashes sift through my fingers. They were so white and clean. Bill had chosen cremation for this very reason. He was proud of his Indian ancestry and believed in purification by fire. The last time Bill brought me here he had shown me where to bury his ashes. Placing his foot on a tree trunk and leaning an elbow on his knee, he looked toward the west and talked about how his "tracks" were all over those states. "I loved it out there," he mused. "Bad things always happen to me when I'm east of the Mississippi (he died in Illinois). I used to try to pick up the world in my teeth and shake it when things didn't go my way. That hasn't worked this time." His eyes smiled down at me. "It's your turn to shake things up now and heaven help anyone who gets in your way."

I recalled Bill had stood quietly for some time, then laughed and said, "You know, once I told my buddy, Howard, that when I died I wanted my ashes scattered over the breaks in western Oklahoma. Howard said, 'Hell, Bill, that would kill all the vegetation out there!' I told him, 'Maybe so, but think of all the pussy willows that would grow in its place.'" That was Bill—taking an emotional or traumatic moment and topping it with a joke.

I placed the canister of ashes so it pointed east and west, and pushed dirt over it with my hands. Bill's words kept returning to my mind. "You will do something with all this," he had once said. "It's too late to help me but you will help someone else someday."

My thoughts turned to others in similar circumstances who also must be suffering in confusion and silence. I didn't know what I could do—if anything, but I knew I had to try. I could not ignore Bill's faith in me. It was time to stop fighting; to release the pain.

Paul Tillich (*The Courage to Be*) wrote that to continue to exist outside the realm of God is a state of non-being—not non-existence, but non-being. For two years, grief had been my companion and my God. It was time to start "being" again, within the realm of God. I asked God to take both Bill's burden and mine and turn them into a blessing for others—something which would give meaning to Bill's senseless death and the rest of my life. I stood up, said good-bye to Bill, thanked God for whatever He would be doing and walked down the small hill to my car. (I could have sworn there was a little dog following me.) With that act of faith, my healing process moved ahead in leaps and bounds.

It wasn't as easy as it sounds here. For the past two years I'd been "running to" and "running from," and for that time, I guess it was as good a balance as any. But now, I had to decide if I wanted to be one of the problems left by Bill's suicide or one of the solutions. Misfortune had befallen me. I had to look it in its face and give it a name; then I could put it—and myself—in the right place.

In order to get in touch with reality and with the present I made a list of questions for myself: "What can I do? What can I not do? What do I want? Not want?" (I *knew* an answer to that one. I had cried daily for the past two years and all it had gotten me was ten years of aging. I *didn't* want more of that.)

Another list of issues to resolve included: my feelings of anger and guilt; the conflict with my family; an understanding of Bill's suicide I could accept; and the ultimate question, of course, what did I want most for myself. I started with Bill—with trying to answer that eternal infernal question of "Why?"

In the weeks following my burial of Bill's ashes, I read every-thing I could find about suicidal persons, but found very little about the plight of survivors. One useful term I came across was "postvention," coined by Drs. Edwin Shneidman and Norman Farberow. It relates to the circumstances and care of survivors who are experiencing the aftermath of a loss by suicide. As I studied the literature about suicide, I began to understand the workings of Bill's mind as he made the decision to end his life.

Now I realized that Bill's obsessive need to "dwell on his suicidal thoughts" did not stem from a desire to be morbid but the desire to save himself. He comprehended the seriousness of his self-destructive urges far better than anyone else. He feared the pulling power of those urges and was desperately searching for help in defeating them. Of course, he was seeking attention. Justified attention. Without that attention, he simply could not face the things he most feared. In failing to recognize this, we let slip by the primary time for saving his life.

Bill's suicide was the combination and culmination of many factors. I discovered Bill fit into the category of those most at risk for suicide: a white male, age forty-five or older, divorced or alone, with a drinking problem, and without a job or profession. Even his ethnic heritage and background were risk factors.

Of Irish, German, Cheyenne and Cherokee descent, and tracing his ancestry to Chief John Ross (a part of the Trail of Tears saga), Bill was the youngest of twelve. Raised on a large ranch in western Oklahoma, he spent his time trying to imitate his older brothers who were all rodeo enthusiasts. Somewhere around nine or ten he tried to teach himself steer wrestling by mistaking a cow for a steer and by using the fence for a hazer. "Most of the time I was in the air," he told me, "somewhere between my pony and the ground."

Bill's father (who tried, but failed, to make his seven sons into a Ross family baseball team) observed all this commotion from a windmill he was repairing. He cleaned up Bill's "skinned bark" at the water tank and began teaching the boy the right way to ride, rope and steer wrestle.

Bill adored his dad, basking in the newly-found attention and special closeness; but lost him a little over three years later when his father died suddenly while on a mining trip. Coming in the back door while his mother was on the phone, Bill mistook her words "heart attack?" for "scout pack."

Bill's scout pack, with scraps of food in it, was missing at the time, and when the cause of his dad's death was shown to be food poisoning, Bill thought he was responsible. "All I remember is that one day, I was a broken-hearted kid of twelve lying face down on the front porch, where I cried myself to sleep, and my oldest brother picked me up and carried me to bed. I remember nothing about the following two or three years. The next thing I knew, I was a man and didn't know how I got there or what to do about it."

Bill transferred his hero worship back to his older brothers, following them to rodeos, working and sleeping in horse stalls and riding the rails. "My brothers showed me how to drink, how to fight and that chasing girls could be as much fun as chasing steers."

"I never got over the loss of my dad," Bill would reflect. "I now know his death wasn't my fault but I still feel guilty and I'm still mad about it because I only had his love and attention for a little over three years."

Even though Bill had not understood all the factors involved with his decision to kill himself, the information I gathered helped me to understand. I believe Bill thought he had lost all he had to live for. He was afraid of going to prison, afraid his marriage was over, and afraid of never returning to his construction work. The day after his death, the judge told a reporter that in view of Bill's good record, he would probably have gotten a suspended sentence. Two weeks later, I received a phone call from a company wanting Bill to supervise a job immediately. I had planned to be reconciled with him the following week. Had Bill waited *one day*, he would have had his freedom; *two weeks*, and he would have had a job in Texas (the place he most wanted to live); *one month*, and he would have had his marriage. He had failed to follow the AA principle of "One day at a time," and could only see the darkness in his own tunnel. He tried everything he knew to help himself but he had lost hope. The tragedy is not so much that he killed himself but that he believed he had to. He made the decision but it wasn't his choice.

At Al-Anon meetings, I learned alcoholics are at great risk to suicide during the first year of sobriety. Alcohol has been their companion, their center of life. Sobriety represents a loss of that familiar life style, no matter how destructive it might have been. I don't think Bill understood his depression was part of his recovery. I also believe Bill gave in to suicide because his self-image depended more upon what he had rather than who he was.

Some people depend upon constant attention, admiration and approval from others for their sense of self-worth. They gain ego-gratification by acquiring material possessions, money, power, position, the perfect wife and children, an attractive secretary, by attention to their own appearance, or by cultivating a certain personality trait, charm or wit.

These people may have trouble developing a real sense of themselves. Their sense of self-worth is achieved by what is reflected back to them by other people and their environment. They constantly demand attention and soak up whatever strength others radiate, often leaving those others feeling "worn out."

Problems arise for these people when they must confront tragedy or disappointment. In fact they may perceive any setback or disappointment as a calamity because they lack the inner resources to cope realistically and objectively. As a result, they panic easily. They fall into their own "pit of lack" and cannot see a way out other than to complain, fight, bully or blame others, retreat into denial, depression or drugs, or give up.

Bill's mind set was like this in some ways. Without his job, without prestige, a pretty wife, a new car, et cetera, he saw no hope for his future and rejected alternatives that did not offer tangibles. Nor did he perceive his own lack of inner resources. He never grasped that difference between himself and others who take the ups and downs of life in stride. Indeed, if he did compare himself to others at all he assumed they were no different than he—just "luckier or meaner." Without a developed incentive to observe others or analyze his own behavior and attitudes, he never learned from his own mistakes, and in the process, deprived himself of inner growth and strength. There's an interesting analogy here between Bill's inner resources and the plane he dumped into the lake. Neither one had a reserve tank of gas.

I decided I would not be defeated in this way. I concluded the answer stemmed not only from the presence or lack of inner strength, but also from recognition of its source. There is mental strength, emotional strength, and spiritual strength. I knew I already had mental strength. I realized my physical image reflected traits of timidity, reserve and defensiveness but in spite of these traits and habits, I knew I was of value and had emotional strength.

For myself, my spiritual strength was the primary provider of the confidence and tenacity I needed for survival and self-growth. It's nice not to be lonely or in pain, to have family approval, and to have nice things, but I didn't *need* these things in order to survive or to love myself. I was worthwhile simply because God created me. My spiritual strength was the backbone of my self-image and sense of self-worth; it assured emotional strength. This knowledge underscored my mental strength.

With those insights I was able to put my own relationship with God to rights, and to gain some understanding of both the extent and lack of Bill's faith.

There's a difference between knowing God and just knowing about God. Say, for example, you're fascinated with Paris but you've never been there. You long to go, you've studied the history of the city, learned the language, memorized the streets, collected pictures. You're an expert about Paris—you believe it exists—but you've never experienced the spirit of the city. You still don't *know* Paris, you only *know about* it.

A lot of people know a lot about God; they believe in Him and in prayer. But there's that special connection—a touching of spirit (when you know that you know that you know)—which I think Bill was seeking those last months but never found. He read the Bible, prayed, went to church and was baptized; all good things to do, but for the wrong reasons. He hoped to please God this way, and in return, get an instant miraculous solution to his dilemma.

He thought faith could do something for him if he tried hard enough, but he never really let go of his security blanket of fear. He couldn't let go of his fear without conditions, and without evidence from God as to His intentions. The sort of faith Bill was trying so hard to find doesn't happen through negotiation, begging, or doing favors for God. It comes from simply believing—from letting prayer flow *into* you as well as reaching out for answers. This special level of belief can occur as a sudden insight or as a gradual awareness.

I believe what Bill was seeking has to do with surrender—with regarding surrender as a safe release; not as giving up to fate, or as a humiliating defeat, or as a frantic struggle. There's a special peace which follows the surrender of sorrow or fear which both frees and strengthens the spirit. This feeling comes after the act of surrendering—not before.

Bill was grieving over many losses. Drinking had been his substitute for facing problems. Now I understood what he meant when he said, "Used to be, when I got into trouble, I could lie my way out, fight my way out, buy my way out, blame someone else or move on to another job. Now I can't do any of those things and I don't know what else to do." Even though counselors and friends pointed out alternatives to Bill, he had never developed other ways to cope and couldn't be sure they would work for him. He had, in a way, lost his "self."

And in the beginning, so had I. With Bill, I always knew I was loved. He had given me a sense of self-worth I'd never before experienced. He did not make fun of my attempts to express myself or interrupt me. He listened to me talk and was proud of my mind. He bragged about my looks, personality, intelligence, talents, accomplishments and abilities to friends and co-workers until they ran when they saw him coming. He thought I was beautiful no matter how I was dressed—or undressed.

Bill's confidence and aggression were the perfect counterbalance for my shyness and fear of people. When he discovered I'd hang back in a store, waiting forever for a clerk to acknowledge me, he'd pull me in front of the salesperson, put his hands on my shoulders and announce in a baritone that carried throughout the store, "My wife wants to be waited on and I think you can do it now." His gaze said they'd better, and they did.

He set about changing my shyness into self-confidence. "You don't ever have to hang your head when you're with me," he'd tell me. "Just carry yourself like a little queen because you aren't put together cheap." This kind of approval was better than all the psychiatrists in the world for my intimidated ego and I adored him.

I was so in need of affirmation and approval that I even saw Bill's insane jealousy and possessiveness as evidence of love. *Someone noticed me.* In my experience, indifference meant the lack of love, so attention, of any kind, spelled love. That's one of the reasons I was so willing to give the marriage every possible chance.

But, in a way, I had become as dependent on Bill's admiration and approval of me as he had been on alcohol. Without him, I had to build a new identity. In order to help myself cope with reality I continued my college education at the University of Iowa with areas of concentration in religion, psychology, and journalism.

I had begun my experience as a forty-year-old-female freshman during an earlier extended separation from Bill. Before attending college I had held a small county job. While still employed at that job during the day, I also had volunteered to design and paint scenery for a community pageant. The scenery consisted of a thirty-foot long reproduction of a small town main street one hundred years ago. I had never done anything like that before but loved the challenge, and with some other volunteers, worked at it every evening in a large building owned by Hope Dunn. One day she brought out coffee, sat me down and started to talk.

"You have too much talent and potential to continue in the job you now have," she said. "Have you ever thought of going to college?" Of course, I had always dreamed of that but never thought it possible. "Well," she said, "if you can keep yourself there, I think I can help get you started with a P.E.O. grant." She didn't have to repeat the offer. I enrolled the following semester.

Now, as I worked slowly but steadily for my Bachelor of General Studies degree, I earned scholastic honors and was presented a number of awards, including the McCall Life Pattern Award and the Ella Cabot Lyman Foundation award. I was also published in the journal, *Death Education*. With these achievements I began to feel as if I were worth something on my own after all. I was finally dealing with the issue on my list concerning myself.

Although these insights, experiences, accomplishments, and information from books were helpful, I still needed to meet other survivors. I attended some widows' and single parents' groups but felt somehow different. Other widows did not share my sense of anger, shame, and abandonment. Their husbands had died by "natural" causes, such as cancer, whereas my husband had died by his own choice. These women did not feel the need to make "amends," as I did. I had more in common with women who had been divorced. It became obvious to me that survivors of suicide were unique and needed a support group of their own.

I told one of my professors that I had just buried Bill's ashes and she was astounded. She had known me for nearly two years but had not known I was widowed that way. When I mentioned that there should be a support group for suicide survivors—something like Al-Anon—she said, "Well, Betsy, if there isn't then you start one." She gave me some names to contact, and I did. Encouraged by Prof. James Spaulding and Prof. George Patterson, and assisted by Sally Smith at the Campus Ministry Office, we planned a meeting with announcements in newspapers and on radio. Marlene Perrin of the *Iowa City Press-Citizen*, and the campus newspaper, the *Daily Iowan*, each ran a full story. To my surprise all sorts of people responded to the announcement and showed up at the first meeting. Some drove many miles to attend the meeting; some said they had waited for years for an opportunity to share with other survivors. We knew we wanted to continue meeting.

During these meetings, powerful things happened. A bond developed among us—something akin to blood ties—perhaps an accepting family substitute. Our most important experience at those meetings was the value of retelling our stories. This helped us understand and accept what had happened.

Resolving grief rather than avoiding it is hard work for those who choose to work through it, but it is well worth it. To my way of thinking, the process resembles childbirth. Once the labor pains start, there's nothing to do but go with them. You can't change your mind, postpone them, or turn back. You can't detour around them or give them away. The only way to get relief is to *work with* the pain. At the meetings, we learned that grief is not an illness, not a weakness, not a mistake, not self-indulgence, and not a medical or emotional dysfunction. Rather, grief is a necessary and healthy process which we learned to accept and experience.

From the very first meeting in the fall of 1977, we realized the need for a national organization and public education. In February 1978, our group, called Ray of Hope, inc., became the first non-profit organization of its kind, so named by the group because those who suicided had lost their ray of hope, and because we, through the group, had found our ray of hope.

That first year saw a great deal of experimenting and re-organization for Ray of Hope, as there were no other survivor support groups at the time to use as a model. With the help of my son, Daryl, as one sounding board, and Joyce as another sounding board and errand-person, we put together a logo, a brochure, by-laws and articles of incorporation. We borrowed concepts from Al-Anon and Make Today Count. In Burlington, Iowa, I met Orville Kelly, who, dying of cancer, had founded Make Today Count (the first support group for cancer patients and their families) and had authored a book by the same name. Orville instructed me in how to organize a non-profit group, plan the meeting format and how to contact the proper officials, professionals, and media.

I followed his advice and found an attorney who volunteered the legal work to incorporate Ray of Hope. My uncle, Bob Spera, advised me on how to select a board of directors and handle the finances. A psychiatric nurse, Ronnye Wieland, offered to co-lead the support group and to instruct me as a leader, as I had no experience or training in the role as yet.

Two things I discerned early on was that part of the survivor's grief is more of a crisis situation than a chronic condition, and that the main purpose of a support group is to meet that need. I used those points to shape the structure of the meetings. At first, Ray of Hope received a great deal of attention here in Iowa. I was besieged with requests to speak at hospitals, churches, schools, funeral homes, civic groups, on radio and television.

Tom Eisen, a reporter for KGAN-TV in Cedar Rapids, Iowa, interviewed us for a two-part special on the evening news. In September, 1979, Tom and others at KGAN arranged for the support group to appear on Phil Donahue, together with Dr. Ari Kiev, author of *The Courage to Be*. At that time Dr. Kiev consented to speak at a conference on suicide postvention if I could organize one.

Following the Donahue appearance, I received mail from people all across the country wanting to know about suicide survivors, Ray of Hope, and how to form their own groups. In November, 1979, with guidance from Professor Herb Exum in the counselor education department, we formed a committee to organize a national conference on suicide prevention and postvention.

A national organization, the American Association of Suicidology, had met for several years to exchange information concerning suicide, but apparently had not yet explored the plight of survivors at any great length except for studies and presentations primarily by Dr. Albert Cain, Dr. Irene Fast, and Mrs. Iris Bolton.

As a result, this conference of October, 1980, co-sponsored by the University of Iowa College of Medicine and the Iowa Mental Health Authority, attracted several hundred participants from crisis centers, mental health agencies, social services, the clergy, funeral directors, police departments, emergency care units, school counselors, and hospices. We ended the conference with a panel of people who represented each of these services. A highlight of the conference was daily Ray of Hope survivor model meetings.

Featured speakers at that conference included Dr. Ari Kiev, Cornell University; Dr. Albert Cain, University of Michigan; Dr. Calvin Frederick, National Institute of Mental Health; Iris Bolton, Link Counseling Center, Atlanta; and numerous professors and professionals from the University of Iowa and surrounding area. Cassettes of their presentations were made available.

Today, around two hundred survivor support groups exist, many modeled after Ray of Hope. One bereaved widow at that conference was Teresa (Knight) Crowe who helped establish the well-known Survivors of Suicide Group at the Suicide Prevention Center, Inc., in Dayton, Ohio.

Also presented for the first time at that conference was a booklet I had written in 1979 entitled, *After Suicide: A Unique Grief Process.* That booklet has been greatly copied in the years since but in a way that is all right—it means what I wrote was valid. This book is the third expansion and rewrite of that booklet; one of which was a manual, ©1986, by the same name as this book. A study questionnaire concerning the after-suicide grief process which was distributed at the conference is still being used.

Ray of Hope was the beginning of a healing process for many who struggle with suicide in their families. For me, it was more— it was the answer to my prayer and a renewing process.

For nearly four years after Bill's death, I knew an important part of me had also died. The tiny bit that remained alive had retreated deep inside me, into an icy, protective casing, while my mind searched for reason and order. Had that fragile, vulnerable bit been wounded, nothing would have been left. But it was strong enough to survive while I healed in other ways.

A great part of that healing came with the understanding and insight into my family situation. At one point, I realized I was grieving more over what I perceived as family rejection than I was over the loss of Bill. I talked about it with my Pastor.

"I want their support so much," I said, "but the more I beg to be included, the more I feel as if I'm left out and told I deserve it. I'm accused of doing and saying things I haven't done or said and it seems as though no one is willing to believe otherwise—or even listen. I feel frightened just like I did when I was a child. I felt pretty much accepted while I was married the first time, and even safer when Bill was alive, but now that I'm alone again, this change in attitude toward me actually feels like persecution. I can understand why they feared Bill, but why is that reason to reject and malign me and my children and interfere with our relationships?"

"Well, it both does and doesn't really have that much to do with Bill's suicide," he told me. "If the rejection has always been there, this is simply another reason to express it, and without the protection of a husband you are vulnerable—so it will be more open.

Think about *all* the things, both past and present, that you may be reacting to now. If there are any skeletons in the closet of your memories, bring them out and look at them in relation to this."

Skeletons in my memory closet? Oh yes, like every one else, I have several, but one in particular came to mind; one of the times I was shut in a closet as punishment for talking back or some similar offense. That's a very symbolic punishment with a clear message of "We don't want you around." Now, I realize this act of separating oneself from a child in times of stress is the action of a troubled and trapped parent, one whose own power to offer help through love and healing is frozen, so they lash out at the object of their frustration, or in my case, put it out of sight in the closet.

Outside I could hear my mother saying to my younger brother, "Yes, I know she's crying but just ignore it. Don't listen to her. Pretend she doesn't exist. She's got a mean streak just like Grandma Miller." I didn't know what a "mean streak" was—I later looked at myself in the mirror but couldn't see anything like a streak. I liked my Grandma Miller so didn't mind being compared to her at all. She was tiny like me. Her eyes were sad but she smiled at me and gave me pretty pictures which she cut out of magazines.

I was used to people pretending I didn't exist. I'd heard that admonishment to others often enough before (and since) but it was the tone of voice—the contempt and scorn—that left me stunned, mute and trembling. I was so afraid of adult voices and never knew what would set off complaints or criticism or when. I thought I really was whatever the voice implied. It would be many years before I learned it was the owner of the voice who had the problem, rather than myself. It was easy to understand that intellectually but it took a long time to believe it.

The other thing was the dark. I was so near-sighted that even close-up objects in the dark looked frightening. Also, my older brother had often delighted in telling me the "bogeyman" would get me in the dark, and I was still young enough to believe it.

The closet was one of those long dark ones under the stair steps and I crept into a corner, trying to stifle my sobs. However, my fear and trembling increased as I watched in terror while a small light appeared in the darkness, began to grow larger, and started to move toward me. Then, I saw that it was Jesus. I recognized him because he looked just as he did on my Sunday school papers. Smiling, he knelt and picked me up, then sat down in a basket of

42

clean un-ironed clothes and leaned back against the wall. I went to sleep on his lap with his arms around me.

It was so good to be held like that. I believe the strength of that protecting presence has always been with me. As I look back, I can see many "guardian angels" in my life. To list only a few, there was: a hired girl who held me on her lap and played with me; my uncle Jerry who carried me on his shoulders; the fourth-grade teacher who discovered I frowned because I couldn't see, not because I was "always mad"; my aunt Genevieve who once included the celebration of my birthday together with a party and cake she had for one of her kids; my aunt Edie who treated me to ice cream after I was in a tap dancing recital; an unfamiliar young couple with their baby who suddenly appeared and gave me a ride home from school just as I was about to lie down and rest while struggling through a snow storm; and Anna Geppert, a landlady who taught a young wife and mother how to look at others with empathy and compassion—to think and see within and beyond myself.

While I was still young, I protected myself with an almost catatonic withdrawal from the possible disapproval of adults and other children. I spent a lot of time repeatedly drawing pictures of pretty girls. I am not an artist, so I think the drawings were my way of saying to myself—"You—Eleanora—are alive, and are a girl, and it's Okay." My psychologist later told me drawing was indeed a safety outlet for my shaky self-image and social frustrations. And I watched people a lot. I learned to read faces, actions and voices, and to sense vibrations by looking deep into a person's soul, although, I have discovered that makes some people uneasy.

Years later, I met the woman who had been my first grade teacher in a tiny rural one room school. "You looked so tiny, frightened and forlorn," she said, "At first you wouldn't talk to me and jumped when I talked to you. Then, you just watched me. At recitation time, I asked the questions and I answered them. Sometimes you'd nod yes or no. One day in December I was drawing a barn on the blackboard and you said, 'I can draw a better barn than that', and you did. You never spoke to me again that school year."

Well, she was an adult and I had to watch her for a time before being sure I could trust her voice, and that she wouldn't touch me. Once I knew I could, there was nothing more I needed to say. In those days, I didn't talk much to anyone. I had learned that if I asked for something I'd probably not get it, or, someone else would.

43

When I was older I discovered I could protect myself in several other ways as well. I escaped family interaction through day dreaming or reading; substituting the lack of family acknowledgment and approval by gaining those very things from others through art work, good grades, 4-H awards, etc.. I thought if I achieved much and asked for little, I could be loved and accepted as much as were my brothers. I ignored being ignored, and pretended I felt no pain. I watched my brothers receive bikes, radios, record players, clothes and cars; I saw their emotional and comfort needs being met, and pretended I didn't want those things also. All this pretense of not caring was a cover-up for the feeling of not measuring up, for the shame of wanting my needs met even if I "didn't deserve it", and the fear of being shamed more if and when I spoke up.

I had to do something about all this unnatural and unhealthy shame and I had to find out why I felt so guilty, responsible and grief-stricken over the suicide of a man who had frightened and harassed me and my son. Why did I go from one rejecting and verbally abusive relationship and marriage to another? And why was I so needy and at the same time so afraid of certain people, afraid to speak up and to defend myself, afraid to be hugged or touched, afraid to reach out to people? I'd find out if it meant dragging every crumbly, moldy, dusty skeleton out of my memory closet.

I went to work. I discovered that you've got to be careful about ignoring your memory closet; those old skeletons have a way of rattling around until you spend all your time holding the door shut. Sometimes they slip out under the door when you aren't looking. They can pop up and surprise you when you least expect it. They can hide in the shadows waiting to haunt you when your guard is down, and sometimes they follow you around in such a way that you don't see what they are doing to you, but other people do. That's not the way memories are supposed to behave.

So, show them who's boss. Open the closet door. Invite them out. Look them over. But look closely. Look for bits of mold or infection on your memory skeletons, and if you find it, set those bones aside. Take time to clean off the mold or infection caused by strong negative emotions. Even though we may consciously forget an early traumatic event, our subconscious remembers the emotion of that event, and as a result, it often controls our present and future actions and opinions more than we realize.

That mold or infection could perhaps be seen as evidence of active "spirits" that might cling to troubled memories. The leader of this gang is probably named Fear or Self-pride. His followers may be any combination of guys named: complaints, jealousy, self-pity, spite, rage, anger, scorn, deceit, resentment, vindictiveness, envy, bitterness, conniving, arrogance, bigotry, denial, idolatry, greed, or (one of the most curious) grudges.

Have you ever noticed how some people proudly display their "spirit of grudges" like a badge of honor? I know a large family who specializes in grudges against one another and in-laws; continuously clutching a list of relatives they don't call, see, write or speak to. They even marry people with pre-existing grudges and gladly shoulder the new ones. I once saw one of them walk out of church when another family member walked in. When they do encounter the detested object of a grudge, they tilt back their head, narrow their eyes, and shoot a withering look over their glasses and down their nose, sweeping this chilling gaze from your head to toe to head to toe again, before haughtily turning away with an indignant "sniff" or "hummph." It's quite a show, and actually, no mean trick when you're only about half the size as the object of the grudge (which is sometimes the case).

Carrying a grudge can serve a purpose; it provides an excuse for being angry, for continuing a vendetta, for blaming others and avoiding one's own guilt, for labeling one's self as a victim, and for hanging on to a state of unrepentance and unforgiveness. It can become addictive. Like the alcoholic, a person addicted to self-pity or a grudge will create or interpret a situation or crisis which justifies going out and getting another bottle of booze (or finding something else to resent—as the case may be)—so they can then indulge in a hang-over (or pity-party—as the case may be). Like the alcoholic they will destroy the reputation of themselves and possibly others to satisfy the addiction. The trouble is, all this only brings temporary satisfaction because the craving (as with alcohol) for a new grudge (or self-pity) will always return.

I think Christians need to be very careful that they don't use God or religion as a justification to indulge in grudges, self-pity, unforgiveness, judgment and self-righteousness. An example is the comment, "Well, obviously so-and-so is a bad person so I never have anything to do with him/her because God doesn't want me to." A little more sneaky technique is to add, "Oh, he/she can call or see me but I will never call or visit him/her."

It may be true God prefers us to be selective about people, but it is an insult to Him to use Him as an excuse to avoid someone of whom we are jealous, want to get even or have a vendetta. It's no wonder some people regard Christians as hypocrites. One might consider asking oneself, "What good is this grudge doing for me? Do I really want to demean myself by carrying around something this ugly?"

These nasty little spirits, sticking onto our memory skeletons, can keep a body so busy kowtowing to them that there's not time left to enjoy life. They suck a person into their skullduggery until his or her soul is dead long before the body reaches a decent age to die. So, clean off the mold and infection and throw it away, not the bones themselves—you need them.

Think about it. Without the skeleton you are currently hanging around on, you'd settle down around your feet in a lumpy pile with nothing but your little ole eyes bugging out. Times like that, an extra set of bones might come in handy. Sometimes, we need our past memories, even the bad ones, as a structure to climb up on, look about, get our bearings, and go a different direction.

One of the first skeletons I tackled was that of my constant thoughts about Bill. They had assumed a haunting presence in and of themselves. This really came to my attention one day when I was wandering through a mall. Window shopping had been a favorite pastime for Bill and me, and I had paused in front of a display of men's wear. Suddenly, I heard myself saying, aloud, "That suit sure would look good on you." I hear a gasp and turned to see a man and woman standing nearby. They were staring at me, wide-eyed and open-mouthed. Then, as one, they turned and scurried away. I had been so absorbed in the feeling Bill was beside me that it had become too real for that couple's comfort.

On the way home that day I talked to Bill as if he were in the car beside me. I said something like "Look, you're not here anymore and there's no way you can be here again so you've got to stop trying, and I've got to stop encouraging you. I will always love you. I know you love me and didn't want to leave me, but you did. And since you did, you have to keep going. Maybe there's someplace you're supposed to be, and something you're supposed to be doing. You can't be part of my existence anymore and I'm not part of yours, so instead of wishing you were here, I'm telling you to go."

Maybe that conversation was silly but it seemed to help. Eventually, the memories ceased their haunting aspect and became a precious comfort.

One skeletal memory in my closet was both confronted and healed in a most unexpected way. I was attending a retreat in Texas, sponsored by Ruth Carter Stapleton, author of *The Gift of Inner Healing* (Word Book Publisher, 1976) when I met Helen, a woman about my age. We looked so much alike we could have been twins. This was quite unnerving to me because I had had a twin who died during my mother's sixth month of pregnancy. At birth, its gender could not be determined but I have always believed it was a sister.

My mother told me about my twin when I was about ten years old. In the years prior to that, unaware of the fact, I had created an imaginary twin sister to play with when I was alone or frightened. I had, in fact, longed for a sister so intently that I once dared to beg my parents to go to an orphan's home and adopt a girl my age.

The longing never left me and when my daughter, Becky, was born, I felt as if God had somehow answered that need. She was, indeed, as much my pal as my daughter in many ways until the divorce when she was fourteen. Aware of the nature of my bond with my daughter, my ex-husband knew that to break that bond was the best revenge he could get, and had assured me he would do so, "with the willing help of my sister, your younger brother and his wife." The timing was perfect because Becky was just at the age where a girl is easily embarrassed by her mother.

As I told Helen about the loss of both my daughter and my twin sister I started to cry, and embarrassed, I turned to leave. She stopped me, "No, don't go away," she said. "Let's try something. Pretend I am your twin. What would you say to me?"

I stared at her for a moment, then almost yelled, "I'm so mad at you for leaving me to face the world alone and I feel so guilty because I was there when you died; I *saw* you die. I watched you suffer, but I couldn't help you and I miss you so much." As much as I tried, I couldn't control the choking sobs between words, but as Helen hugged and comforted me , I felt the release of the terrible sorrow which had been buried for over forty years. In a twinkling, I realized that from birth I had carried a loss never before recognized, a grief never expressed and a guilt never purged.

This experience had such a profound effect upon me that I

began to wonder about other early experiences in my life I had heard about but didn't consciously remember. Upon my return home I began therapy with a psychologist, Dr. Deea Stewart, who used a variety of techniques to reach the source of unidentified and unresolved fears and feelings. We focused on some stories I'd often heard my mother tell about my infancy and childhood.

Apparently, my mother was unable to breast feed me as she had my brother, so I was put on a four-hour interval schedule. I was to drink four ounces of milk between every four hours of sleep. But, I didn't co-operate; I neither slept the four prescribed hours or drank the four prescribed ounces, much to my mother's distress. After some weeks of this, she complained to the doctor that I only slept for two hours, then cried for two hours until she fed me and that I only drank two ounces before falling asleep, and "she's so thin and scrawny."

The doctor replied, so the story goes, that, "Of course the baby doesn't drink four ounces of milk; her stomach isn't big enough to hold more, and of course, she wakes up early—she's hungry—so she cries until she's fed, and of course, she soon falls asleep. She's exhausted. And yes, she's thin, because you're starving her to death."

It's my understanding that she then fed me when I needed it but a few months later, my "mean streak" surfaced again. I learned that I could toss objects, as babies tend to do. Apparently I threw my toys and bottles out of the play pen, laughing at the time. When the second bottle broke, my mother says she said, "All right, young lady, if you're going to do that, you just won't eat until you're hungry enough to use a cup."

Over the years, I tried to laugh along with my older brother, his wife, and my mother whenever she told this story and would add, "That sure fixed Eleanora. She never threw anything and laughed about it again." But inside I didn't share my family's amusement. Just hearing the story—it didn't sound so bad, but the way I physically reacted puzzled me. Sometimes I felt faint, my hands shook or my stomach hurt—and always—I felt such a vast ache in my heart at hearing any of these "funny" stories of my infant and childhood distress, misbehavior and punishments that I often had to leave the room until I recovered.

With the help of my psychologist, I could see a pattern to these physical symptoms. They occurred whenever I perceived that someone seemed to get a kick out of the pain, fear, trouble or distress I had experienced (or was experiencing). I recalled when we were children my older brother liked to amuse himself by destroying other people's things, and my aunt Edie often said of my brother, "He was really spoiled, and never knew the meaning of the word 'No'." Usually, my parents laughed it off when he broke my younger brother's or my toys (or hurt us) rather than stopping him. I recall feeling sick with fear some of those times.

In retrospect, I realize that my father usually looked uncomfortable when the others were laughing at some story of my suffering; but in my mind I felt I was being ganged-up-on by *all* of my family, and many years passed before I learned to avoid those situations if I could, rather than try to fix them.

Also during therapy—through hypnosis—I was able to recall many infant and childhood events—including those connected with nourishment—and the feelings surrounding them, and came to understand many of my puzzling emotions and reactions. I learned that a baby's sense of trust is either developed or destroyed in the first weeks and months of life when the primary need for survival (nourishment) is met, along with the warmth, comfort, and the gentle handling which makes an infant feel safe.

During those hours I lay crying from hunger, distress, discomfort and the accompanying fear of frightening sounds and handling created the basis for my deep long-term fear of people, fear of being touched or hugged and fear of defending myself, and heightened my awareness of people's tone of voice and its implications.

The punishment I received for expressing myself as a normal baby discouraged autonomy (self-confidence) and reinforced the message that it was useless for me to *expect* to have my needs met in childhood—that if I were, indeed, to survive, it would be on my own and by happenstance.

The result of these infant experiences, harmless as they may sound, were serious enough to result in what is called "early attachment disorder," which affected my ability to love and trust without fear, and created the feelings of dispair and helplessness.

Deea warned me that it might be a long road to well-being, and it was. Although therapy was stressful at times, it explained a great deal and revealed so many possibilities for relief and release. I learned that the *lack* of nurturing care and guidance can be as harmful as broken bones; perhaps more so in some ways, because it can be so insidious. Physical abuse resulting from an angry reaction is doubtless harmful, but, calculated abuse can be especially cruel because it is deliberate. There's a subtle, but important distinction between indifferent neglect and deliberate deprivation. It may seem one way and be another.

I struggled with that concerning my mother's way of leading me to believe things; that I'd be told the truth about family plans, that she'd call me when she and Dad came to town, that I could safely store some antiques in her house, that she was saving my Aunt Leora's diamond ring (which my aunt had willed to me) or other family heirlooms especially for me. I eagerly believed each promise. Sometime later, I'd find I wasn't informed of plans because they "forgot", or, "didn't know if I was home." My stored items (a tiny chest of drawers, a drop-leaf end table and a braided rug), the ring and other promised heirlooms either disappeared or someone "took them," or, they were given to someone else with the comment, "Here, you take this so Eleanora can't get it."

I felt like a hungry puppy, who sees food offered, believes it can eat, then finds the plate of food yanked away and gets whipped for starting to eat. It was pretty difficult to believe this repeated action over the years was not deliberate and malevolent. It wasn't the lost objects that hurt so much, but the action itself of offering—of enticing me to trust and hope—then of taking away.

"But, what do I do," I cried to Deea, "when I feel so unjustly tricked and discredited."

"It *is* unjust," she replied, "to destroy you in the mind of others, to pit you against one another through envy and distrust, to be subjected to family indictment, accused and punished for things you haven't said or done. It *is* unjust to promise a person something, then withhold it and also scold them for objecting when the expected promise isn't met. It *is* horrible to be or feel ostracized by your entire family because of one person's hell, but that's the way of closed dysfunctional families. Any disturbed leader of controlling figure of a family or group will naturally attract or create a dysfunctional following. Some followers don't know why they are rejecting or hurting others—they just know that because the leader (or Dad or Mom) does it, it must be the thing to do.

Closed families operate on old fears. Your parents may have, early in life, accepted and believed some terrible messages about themselves and they continue to operate on them. But, remember

50

this," she added, "It's not really you they hate. What they do hate is what they have decided you represent—they hate whatever ugliness in their own lives or selves they have transferred onto you, although they would probably deny that. And the longer it isn't confronted, the longer it will continue; and the more there is to cover up, the more you will be made to look bad rather than for others to admit they've been mistaken. Closed families tend not to give others a chance; they don't check out facts and usually believe what they want regardless of what the person says or does. Denial—and denial of denial—is the only way they know how to fight for their own survival. However, I realize that just explaining and understanding the situation doesn't repair the crippling damage that has been done to you."

"You, for example," she continued, "don't have to believe something is wrong with you just because your parents or family believe it or say it. If others believe negative assumptions about you without giving themselves or you the benefit of a doubt or without confronting the facts, that's because of their sickness. But, you can choose to operate from a different point of view." She was right. I would have to heal myself because the past couldn't be undone, but the explanations and understanding *did* help me begin to forgive.

I knew I had to forgive in order not to pass along harmful feelings—to avoid placing my children in bondage to my own negative emotions. I also knew that I had to empty myself of bad feelings in order to make room to feel forgiving—that the act of confession and repentance leaves open space for new habits of behavior. It is not enough to just intellectually comprehend this.

For example, the Alcoholics Anonymous principles of confessing to a higher power that one is powerless over alcohol, of admitting this to others, and of being open to receive help, all requires action. Consider further, that if we are also powerless to control feelings of abuse and victimization, we will then be an abuser or victim as long as we are beset with negative feelings toward our victim or abuser. It's not enough to just say, "Forgive me," or, "I forgive you." You might ask yourself, "What would I be doing, saying or feeling if I really have forgiven?" It's action and affirmation that breaks the cycle.

I knew this had happened for me when I could recall the former painful incidents without feeling any painful emotion. I knew I had forgiven when I no longer felt the hurt or a desire to hurt back.

Finally, I understood why it had been so difficult for me to teach my children problem solving and coping skills; I had just not learned them myself. Clearly, and excitedly, I could see the basis for parallels and implications between so many losses and rejections; and the self-defeating ways in which I reacted to all of them.

At last, here was a pattern which I could use to examine my feelings and actions. The resulting self-knowledge supplied references and points of direction on which I could base conscious, deliberate changes in thought, beliefs, and behavior.

In their book *Happiness Is a Choice*, (Baker Book House, 1978), Frank Minirth and Paul Meier claim that once we are into adulthood we are the primary source of much of our own unhappiness until we grow in wisdom; once it develops we gain insight into our own self-deceit, happiness then becomes a choice. This can occur by yanking the bad "memory skeletons" out of the closet, cleaning them, and putting them back into the closet. With that in mind, I pulled out a twenty-year-old one marked "First Marriage."

My first husband and I had no idea of what was really in each other's mind; not at the time of our marriage nor anytime afterwards. Barely aware of our own real needs, I believe we married out of loneliness and need rather than mutual, mature love and respect. Habit and duty helped hold the marriage together. We both meant well, but because of our backgrounds (he was the child of an alcoholic parent) we both lacked skills in communication and personal interaction. I was comfortable; I liked being a homemaker, but, I think I was more *alone* during that twenty-year marriage than I have ever been while living alone. I think he was too. That loneliness and frustration resulted in depression for me.

In 1962, two months before David was born, I entered a psychiatric hospital to be treated for prenatal depression and complete physical and mental exhaustion. Pregnancy was not easy for me. Following the birth of Daryl, who nearly died, the doctor told my husband that I was too small to continue having babies. However, Becky's birth, two years later, was much easier. But, with this third pregnancy, my weight soared from 94 to 167 pounds. I had toxemia and varicose veins. I couldn't sleep and could barely walk, but helped move into a new home one week before Christmas (in my sixth month), made the 600 mile trip to and from Iowa at Christmas, and got the older kids settled in a new school after Christmas. I hoped this baby would be a boy because my special little Grandma Miller was dying and I told her I'd name the baby David Ray—Ray because it was her favorite boy's name. I also liked the idea of having another baby to cuddle—but I sure needed some rest first.

My doctor prescribed at least four weeks of rest and daily counseling. At first, the experience was heavenly. I was pampered, complimented, respected and people listened to me. Really listened. There for the first time in my life, a counselor told me that I had the right to respect and affirmation the same as everyone else; that I was just as good as my brothers and two sisters in law (I had already accepted the fact that my mother considered them "her daughters"). I was amazed. It just never occurred to me that I could even begin to measure up to my brothers, or was just as deserving. I always thought they were both so very special and not the awful burden that I was. I began to see myself with different eyes.

He also told me that I was not responsible for all my parents' problems and all my husband's moods. "Your father loses his temper because he lets himself, not because you make him do it," he said. "Your mother shook you till your head hurt when you were little because she chose to, not because you made her do it. Both your parents claim you tell lies, and are mean and bad-mouthed because it's the way they cover up their own actions and guilt in order to protect themselves, not because you are. Your husband pouts and intimidates you because he chooses to and because he gets away with it, not because you make him do it. They are responsible for their own words and actions. Not you."

"But," he continued, "if your husband and parents keep modeling the idea in front of your children that you are an object of contempt and are to blame for everything, your children will eventually see you the same way and will copy the technique of blaming, ignoring and making fun of you. Things will change only when you refuse to believe the worst about yourself and refuse to respond the way you have been. You have a choice just as they have, and are just as responsible for your choice of action as they are for theirs."

What a revelation that was to me. Here I was, thirty years old, and didn't know something that simple. But I learned quickly. I went home from the hospital with a new vocabulary; words and phrases such as, "Do it yourself", "I don't care", and the most unforgivable of all—"No." Sometimes I practiced saying "no" when

I was alone just for the sheer joy of hearing myself.

However, before I went home, my husband decided that four weeks was too long for me to be away from my "wifely duties," and while my doctor was out of town he persuaded a resident physician to use treatment which would enable me to be released earlier. My doctor was furious when he returned to discover that the resident had, although against her better judgment, authorized a series of five electroshock treatments. And I was seven months pregnant! I never even knew what was coming. No one told me. They just got me out of bed one morning, took me into the room, and zap.

On the morning I went home, the resident physician stood in the hospital entry, watching us. Just before leaving the building she 'ad asked me, "Are you sure you want to go home now?" "Yes, she is," my husband replied for me, while I nodded assent. Inside I was screaming, "No-No, not yet! I still don't know what to do—how to act!", but said nothing. At the curb I looked back. She was still watching. I was still silently screaming.

I went home ahead of schedule all right, but shocked into a changed person as well as shocked out of depression. My energy was renewed, and a positive self-image had taken root, but so had a new concern.

I had to take a good look at this man whom I had previously so meekly and willingly served, trusted and respected. Here was a man who was quiet and stoic, but steady, intelligent, industrious, witty, a good provider and usually good natured. I also saw a man who had jeopardized the life of our unborn son by subjecting me to violent treatments that may have caused brain damage to either or both of us, simply in order to keep me at home. (Both David and I were later found to have difficulty with memorization. David's problem showed up when he was learning to read and mine became evident when I was a college student. Although I could still handle concepts, memorization required extra effort.)

Not only did my trust and respect for my husband vanish, it turned into fear. I reacted the only way I knew how—by pretending that everything was fine, and by withdrawing from him emotionally. I *knew* that I had a right to have those feelings but I had left the hospital before my counselor had a chance to help me learn the conversational skills I needed to discuss those feelings. I didn't know what to say to my husband and was afraid to try.

But, my newly found confidence was working in other ways. I

helped develop the church library, taught Bible school, began to visit with neighbors and other women, attended an art class, and took a part-time job. However, the more I gained courage to venture into the world on my own, the more my husband saw that as a threat—a loss of control over me. He reacted with criticism, assumptions and belittling, a technique which, at one time, would have stopped me dead in my tracks. But, not this time; I'd cut my teeth on that stuff.

I chose a different way to react—more independence and passive resistance. This was the beginning of the end of a marriage that might have been saved with proper counseling to develop the knowledge and understanding to face our fears and to welcome positive changes.

He stepped up intimidation with statements such as, "You're getting old and ugly. You aren't as smart as you think you are. You're not an obedient wife any more. Your kids don't love you. No one likes you," and the topper, "If you don't change back like you were, you're going to go crazy or kill yourself, but if you leave I'll make sure you lose the kids." To me, this was proof that my fear of him which began with the shock treatments was indeed justified. He never seemed to realize that by trying to save our marriage with threats and force, he was only destroying it.

One day I told Daryl, our seventeen-year-old son, his dad and I would probably divorce. He said he'd been expecting it and he would be okay. I put the two younger children on a bus to their grandparents in order to protect them from whatever might happen, packed a suitcase, wrote a note, said good-bye to the plants, and walked out. You see, I still had not really changed my usual way of coping; I had just found the courage to do the same thing a different way. I retreated physically, rather than to withdraw emotionally. Although I had learned I could make a choice or decision on my own, I had not learned how to think it through.

As a result, chaos followed. My husband took the children from my relatives and hid them with his relatives until I discovered where they were. They then returned home with him where he changed the locks, got an unlisted phone number, returned the mail I sent the kids, and finally called to tell me that none of them ever wanted to see me again. I couldn't believe that and tried to see David at school but the teacher stopped me on my husband's orders. So, I waited until the next morning. My husband and the older children left David with a baby sitter for ten minutes before he took the bus to school. The baby sitter saw me coming and locked the door. I broke the window with my fist and gathered up David's clothing and the silverware (because that's what I'd seen in the movies). While I loaded the car the baby sitter scooted David out the front door and down the block to the bus stop. When I realized what had happened I jumped in my car, drove to the bus stop, and was able to pull David from the line of waiting children. When in the car, David said, "I can't be with you, Mom. If I go with you Daddy will spank me." He didn't realize he didn't make sense. We returned to Iowa where I enrolled David in school.

Two weeks later my husband again took David, this time from school to his sister's home, where he phoned me to say I'd never see David again. With my parent's help I went to retrieve David a second time. I broke another window with my fist to get into the house, but before we could leave with David my dad hit my husband on the jaw while my mother grabbed David and left. At the custody hearing the judge said, "This woman has been very much maligned and manipulated, and if she is willing to go through that much to get her son she deserves to have him." I got custody of David, but Becky, thoroughly confused by now, chose to stay with her dad.

Neither my husband nor I had the presence of mind or social aplomb to explain our position to ourselves, to each other or the children, so it must have looked to them as if they were suddenly, and for no reason, rejected and abandoned by both parents, as well as at fault for their own predicament. It's a miracle families survive things like this and no wonder so many of them don't. This is why marriage and family counseling or a mediator is so valuable.

I think it was more difficult for our children to accept my position in the divorce. Their father had always been the vocal parent and often absent; his behavior was already unpredictable. But I was always there. I had been the typical "super-mom"; providing rides, money, stylish clothes, a clean house, well-balanced meals, and social and educational opportunities. Even though I might lose my temper with them I was still the available parent.

With their father, and in public, they saw me as pleasant and subservient. I did my crying when I was alone or in the bathroom at night with the door closed so no one could hear me. At the time, it never occurred to me that my husband was also a disturbed adult.

56

Only much later did I recognize as abuse, my husband's attempts to undermine me to the children, to convince me I was worthless and crazy, to force me into unwanted sexual acts, and to try to sabotage or prevent me from having hobbies and friends. I really believed no one should know when I was in pain or confused. I never thought about the irrationality of that; I'd learned long ago to hide my pain for fear of more pain through disapproval. There's just no hurt like being hurt more when you're already in need.

But, if the children hadn't had the image of me as always strong and always nice, it might not have been such a shock to them when I moved out. This action from the consistent parent was a greater betrayal because it wasn't expected. Their protector had deserted them, leaving them at the mercy of what they perceived to be the less dependable parent. It looked as if I had deceived them when my only intent had been to protect them from marital problems which I believed were all due to my own failures.

This has to be a factor as to why older children often seem to turn against the "good" parent—the one who never complained. Our children took my unexpected action as evidence of insincerity and as a personal rejection of themselves and responded by rejecting me. The more they rejected me, the more unsure I became of them and of myself, and withdrew even more.

It's a classic situation and an unscrupulous or grudge-carrying parent can take unfair advantage of this by maligning the absent parent with insinuations, vague remarks, body language (rolling eyes, shrugging shoulders), and/or outright dismissal. It's then easy to plant the sort of suspicion which can destroy a relationship with only a gesture, implication, or insinuation.

Sometimes the parent who appears to withdraw after a divorce mistakenly—but honestly—believes it is in the child's best interest. Possibly out of guilt, or possibly out of misguided concern, they try not to cause any more conflict in the child's life, and unfortunately, that silence may be misinterpreted by the child, or encouraged by the other parent to be seen as "lack of caring."

I once heard this situation compared to the story of King Solomon and the two women who each claimed the same baby as her own. When Solomon suggested dividing the child in half, the real mother was horrified and cried, "Oh, no, let her have him." She was willing to give up her baby rather than see him killed.

Sometimes the parent whose love is the most responsible

meddles the least. That's not the same as the parent or person who refuses to speak, make any contact, never writes or calls, and makes no attempt at all to understand, reconcile or forgive, and all without any explanation. That action, if indeed deliberate, is the cruelest of mental cruelties when directed toward a child, parent or spouse.

The responsible response is not one of total withdrawal or total smothering, but a balance of unconditional love, acceptance and attention—a message which says, "I'll always be here for you no matter how you feel about me or how you treat me," rather than, "I'm on your side only if you accept me and reject him (or her)."

I had married Bill two years after my divorce, while my two teenagers were still in turmoil. I was trying very hard to rectify my relationship with them at the time but with little success. "What can I do?" I wailed to Bill. "Well, you just love 'em, honey," he had answered. "You just love 'em, and wait for them to know it."

Following Bill's comment, I had confronted Daryl, who had suffered the most during childhood from his father's and my anxieties. I had explained to him that it was important to me that he not go through life "dragged down" by crippling memories, and invited him to tell me everything that I'd done or said throughout his life that had hurt or angered him. I wanted to understand how he thought and felt and why. I listened to everything he said without interruption except to affirm or acknowledge, and asked only that he listen to me in return. He did.

I told him, "While I may not be the parent you wanted or needed, that doesn't mean I don't love you. There were things I thought I had to do in order to survive; I may have reacted out of fear or ignorance, but it was never my intent to hurt or deceive any of you. I've never plotted to deprive you of anything or laughed at your pain. Yes, you've suffered in some areas, but if you think about it, you may see that you have profited in others. In any case, it serves no purpose for you to carry endless resentments other than to make yourself bitter."

I explained to him what sort of a mother-son relationship I'd like for us to have if he could or wanted to, and gave him permission to refuse any part or all of it. I didn't mean it was okay to treat me shabbily or disrespectfully (certainly I wanted to know how he was, and to be remembered on Mother's Day). My goal was to offer him unconditional love and acceptance, and his right to accept or refuse it without incriminations, demands or expectations from me.

58

I gave him time to think about it and test me. As a result, our relationship took a major turn and is still healing. The time and risk invested were worth it. During those times just before and after Bill's death, Daryl was more than a son; he was a best friend.

Sometimes, we can clean up those skeletons ourselves and sometimes we need the help of God and others. A counselor-friend guided me through a process of healing of the memories concerning one very painful childhood Christmas-time memory. I recalled I had spied a large tricycle just like the one I wanted under the tree. Thrilled with delight, I ran toward it, but, before I could reach it, my mother stopped me and said, "Maybe that's not for you. (It was, in fact, for my little brother.) This is what Santa left for you," she said, and held out one of my long brown stockings filled with willow tree branches shaped into switches. My father pulled one of the switches out, when, hands behind me, I backed away from my parents and refused to take out the switch and hand it to him myself. When my maternal grandparents arrived later for Christmas dinner, I heard my grandmother ask, "What's wrong with Eleanora? She looks funny and she won't let us touch her." "Oh, you know how spoiled and contrary she is," my mother answered, "She's mad because she didn't like her Christmas present. Don't pay attention to anything she tells you. It's all in her head."

My friend helped me to imagine the scene with a different ending. In this case, we visualized God in human form who stepped in front of my parents, caught their hands, took the switches away from them, and said, "*No! you will not hurt my child!*" We then visualized God holding and comforting my parents as well as myself, because they couldn't have done that unless they were troubled themselves. If I could see God forgive them, then so could I.

Imagery of all kinds is centuries old and has often been believed to have various degrees of power. We have to be thoughtful when using this technique of healing of memories because it is part of a process, not a cure-all for all disorders. But, used this way, coupled with special prayer, it was very helpful to me. I can still remember the Christmas incident in my mind, but can no longer feel the pain in my heart.

With this memory healing, I knew it was time to confront and try to understand my relationship with my parents and brothers. I thought about my parents' background and realized that both of them had been victimized, as well as had my father's parents before him. My grandfather's back was injured at birth (in the 1880s), leaving him physically deformed, and the object of curiosity and ridicule throughout his childhood.

A similar fate affected my grandmother. At age three she lost an eye when her father, in a drunken rage, knocked her into a knitting basket. A few years later she was orphaned and sent to live with a maiden aunt and bachelor uncle who were twins, both unmarried. Already raising one orphaned niece, they didn't want another. My grandmother was young, alone, uneducated, naive, disfigured and unwanted.

In that day, people with disfigurements were often ignored, hidden away, abused or tolerated, rather than taught to overcome their handicap, so both my grandparents were rejected people, filled with anxiety, fear, shame and anger.

My grandmother, a petite, bright, artistic, curly-haired blond, found herself pregnant with my father at age sixteen, with no alternative but to spend the rest of her life in a tiny, four-room farm house. At the time of her death, she could count on her fingers the number of times she had been out of the county. She directed most of her repressed rage, grief and frustration upon my father.

In fact, all my mother had to do to make my father see red was to point out that I resembled his mother. It always worked; he would remember the pain of his childhood beatings and react. Just as my grandparents projected their pent-up rage and emotion onto him, my father projected much of his onto me when it was brought to his attention, and out came the razor strap. Somehow though, even while still a child, I seemed to know in my heart that he was not really angry with me but was striking out at something else.

My mother's home life was quite different from the actively violent atmosphere my father and his brothers experienced. Her family's life style was one of being proper and well-bred to a fault. Most important of all, no one ever *confronted* anyone about anything because that would not make a good impression; it was better to say what sounded right to others. A great deal of approval was bestowed on those who gave lip service, made a good appearance and gushed fine-sounding phrases. You could say anything at all behind someone's back, no matter how untrue, malicious or scandalous it might be, but *never* to their face because "it might hurt their feelings." If at any time an apology was necessary it was important only that the apology be made and accepted on the surface. Any remaining discontent was glossed over. Judgments and opinions were formed from assumptions and by jumping to conclusions rather than from truth or fact. They truly never realized that what they thought to be considerate and proper was actually deadly polite deceit.

While I was still a child, I observed that these relatives were very competitive for attention. At gatherings, they spent a great deal of time arguing over who was the poorest, sickest, had the most (or least) and who knew the most (the winner was usually the one who talked the loudest or longest). Another chunk of time was spent in bashing whoever was too absent or too dead to defend themselves. Once all that was settled people relaxed, enjoyed themselves and could be quite interesting.

To complicate matters, my mother became ill with smallpox at only six weeks of age. The doctor had pronounced her dead when an aunt who was there at the time disagreed and ordered two large basins of water—one hot and one cold. She then dipped the baby into the basins, alternating between the hot and cold water. In a few moments the shock of the extreme temperature exposures began to work, and the baby began to wail. The baby, later to become my mother, had almost been buried alive.

One can look with horror at what nearly happened, but I believe her experience with the basins of water were much like being reborn. God must have considered her very special to have wanted that much for her to live.

She recovered, but the pox left huge red pits on her face where it had not been bathed in the water. These scars faded with time but as a child they caused her great suffering as an object of torment, teasing, ridicule, and shunning by other children. Her own younger sister often joined in the jeering. She was left out of games, called names, chased or avoided. Older kids often threatened to "sell her to the Gypsies", and once tied her to a bridge support while the water was rising. How she must have wished they would fight with one another instead, and longed for a chance to exchange places and be the one with a crowd of followers who would be on "her side" to help her pay them back. Surely, she must have wished her tormentors didn't exist. There is no pain like the pain of not being accepted by one's childhood peers.

My mother's parents were not physically abusive but must

have been embarrassed with this disfigured child who was an object of curiosity. But, either unable or ashamed to admit or express any negative feelings, they overcompensated, unaware of a subtle but strong underlying message that quietly and politely shamed her for being as she was.

Their response to her distress over the teasing was to tell her, "Now, don't say anything back. Just let it go in one ear and out the other. Pretend it doesn't bother you." When she complied, she was told, "Now that's how good girls should act." (What her parents *really* meant was, "Good, now you won't bother *us* with this.) She had to repress justifiable rage to a monstrous degree, rather than learning how to deal with other children and her own handicap.

When her sister romped outside with other children and my mother was left to sit in the windows and watch, her parents (especially her father) gave her pity rather than encouragement and skills to overcome her affliction. When her younger sister received new clothes because she wore them out, my mother got new clothes because her sister did. Her sister received attention from their mother when she laughed and joked; my mother got their mother's attention when she was disruptive, emotional, sick or hurt.

To my mother, pity and material things came to mean love, so she had to devise ways to get them and learned how to use self-pity and material possessions as a way to control others, or to pit family members against one another (especially the women). Unable to consider herself lovable as she was, and unable to reach inward for the self-confidence that makes one feel accepted and comfortable, she had to reach outward —through illness, histronics, or manipulation—to gain the pity and attention she saw as acceptance and evidence of love.

Being shamed for the way you look is much the same as being ashamed for existing. For some people the way out of shame for existing is to no longer exist, such as suicide. Some people deny they have any negative feelings or thoughts. Still others may adapt any method of behavior that either overwhelms people and throws them off guard; or redirects attention *away* from their own "shameful self" *onto* what they *have* or *do*, or, onto others. When a person believes he or she must fight to survive—must always be on guard against being attacked, it's pretty hard to think about anyone but yourself, and is easy to become self-centered, suspicious and subject to panic attacks.

My mother developed a wide variety of diversionary, offensive and defensive tactics, and built an inpenatrable protective armor around herself. But behind it all is still a lonely frightened angry girl child crying, "Please love me. Please let me play too. Please don't hurt me anymore."

My mother erected this defensive armor against an outer world she perceived to be cruel and threatening and against a real inner world she couldn't or wouldn't face. From there, she could survive despite her childhood tormentors. Behind an armor of denial, guilt and paranoia, she could—through transference and projection—recreate a situation and symbolically get back at those phantoms of childhood tormentors by instigating dissension and distrust among very real people, such as family members. Perhaps she fears that if she were to confront this monstrous rage and guilt, it could shatter her armor; that in order to survive, she must disregard scruples and conscience. Also, by transference, perhaps, she could hang on to an unforgiving spirit toward those early tomentors.

Her parents' neglect (whether from ignorance, indifference or intent) to help her develop insight into her own emotional turmoil prevented her from developing a sense of self-worth and pride and of the ability to handle life without strife, rather than learning to focus on her many talents, her love for beautiful things, her stamina, strong spirit and intelligence. Without having been taught to be accountable through self-assessment, her resulting actions and choices risked being based only on her feelings, not objective judgment. Early psychological and mental wounds, when left unattended, can produce a closed person, filled with jealousy and guilt, afraid of growth or change, who represses remorse, or who is possibly subject to paranoia or sociopathic tendencies. This can lead to a crippling selfishness where one never sees one's own guilt.

As long as one fails to forgive, the appetite to avenge will not be satisfied. But, it seems to me, that regardless of the past and its influence or lack of, there should come a time of accountability; when excuses and pity should be put aside. Perhaps the greatest mistake one can make is to be *unwilling* to be open to insight and self-assessment.

It is normal to be angry with the one or ones who shame or ridicule us for having a defect, for not measuring up, or whatever. It is normal to be angry with oneself for having the perceived defect. It is also normal to resent being unable to express those feelings—

whether from inner fear or outward circumstances—and to resent being unable to retaliate against an injustice or oppressor (which happened to my grandparents, parents and myself).

Unfortunately, it is not unusual for one to project that frustration and shame in devious or vindictive ways upon someone who resembles one's self or symbolizes the resented persecutors from the past. After all, that repressed rage has to come out somewhere.

Suppressed rage, from this kind of early teasing, can sink its fangs into a child's spirit, gaining a life-long stranglehold of hate. Sometimes, hate festers until it kills someone; other times, instead of outright killing, it compensates by finding a symbol to deprive of the things that give life. Then, the suppressed rage is compounded by suppressed guilt.

For example, to pretend that I "didn't exist" was symbolic of pretending the childhood tormentors didn't exist. In hurting me or laughing at me, she could at last experience the satisfaction of hurting or laughing at them in return. Perhaps, she imagined what those girls might have felt if she were to die while they were teasing her. I think that's what she may have meant the many times she said to me, "You'll be sorry, someday. When you see me in my casket you'll know you killed me." When I sat alone in my trailer, longing to be included in some family gathering, it was the reversal of her experience. Now, she was part of a crowd and the symbol of her tormentors was left out and alone, watching from the window.

I could understand why I would seem a likely symbol because among other things, I was born in the middle of the coldest winter during the Depression, following an uncomfortable pregnancy; and I was small, as were the threatening females in both my parents' lives. My mother has stated that just hours before I was born, the doctor had told her she was going to have a girl and her response was an emphatic and furious, "Oh, no I'm not!" (She has very definite opinions and does not easily change her mind.) And here I was a girl after all, like her sister and the other little girls who whispered and snickered. This would explain why she so desperately wanted another boy and was so set against having a girl. A girl would be an extension of herself as an unacceptable little girl. Also when a woman feels very strongly against one gender and has bonded in her mind for nine months with the opposite gender, the resulting disappointment could easily become an intense love/hate attitude if she lets it.

Apparently, I was also an eyesore, anemic and skinny because my stomach often hurt too much to eat. My nickname was "Bones"; my nails were chewed to the quick; and I looked like a "peeled onion" my mother would say—not pretty like my brothers.

For most of my life I tried to make things easier for my parents to make up for having been born and for being a girl. My first husband realized I felt a need to make up for this and for what it had cost them to raise me, and he tried to help me by agreeing to use his vacations throughout our twenty-year marriage to help my parents with farm work, remodeling and so on. But, after sixteen years, he called it quits. "Your dad always thanks us for our help, but I am tired of being a free work-horse for your mother with nothing but complaints and fault-finding in return," he said. "Your older brother has never lifted a finger to help me like your dad and your younger brother do—so now it's his turn. I know you hope they will see that you love them, but can't you see—your mother will never give you—or me— credit for the time and income we've given up so she can have the remodeling she wants. She's good to you now because you've got me to do things. Without me, you'd be dirt again and of no use to her."

I heard him but couldn't believe the rapport I had finally achieved with my mother (after becoming a wife and mother myself) wouldn't last, that it was simply because I had a husband and not for myself. Still in the back of my mind was the hope that maybe now, I will be good enough; that my love for my parents would be as pleasing to them as was my brothers' and my two sister's in law.

Dr. Stewart told me that her suicidal and depressed patients suffered as much from feeling that the love they tried to *give* was as futile as the love they wanted to receive. We all need to love someone as well as to be loved. For example, to *accept* a child's love only "on condition" is as harmful as to *give* love only "on condition." When love given is thought to be rejected, it can be interpreted by the giver as just another way of being an unacceptable person, and provides more reason for shame and suicide ideation.

This dysfunctional behavior called scapegoating is as unfair to the favored person as it is to the unfavored. Favored siblings may witness the abuse and believe they must keep it a secret, thereby becoming unwitting accomplices—which in turn, encourages their own denial or disregard of the situation. Some favored siblings (or persons) may find themselves in a position, where, in their own best interest or out of fear of disapproval, they feel they must conspire with the troubled, abusive parent or person. To defend the unfavored would be to risk their own favored position, which is usually rewarded by taking advantage of their greed with gifts, cash or real-estate; or is reinforced with claims of, "you are the only one who cares." The favored are then caught in a double-bind; forced to choose between their conscience and their own need for acceptance.

This shame-based attitude is a major contributor to the dysfunctional family. In this double bind of shame, all are persecutors and all are victims, claims John Bradshaw in *Bradshaw On: The Family*. He says that some parents do to their children what they wish they could have done to their own abusive parents. But with forgiveness, he adds, "we can love our parents as the real wounded people they are."[4]

For me, knowledge is always a key to understanding and forgiving. Knowing my parents' background, I could empathize with the pain they had suffered. That knowledge explained what had happened to me. I could understand, sympathize and make allowances—but it didn't justify anything, excuse it, make it right or stop it from hurting.

Then, as I said, sometimes God takes a hand in the healing of old memories when He knows we are open to His help. It happened when my father was hospitalized for observation and tests regarding a heart problem. One morning he called and asked me to come and see him. "No one else will be here today," he said. Surprised, pleased and curious, I went to see him. He seemed ill at ease but glad to see me. We discussed his condition, the weather, and all the little chores on the farm that he had finished up prior to this hospital stay. "I got the porch trellis fixed but didn't have time to dig up the garden," he said, then fell silent.

Finally I said, "I was really surprised when you called me. Do you realize we've barely talked to each other since I graduated three years ago, sold my trailer, and moved into town?"

"Yeah, I guess that's right," he answered.

"I figured you and Mom disapproved because I went on to graduate school. I know you approve of education because you went to college for a while—and there are nieces and cousins who are getting an education. I never could figure out why you were so opposed to my being in college."

"Well," he said, "it seemed like it should have been the boys—Mom and I gave them everything we could and they didn't get to go." He paused. "We also thought you were too old. But I noticed several other older women in your class." He paused again, started to say something and then stopped. "Is there anything you want to talk about?" he asked, finally. I couldn't believe my ears. He usually stopped me from talking—now he was encouraging me. I decided to take advantage of the chance and took a deep breath. "Yes, there is something I want to ask about. I've never understood why you, Mom, my brother and his family all went out to eat after my graduation ceremony and didn't want me to come along. That really hurt." Sitting there in the hospital room, waiting for him to answer, I could remember the incident as if it had just happened. My parents, brother and his family were standing in the lobby following the ceremony when I joined them, carrying my cap, gown and certificate. We stood around and talked a bit, and then my brother said, "Well, we're going out to eat." He hesitated. "What are you going to do?"

My breath caught in my throat. Then I stuttered, "What do you mean? Are you saying you don't want me to come along?" They looked at one another and finally my mother said, "We figured you had other plans with some of your *special* friends and all."

"No, I don't," I said. "I just assumed I'd go with all of you." More silence. "Well, I guess you can come if you want to," said my brother.

"No-no," I said, tears welling up in my eyes. "I have places I can go and things I can do." "Well, let's go then," someone said briskly, and like a flock of birds, they were off.

I don't know how long I stood there. I had been so excited—so sure I'd done something right in proving I could take care of myself—so sure they would share this triumph with me. But, it had happened again. I had fallen right into the role of rejected Eleanora without the nerve or foresight to have reacted any other way. Why hadn't I laughed it off and gone along anyway? I despised my helplessness and willingness to be so easily manipulated. "When am I ever going to learn?" I asked myself. "Here I am, over forty-five years old and still trying to earn my family's acceptance and approval."

Then suddenly, while still standing in the lobby and watching them head toward the door, I had found myself being drawn farther back into time to a similar feeling of bewilderment and desolation. I was almost five years old and was standing on a wooden porch behind my mother, watching her play with my year-old brother. Just learning to walk, he was toddling around her; they were laughing and hugging each other. I wanted with all my heart to join them but held back, fearing something—I don't know what.

Finally, the desire to show her that I loved her too was so strong that it overcame the great knot of fear in my heart. Looking back, I can see (rather than feel) myself walking forward, putting my arms around her neck, and kissing her cheek. "Oh, no," she yelled, disgustedly, jerking away and upsetting my brother who started to cry. "Watch out, will you—what are you trying to do!"

She shoved me back with her arm, picked up my brother and ran into the house. As the screen door closed I heard her saying, "There, there, now. That was a bad sister. We'll leave her out there and Daddy will spank her when he comes home."

The memory of this intense feeling of despair overwhelmed me again, standing there alone in that huge lobby, watching the door my parents, brother and his family had gone through. I felt erased—blotted out. Tears finally streamed down my face as I sobbed for both the lonely and bewildered little girl and grown woman who stood—stunned and mute—staring at closed doors—their anguish and heartache a monstrous hovering thing.

"Why am I trying so hard to be part of this family?" I wondered. I'm no longer a dependent child. What, other than blood ties, keeps bothering me? "Could it be," I asked myself aloud, "that it's important to me to be accepted *simply because I'm not?*"

As I pondered that question, I felt something snap—and then a tugging and pulling—an insistent moving away—like the shedding of a lifetime. Something tremendous was happening to me and for me. In a new light I saw my belief that "if I changed my attitude toward them they'd change their attitude toward me" begin to fade away; and be replaced with the knowledge that what I needed to do was change my attitude toward *me* —and separate my real needs from what I thought I wanted. With that insight, I was finally, fully released from something and found I really wanted to live my life for me, at last.

There in the hospital room, I recalled those two moments of rejection and the extreme opposite changes they had brought about within me. "But, it wasn't right to leave me there like that," I said aloud to my dad, pulling my mind back into the present.

"I know that now," he answered, thinking I was referring to just graduation. "Mom and some of the others said you didn't want to be with us because you think you are so much smarter and better than the rest of us."

"That just isn't true," I said. "I wanted to be with my family."

"Where did you go?" he asked after a short silence. "I went to Faye's house and helped her." Faye was a friend, who, together with Joyce, had planned a graduation reception for me that afternoon. "Well, we came to that, didn't we?" he asked.

"Yes, you did and I was glad to see all of you," I said. "By the way, do you remember what my aunt said to me there?" He didn't. "Well, as she was leaving, she said 'Now, Eleanora, do you think maybe now you can settle down like a woman your age should, and get a job, maybe in a factory or something?'"

"Oh?" glanced at me sideways. "I didn't know she had actually said that to you." Apparently the subject had been a matter of family discussion, for my dad was surprised not at what she had said but that she'd said it to me.

"In fact," I told him, "I probably would have found a job then if she hadn't said that. I had been undecided about graduate school, but, because of that remark, I enrolled the following week." Suddenly, he was chuckling and his expression surprised me. I had a startling thought that perhaps he had never really disapproved of my spunk after all, maybe he felt pressured to go along with the "family tide." Then I recalled other times when we were alone like this and had talked—when he didn't seem to be mad at me at all as he was when the family was around.

Now, I saw he was inviting me to talk again. I plunged ahead. "You were right when you agreed I shouldn't have been left that way," I said, "but I wouldn't have done a lot of things if it hadn't been for events like that in my life. I've always felt as if you and Mom did all you could to keep me from existing in the minds and lives of the family, and when I protested, you blamed or punished me. I can't help it I was born a girl—I didn't create myself. But, how long and what more will it take to get even with me? Does anyone realize how self-defeating it is to make people "choose sides" against me, my children or anyone for that matter? How long will it be and what will it take for the family to want to understand, reconcile and repair the damage to everyone?

My dad continued to sit quietly and listen—not scolding me as

69

he usually did when I tried to talk. The only sign of concern was the way one hand jerked as it often did when he was unsure of what to say.

Finally, he looked up. "But what could I do?" he blurted out. "I know things have been done and said that weren't right, but, what else could I do?" Having finally gotten up the nerve to speak, he continued in the same forceful tone of voice. "I want you to know I've told Mom all three of you kids are to know all about everything so you can all three work together to take care of her—that all three of you are to be treated *exactly the same*—and she *promised* it will be that way." He had enunciated each word and watched me intently as he spoke—imploring me to understand.

And I did. My father was, by nature, a fair and just man, as well as unassuming, unaffected and unpretentious. It was not in him to be deliberately scheming or conniving. He was telling me he had not willingly compromised those values where I was concerned; that it had not always been his choice to act as he had during family dissension, but he had held back, not knowing what else to do. I realized that, as a parent, he had felt as trapped by fear and ignorance as had I as a parent. He had both protected me and pacified my mother as much as he could. He was also promising me I need not fear I would be disinherited as he and my mother had often threatened; he was saying—promising me—that no one, not myself or my children, would be cheated in anyway. He was assuring me he was still concerned about my welfare. (I recalled the times I had found garden vegetables on my door step and how he had co-signed the loan for my car following my divorce.) These were the best ways he knew to make amends and let me know I was as important to him as my brothers.

With that understanding I experienced a *flooding* reversal of need—from needing to make a point to needing to reassure him it really was okay. He didn't owe me an apology about anything. "Believe me," I said, "I really do understand."

Having both had our say, we sat quietly and made a couple of attempts at small talk. Then I had an idea. "How would you like to talk to Becky?" I asked. "I can call Florida from here and have the call charged to my number." He was delighted. Becky has a way of sparkling at people, especially this grandfather whom she adored.

My dad had always had a special rapport with my daughter; he seemed to be comfortable with her in the way I want to think he would liked to have been with me.

Watching him laugh and chatter on the phone with Becky, it occurred to me that maybe God gives some people the gift of long life because they live it so well; maybe others live on and on because they are being given every chance to repent and make amends. It must be horrible to grow very old, sick and alone, and still be filled with suspicion, self-pity, malice or a vindictive heart, and to die without peace of mind and a clear conscience.

If I added together all the ages of both my parents and myself it would come to over two hundred life years where each had been given a choice—free will—to live life in enjoyment and thanksgiving for each and every family member, or to spend that time in unresolved, unconfronted, misdirected and disabling fears, resentments, self-pity and jealousy over real or imagined injustices. What a waste to not reach out for the former. My father, as best he could, had taken advantage of the opportunity to make amends before it was too late.

"I'm leaving now," I said, interrupting a chuckle over something Becky had said. "Talk as long as you want." He grinned at me and waved. It was the last time I saw him alive.

With that experience—when my father reached out to me that way—the noise in my memory closet settled down. I could sit back and reflect.

I realized that Bill's suicide, my childhood, my first marriage and the current family situation all had a big factor in common. It seemed to me they all contained some form of unresolved abandonment; all deliberate withdrawals from my life by someone I loved and whom I wanted to love me. It's no wonder I missed Bill so much and felt such dispair and anger for so long following his death. Bill had been not only my husband and lover, but the substitute for an entire family. With him, I was noticed—I *belonged*—and I was safe.

Safe, in the sense that Bill's love for me was out of a desire to protect me rather than control me. Fourteen years my senior, I found in Bill the parental nurturing traits of affirmation, encouragement and willingness to accept oneself and others as they are. With him, I experienced the laughter, games and bantering companionship of siblings without every comment being taken as a personal insult. I could fuss over him as I no longer could over my kids—and, he liked my being a girl.

In addition to fun he gave me "loyalty"—not just lip service—

but real loyalty; the kind where I knew that if anyone attacked me verbally in his presence, he would come to my defense. I'd always envied that in other families. With Bill, I experienced the ability to trust that this loyalty would always be there, regardless of his drinking. I knew he wouldn't lie about me or make fun of me.

After his death, I felt as though I'd finally found this kind of family trust and comfort, only to lose it in just a few short years. But that was not the only reason I worked so hard to save the marriage. One of the most valuable insights to come from that time of reflection was to realize I was not a weak, needy person who was asking for or wanting abuse all those years, but rather, I was strong enough to be willing to work for and toward *all* relationships I valued regardless of resistance and untruths.

Grieving over the loss of Bill was easy in some respects compared to grieving over the loss of acceptance. It helped to know I was resolving more than one issue in my life. Bill's death had unleashed this other hidden heartache which may never have had the opportunity to heal otherwise. Together, the two grieving processes were tough but they had to be experienced in order to break the bondage.

Generations of feeling trapped and frustrated, of covering up honest feelings with polite lies, stored-up excuses and misguided shaming—had finally driven one of us to the limit. I could no longer be part of the game of judging one another with assumptions and insinuations, and then of denial of doing it, as others seemed content to do. I had to break free—to confront the shame and the shamers head on—and Bill's suicide had given me the insight and desire to do so. I realized if I had not been forced to deal with my childhood and other losses I would probably not have developed the insight and compassion to begin the ministry of Ray of Hope. In that sense, I could thank God for my past—not for the pain, but for what I had become and could now do because of it.

The entire experience was the catalyst for an incredible soul-searching experience. I spent a great deal of time searching for triggering factors, underlying causes, and the meaning of priorities. Gradually, I realized that I was beginning to perceive things differently—realizing that relationships were too fragile to jeopardize, and time too precious to waste with petty judgments. I learned not to blame people (myself included) for what they didn't know or couldn't do. In my great need, I'd been looking to my earthly family for the total unconditional love and acceptance only my heavenly father could give. I could not expect that from anyone but God, and from God, I had a right to expect it.

It was time to get my expectations and priorities straight concerning others, myself, and God. I had been to hell and back, and I knew where heaven was. Hell was living in the presence of hate, of destructive feelings and forces; heaven was living in the presence of God's love, deliverance and healing. In order for forgiveness to come full circle, I had to give love fully even if it was not given in return. When I felt as free with my family as I did away from them—when I no longer felt as if I had to walk on eggs around them—then I was free of being the underdog.

I learned a great deal about myself. I discovered strengths and resources I didn't know I had and maybe would not have developed otherwise. I had not realized the extent of my mental toughness. Now, I figure I have calluses on the brain. God help the doctor if I ever need brain surgery, or he'll never get through the scar tissue. But that's O.K.—it means that something has pushed me beyond insurmountable odds which could have destroyed another. A lot of that toughness was born in anger (another issue on my list of things to be resolved).

Anger is interesting. A friend once said, "People told me to get angry. So I did, and it just made me mad all the time. I got so sick of the misery I couldn't stand myself." There's a Sanskrit wisdom that says the anger of a good person lasts an instant, that of a meddler for two hours, that of a base man for a day and a night, and that of a great sinner until death. In Ephesians, the Scripture says to be angry, but not to sin. The feeling of anger is normal; the way it's dealt with can hurt oneself or another. That's sin.

Undirected, misdirected, or denied anger can turn into a ball of energy that burns us up inside. We sit and burn until we are a shell of ashes. Then when insight and an idea are at hand, we can do nothing because we are only ashes. Perhaps this is the meaning behind the idea that hate hurts the hater more than it does the hated.

I believe strong denial of anger (or guilt or hatred or whatever) is often evidence of its existence. Better to mobilize all that energy. Summon it. Harness it and direct it toward correcting an injustice. Make it useful in a positive way.

Following Bill's death, I had lost that exuberant innocence one has when life is everything—when death is only a fantasy and you're sure you really are immortal. I had encountered mortality head-on in a sobering but realistic way which caused me to question the sanctity of life. I had lost the will to fight for the sheer fun of it. I wanted that exuberance back. Not to fight for the fun of it—but to fight for the right of it.

With action, the anger dissipated. Resolving guilt wasn't much different. I was just so sick and tired of having it, and that helped. I knew, however, that guilt (like anger) also had to be transformed into something else. John Bunyan said his sense of guilt intensified his pain but eventually became his deliverance. In that sense, guilt can be used to bring about a needed change.

Thank God for good guilt; it leads to growth. When one has the capacity for guilt, it means they also have the ability to feel empathy, compassion, and love and respect for self and others. With proper channeling of guilt, we can promote healing and growth; with denial of any guilt at all (i.e. "Now, don't feel guilty.") we risk the danger of creating a people without conscience—either guileless or ruthless. It's important to make a distinction. The same is true concerning shame. Shame is feeling bad about who we are; guilt is feeling bad about what we do.

It's the wrong perception and wrong use of guilt, such as using it to shame someone, that destroys. When I thought of blaming myself for Bill's suicide I was overwhelmed with a guilt I could not rise above. When I realized I could take responsibility for any or all of my actions (intentional or unintentional) which may have influenced Bill's decision, I experienced a new power and freedom. Many different things and people influenced Bill's decision, but no one thing or person was to blame. Being responsible and taking blame is not the same thing. (I think that's what some people are really trying to say to survivors when, in an effort to offer comfort, they say the suicided person "had a choice.")

Just as it had not been possible to build my first marriage on self-abasement and apology, nor the second one on someone else's strengths, neither could I now build a future for myself unless I stripped away all that fogged my mind and spirit. I had heard it takes an extraordinary person to incorporate the limits of pain and rise above it. I decided I wanted to be extraordinary if I could.

Surely, my children felt as rejected, betrayed and abandoned by the divorce, as I did from what I perceived as parental and family disapproval, scorn and contempt throughout my life, but in their lives as well as mine, the adverse circumstances gave them a strength to be proud of. They each possess a sense of self which is not affected by anything they perceive as bribery, flattery, guilt trips or coercion from anyone, including family, and I respect that even if it separates us at times. They are self-sufficient, tolerant, open-minded survivors, not whiners, complainers or manipulators. True, they got there through adversity and necessity rather than informed guidance, but they got there, scar tissue and all.

I believe we do not exist to the fullest unless we know ourselves. Some people cope by seeking insight; some cope by avoiding it, but without insight, we rob ourselves of honesty. If we are not honest with ourselves, the lies we tell ourselves will go with us into death. I want all my family, my children, and my mother to be free of that. So I continue to involve myself—if only through prayer.

The primary question—what I wanted most for myself—was easy to answer. I wanted that quality of spirit which comes with knowing I have both given to life and taken from it graciously.

I wanted the peace of mind which comes with knowing that one has a destiny—with knowing these things I must do are more important than I am. This destiny is the continuum I leave to my children. It's a cord—a center—something they will carry on, even if they don't realize it.

I knew I had that peace of mind and spirit when I realized something had melted the icy casing within. My earlier resolve to never again allow myself to love anyone so much that I could hurt so much was gone; I was willing to be vulnerable again. I knew I was a new person, operating on a different level of consciousness. I wanted to reach out and hug heaven.

Ray of Hope's ministry is a gift from God—to others through me. This new sense of self-worth was Bill's gift to me; it reflects his faith in me when he said, "Walk tall and hold your head high, little lady. You're a Ross now."

—*Eleanora "Betsy" Ross*

Other Voices Speak

A Journal

In March 1979, my husband killed himself by taking an over-dose of an antidepressant drug for which he had written his own prescription. He was a doctor—a psychiatrist. Although he helped heal the minds of others, he was unable to heal himself.

He had attempted suicide several times before. As a result, I lived in constant fear and was overwhelmed and frustrated by my own helplessness. In 1977, two years before his death, I began to keep a journal where I poured out my feelings of anger, self-pity, love, confusion, and pain. Excerpts from the journal, as I look back at it almost ten years later, show the subtle transitions that took place as I struggled to survive. These bits and pieces tell my story much more honestly than any words I could possibly write today.
SEPTEMBER 1977

My heart stopped when I heard an announcement on the radio that a young man had been killed in a car accident this afternoon. My husband didn't go to work this morning and all day I've been waiting for the call that says he's in the hospital again or even dead. I often feel like this but even more so on those days when he doesn't go to work. Whenever he's home alone, I worry about what he's going to do. It's not an easy way to live. I don't know how to handle it except to keep trying to live the rest of my life as normally as possible. I've almost accepted the fact that it will happen someday but it doesn't make the reality any easier to face.

I may not look it to other people but I think I'm going crazy.
OCTOBER 1977

How do I feel about all of this? And why am I staying? I've reached the point where all I feel when I'm with him is anger and fear. I don't want to go home at night. I dread weekends. I feel totally exhausted all the time. All I want to do is sleep. I can't even cry any more. I scream and scream inside. But I can't leave.

I don't know how much more I can take. I stand it by blocking it all out. My mind throws up barriers to stop the pain he's inflicting

Note: These first two stories, "A Journal" and "Nightmare", point to the need and value of sensitivity and empathy in marital or divorce counseling, especially when suicide is threatened. The primary goal should be to help the couple and family through the crisis before that of saving the marriage.

on me. That's all he gives me these days—pain. I'm constantly waiting for the call that says he's killed himself. I expect to go home some night and find him dead.

NOVEMBER 1978

It seems strange to me. Why do we tiptoe so carefully around each other's feelings, steering clear of each other's emotions? Why do we keep this glass wall between us? Are we both so fragile we can't face each other without fear that one of us will break?

Are you afraid of me? I'm afraid of you. That sounds pretty strange, doesn't it, after more than seven years of marriage? I'm afraid of being swallowed alive by you and yet, no one has ever meant as much to me as you do.

MARCH 1979

He did it. I wasn't there.

MAY 1979

The pain is so great sometimes, it is actually physical. At other times, I feel nothing but an overwhelming numbness. I always thought suicide wasn't the answer for me, but now, at times, I see it as a reasonable alternative for myself. I hurt so badly that I don't think I can stand it. I wonder why I should have to.

MAY 1979

It bothers me a lot that he was alone when he died. I wish he had let me be there. I wish I hadn't called the police so soon. I wish I had held his hand and talked to him first. I want to erase that lost, empty look on his face and make myself believe he achieved what he was looking for. I want to tell him I understand, that I know how much he suffered, and I understand his need to end that suffering. As time goes by, I understand it even more.

JUNE 1979

Mornings are so difficult. I'm more vulnerable then.

JULY 1979

Tonight I'm alone with no place to rush. The last few weeks have been frantic with going places, drinking, partying until all hours, being with people, and forgetting. I know this won't last forever. It's just something I need right now.

NOVEMBER 1979

Weep for your colleagues
who said what a shock, and
scurried back to their labs in search of
a reason.

Weep for your friends
who mourned a lost companion and
slipped back to their lovers, thinking they knew
the reason.
Weep for your family
who strangle themselves with blood ties
never so strongly felt, thinking, of course, they were
the reason.
Weep for me,
facing the world alone in agony,
knowing full well there was
no reason.

NOVEMBER 1979

At times like these I sit and cry, wondering why this had to happen to me. What did I do to deserve this? And I ask him, "Why did you do this to me?" Why did he have to go away and leave me to face this messed-up world by myself? We belong together. I don't know if I can make it alone.

DECEMBER 1979

He was fascinated by the pain
he could inflict on himself.
It is my misfortune
that I understand that fascination.

MARCH 1980

Other people in my world have spent more time building their lives, have had more time to make their lives what they want them to be. I feel envious, impatient, frustrated. I'm building, I guess, but the drive to continue is hard to maintain. Suicide? I don't think so. Death? It seems very inviting right now. I have no reason to live. I look forward to more pain, more confusion, more loneliness.

AUGUST 1980

Maybe after all this time, I'm letting go. Everybody else thinks I already have except for my family and a few very special people who know better. It's a very long, extremely painful process. In some ways, I don't want to let go. But I guess my mind and body, nature, God, whatever, view survival differently.

JUNE 1981

Throughout the ten years I spent with my husband, he seemed to be pursued by demons I could never comprehend. He did not seem so much to feel that he was "unworthy" or "bad," but rather that he was a misfit without a niche in this world. He was afraid others would take something from him. He was angry and frustrated by this power, real or imagined, that others had over him. His depressions were painful and frightening to watch but his occasional, almost manic, highs were exhilarating and drew the people around him into whatever direction he went. My husband played a great part in shaping my adult life and was a man whom I loved and respected. Therefore, one thing I must consider is that his choice was rational and proper for him in his thinking.

JULY 1981

His suicide was the ultimate rejection of me and my efforts to help him. There's also the element of my contribution to his death. I am human. I often was angry when he needed sympathy; cold when he needed my love. I built barriers to protect myself from the pain he caused me. When I could no longer cope, when I needed my own private space, I turned away from him. Now I have to deal with the guilt and learn to accept my own human frailties.

AUGUST 1981

I'm angry. What gave him the right to hurt me, his family, and his friends in this way, when we loved him so much? How dare he! I feel cheated and abused. He made his dreams mine and then snatched them away. Why did he do this?

OCTOBER 1981

All goes well in my life. The house I bought is wonderful. I'm getting A's in school and I honestly believe I have a good chance of getting into graduate school next fall. I have as many dates as a young, single woman could want. My friends call me often to ask me to join in their fun or just to talk. My life seems to have a good balance of fun, work, future plans, even security. So what is missing? I recently took part in the wedding of two friends. I want that. I want it back, that special relationship.

MAY 1984

As of last week, I'm no longer a graduate student! I'm fairly amazed at myself. Five years ago, I said I was going to buy a house and go back for my Master's Degree. I did both! At the time, I had no doubts that I could do either or that I really wanted to do this. My third goal of five years ago? To get remarried or at least to find that close special relationship again. I haven't reached that goal yet. I want to love and be loved. That's simple enough, isn't it?

79

DECEMBER 24, 1984

I've spent the day packing, pitching, sorting, and re-reading some of these old journals and I think it's time to make another addition. It's worth noting that almost all of these writings were done when I was at my lowest. I still remember how I felt when I was writing. I also remember how much better I felt when I was done.

It's been five and one-half years since my husband died. I've worked, gone to graduate school, developed a lot of deep, loving friendships. Next week, I will start a new job in another state.

While reading the old journals, I was struck how often, both before and after my husband's death, I doubted my sanity and wished my life would end. I no longer have doubts about either. I want to live for as long as I can. And I'm sane (well, mostly!) I still get depressed. I get frightened. I get frustrated. But I can deal with it. I can cry about it. I can grit my teeth or punch walls, but I can deal with it. It feels good to know that.

I know there will be more bad times. I will lose people I love and wish I had told them, "I love you." People will hurt me, and I will hurt them. I will feel all of those petty emotions—anger, jealousy, envy, guilt, inadequacy, and more—for which I hate myself. I will feel more insecurity and loneliness. But I also know, even if I can't believe it at the time, that I will survive.

My husband taught me so much about life and death, love and pain. Maybe these seem like negative lessons—experiencing them was. But I'm glad this man was part of my life. He taught me about myself. It's a gift I hope I can pass on. So, if right now, I'm scared and sad about leaving my old life behind, there's still excitement and pride. It may not be easy but it's definitely interesting!   *C.S.*

Nightmare

Several years ago, I was a happily married, young woman with three beautiful children. In January of 1979, my husband moved out after I discovered he was seeing another woman. I filed for divorce even though I was convinced we could reconcile.

Three months later, my life changed forever. During our six years of marriage, Jerry had often talked about suicide but I didn't believe him. He had always been happy and outgoing. Then one day, he changed. He began to harass me by following me everywhere I went. He confronted me at work and shouted at me not to worry about support payments. He said there wouldn't be any. That night he came to our home drunk. Although I knew that something was wrong, I made him leave. I waited until he had time to return home before I called him. When he answered the phone, I realized immediately that he had taken something. I called a friend for help, but by the time our friend reached Jerry, he was dead. He had taken pills, then shot himself.

The coroner refused to let me see him. He felt it would be too much for me. I wish I had seen the body. Although I knew Jerry was dead, for a long time it seemed as though he'd just moved away. I made funeral arrangements in a daze. None of this seemed to be happening. I thought I'd wake up from the nightmare. I didn't.

I didn't sit around and brood for long after Jerry's death because I was afraid I would withdraw too much. I began dating very soon.

The first man I dated reminded everyone of Jerry. It was almost like seeing a ghost. Six weeks later, I asked him to marry me. But three weeks before the wedding, I met another man and broke the engagement. Two weeks later, I was married to Jack.

Jack was twelve years older; an alcoholic. I was going to help him and make our marriage work. My family, who had been very supportive throughout the tragedy, was shocked. Jack not only had married several times before, but there had been an inquiry into his last wife's death before he was acquitted of murdering her. I had put myself into another nightmare. For a year and a half, I put up with the lying, cheating, and, when he threw me against the wall, violence. I felt I had to make this marriage work. Finally, I filed for divorce because I was afraid for my children, not myself. I guess I thought I deserved to be punished for not saving Jerry.

I went for counseling. I couldn't tell the therapist how I felt. I was still numb. He suggested I needed sex therapy and volunteered to be my partner. That was the end of that.

I changed. For the next five years, it was as though someone else was in my body. I seemed to be in a far-off corner, watching, yet unable to understand or change my behavior. I went against everything I had ever believed in. Since I needed to be with men, I would go out with anyone who would treat me like dirt. Danger seemed like a magnet. Normal men were boring to me. I needed excitement which seemed to be the only emotion I could deal with.

81

Eventually, I ended up in singles' bars. They became my evening home but only after my children were in bed. I didn't want them to see me like that. It felt so good to have someone hold me. It made me feel secure—for a while.

My family was terrified for me and my children and suggested counseling again. This therapist told me it was fine to have sex with as many men as I wanted. I knew better—it didn't work. I also was a borderline alcoholic. I knew if I continued this way I'd be lost to everyone I loved, including my children.

I didn't care about myself. Why should I? The only man I had ever loved didn't care about me. He had left me. I couldn't yet release my feelings; I was afraid of them. There were so many different feelings, it was like a time bomb waiting to explode. Anger, frustration, despair, fear, and *pain*! I had no self-respect. It had left with Jerry. He took it from me.

Since men seemed to be the root of my problem, I swore off them. I decided I didn't need *any* man to take care of me or my children. I forced myself to clean the house and spend quality time with my children, but it was hard to be with them because they reminded me of Jerry.

My second husband had drained me financially, but that didn't stop me from spending money that I didn't have. I wrote checks knowing there was no money to cover them. Who cared? It was fun. One day, a policeman knocked on my door, arresting me for writing false checks. I couldn't believe it was happening to me. I had always been a good girl! I was convicted, fined, and placed on probation for a year. Subconsciously, I was glad. I was finally going to be punished for *allowing* Jerry to die.

When I was taken to the probation officer, I was crying for the first time since Jerry had died five years earlier. The officer talked to me and made me see that I had done something terribly wrong. He helped me see myself for what I really was, although I didn't like what I saw. Since the probation officer was someone I could open up to, we became close friends.

I slowly began to find bits and pieces of my old self. The old values began to mean something. Although I was tired and drained emotionally, I began to feel whole again. The part of me that I thought had died with Jerry began to live again. Eventually, my probation was cut to six months.

During this time, a girlfriend introduced me to Dan who was

understanding and supportive. He finally got through to me that I was worthy of having someone *love* me. A year later, we were married. There have been a few problems in our marriage and we are seeing a counselor who has already helped us enormously.

One thing the counselor brought out is that I never grieved over Jerry. A period of about two years was almost blank for me. Only recently have I been slowly remembering bits and pieces of the first couple of years after Jerry died. There was a ghost in my mind, Jerry's ghost. I really had never said good-bye or let him go. The good memories were a safe haven. I could go back to feel *those* emotions and relive those times without the hurt of missing Jerry. In letting go, I finally found peace within myself and I think Jerry has, too. But it was hard to do, very hard and scary.

I thank God my children were too young to realize what was going on. It's funny, but anyone who walked into our home would have thought everything was normal. Maybe I can tell them when they are older. I hope they'll understand.

Being a survivor of suicide is lonely. Few people want to know how you feel. Everyone wants to know the gory details. From my experience, not many counselors or doctors know how to help. It seems that we must help ourselves since no one knows what we go though except those who have been there themselves.   *J.A.*

Janice

On November 1, 1984, my daughter, Janice, died of an overdose. She was a talented young woman with a brilliant mind and a career in pharmacy. Diagnosed as schizophrenic, she had pulled herself back from death and depression many times. Twice, she had been revived from massive overdoses that should have been fatal. The last time, she told her dad, "God must be keeping me alive for something. No one should have lived through what I have done to myself." She called those bad times her "dark hole preceded by gray days." She left this poem on her computer.

> Alone, unseen, burdened by despair
> and answering the inner call,
> I stand at the edge with the wind in my hair,
> ready to jump, yet afraid to fall.
> Sorrow and anguish echo hollow tonight.
> Words won't help your understanding.

Soon briefly, I'll soar like a bird in flight
but seeking surcease in the landing.
Power to choose between death and life
looms awesome as I stand
weighing merits of hell and the daily strife.
Gravity tugs to agree with the plan.
Then primal terror of the great unknown
hauls me back from the abyss;
my days go on 'til the fear is gone—
a sure appointment with the precipice.

Janice Stallman

At first this poem made no sense to me. It was just words put together. When a friend had it framed for me, I hung it by the front door where I could read it often. Each time it would become clearer. One time when I was looking at it, thinking about the meaning, I clearly heard Janice's voice say "It's all right. I'm fine, now." That was very comforting—a great load was lifted from my heart.

Janice was on a life-support system for several hours before she died. Since she was very healthy, the doctors asked us if we would care to donate any of her organs. We agreed and as a result, our daughter holds the record for organ donations. A cousin received the pancreas, two different people each received a kidney, one man received both corneas, her heart went to research, and a section of her skin was grafted to a woman's stomach.

We are constantly being interviewed by television and newspapers. I have to admit that old wounds are reopened each time we are asked to speak about this. I believe that hospitals should have a coordinator to work with donors' families and the recipients. This coordinator could offer information and reassurance, and could arrange for the people to meet if they wanted to. When I think of the recipients of Janice's organs, I think of them as five more members of our own family. I wish I could meet all of them in person.

Marie Stallman, Cedar Rapids, Iowa

Randy

My name is SuAn Richardson. I would like to share with you my experiences with attempted suicide, completed suicide, grief, help received, and my association with a self-help organization.

My life changed drastically in 1977. In April, when my cousin attempted suicide for the second time, I became involved in trying to help her overcome her depression. She finally killed herself three years later on her fourth try. On June 9th, my son Randy's 22nd birthday, his girl friend shot herself in my front yard. On August 23rd, Randy shot himself in my home. All these attempts and the three completed suicides within a few months left me with a trauma that I had to work through in order to put my life back together.

Since my mother is also my best friend, we talked daily on the phone to help fight the stress, anger, loneliness and bewilderment we both felt due to Randy's death. We provided moral support to each other. It's so important to have someone to talk with when depression threatens to set in. Questions like, "Why?" "What if?" and many others always seem to keep coming back to mind. Then you realize that there are no answers because the only person who could answer them is gone.

After nine years, these questions have disappeared but the shock still returns to my mind. Recently, I ran into an old friend of Randy's who didn't know he was gone. The look on his face when I told him really hurt me inside, for both of us. I will always have a void in my life that I can't fill. Randy was my only child. I'll never have another child, nor any grandchildren.

I keep busy with a job, my church choir, and Sunday School. Working at a college switchboard brings me into contact with young people every day. My mother works with children at the Cerebral Palsy Center. These activities help both of us live a more complete and fulfilling life.

I'm now interested in working with other people who have been through the same trauma and shock. These people need to talk to someone who really understands their despair, who will not be criticizing as they can tell their honest feelings. Some of my help came from members of my church and people at work. Although these people hadn't experienced a suicide in their own families, they were interested in me and listened when I needed to talk.

I was aware of Randy's feelings of devastation after his friend's suicide. But since I hadn't dealt with this type of death before, he knew I didn't have the same feelings he had or the understanding he needed and desired. When we talked, I tried to understand the hurt he was going through but somehow I failed to comprehend the depth of his loss. How sad for someone so in need of help and understanding not to find it.

Since I lacked this knowledge, I failed to help my son. After his death, I wanted to share what I had learned with others. I discovered that Ray of Hope wanted to start a chapter in Joplin, Missouri, and I became its president. This group gives me a chance to reach out and let people know we care and are available anytime they want to contact us. The meetings help us to understand that what we are feeling is normal.

Since our first brochures were sent out, I have been invited to speak to church youth groups, and to Sunday school and high school classes. These talks are focused on ways to prevent suicides and on helping people understand where the suicide survivor is coming from. Good luck and always look upward and onward to better days ahead.   *SuAn Richardson, Joplin, Missouri*

Danny

On January 3, 1981, my beloved son Danny killed himself. One week before his 25th birthday. I was deeply shocked and ashamed. My greatest need was to talk about Danny and find a reason for his untimely death. But I was alone in my grief because my friends seemed to be uncomfortable with me.

After checking around, I discovered "Ray of Hope." This organization saved my life because at last, I could share my grief with people who had experienced the same emotions. I was not alone anymore. After about a year and a half, I was able not only to talk about my feelings but to be a good listener and help others overcome some of their emotional scars.

It has been more than six years since Danny died. I'm handling my emotions now and have control over my life. I'm not ashamed to say, "My son died by suicide." I still love him. Thank you, Ray of Hope, for saving my life and helping me to be normal again. Thanks also for enabling me to help others help themselves by listening to them.   *Carolyn Trautner, Sperry, Iowa*

Legacy

On a bright Monday morning, I followed my sister, Peg, into the garage for my ride to school. But as I entered the garage, I stopped. Something was wrong. Seconds passed before I recognized what I was staring at—a vacuum cleaner hose stretching from the exhaust pipe of the station wagon to the window on the driver's side. I approached the car. My mother lay inside. She was bundled in her red corduroy winter coat. She looked as if she were sleeping. I shouted and began pulling at the door. It wouldn't open. My sister rushed over and yanked the hose from the window. The door opened. In all the noise and confusion, my mother never stirred.

I was ten when my mother committed suicide. Seventeen years have passed, and although I vividly recall the events leading up to the discovery of her body, much of what happened in the ensuing hours and days seems lost or obscure. I remember meeting my father in the hall on his way to meet the ambulance. We hugged each other, wordless. Later that morning, I overheard him being interviewed by a state trooper and I was astonished to hear that my mother had received psychiatric care several years earlier. The trooper then asked if my mother had done or said anything the previous night to indicate she planned to commit suicide. I remember only that she had seemed unusually happy and serene.

She was buried two days later in a small cemetery near our home. A year later, my father remarried and we moved to another section of the city. He has not spoken of my mother since.

My mother was an attractive, energetic woman in her mid-forties, with prematurely gray hair and candid blue eyes. She was passionately devoted to her family and, like many women of her generation, she defined her accomplishments according to her duties as mother, wife, and homemaker.

My own recollections of her are based more on youthful impressions than understanding. From relatives and from my older sister, I learned that the last years of my mother's life were increasingly marked by change.

During the previous five years, she'd had two surgeries. A doctor told her she was in danger of developing cancer. My father, an ambitious man, was promoted to head a new division for his company. The pressures of his new job made him withdrawn and demanding. Finally, with each passing day, my mother saw her children growing up and away from her.

Although embarrassed by her lack of education, she joined a hospital volunteer service. When she was elected vice-president in a short time, it was confirmation that her talents compared well with those of college-educated women. As she became more assertive, she got into arguments with my father. I believe she began to sense a growing estrangement.

She also discovered that her relationships with women on the board were changing. Some of them resented her, and my mother complained that she was being betrayed by her friends. Less than a year after winning the vice-presidency, she decided to resign.

She died the night before she was to deliver her resignation speech. That same evening, a family argument had particularly upset her. A few hours later, however, she seemed calm. In Peg's last memory of mother alive, she is sitting on a couch in the family room watching TV. She holds a small, smooth stone in one hand and rubs it with her thumb. She calls it her "worry" stone.

Words cannot convey the shock, the disbelief, the numb emptiness caused by my mother's suicide. In the weeks that followed, my family adjusted and our lives took on a more normal rhythm; but we had subtly undergone a far-reaching change.

Peg had recurring dreams where she could not find our mother. I developed a fear of dark windows, and for months was unable to stay in a room at night unless the shades or curtains were drawn.

Years later, Peg and I discovered that we still retraced the events of the night my mother died to see if there was some way we could have prevented her suicide. We felt as if we had failed in some vital, unspoken responsibility. Yet, we also felt this responsibility extended to other members of the family. "I blamed myself and everybody else for not being there when Mom needed us," Peg said.

Peg's guilt was heavier because of the relief she felt. "For several months," she said, "Mom had been confiding in me and I guess I felt that she put a burden on me that I really didn't want. I got tired of being a sounding board."

Many relatives and friends were deeply upset by my mother's self-inflicted death, and in the next few weeks they provided constant solace for my family. Within months, however, my mother's name was dropped from all family conversation. During a recent conversation, one relative who was particularly close to my mother told me that it was the first time in seventeen years he had spoken of her to another family member.

News of the suicide appeared in our city's newspapers. Peg recalls the reaction of her co-workers the following week. "About halfway through the day, a woman told me that everyone at work had been very nervous about seeing me again. She said that I seemed the same as ever and thanked me because it made them feel a lot better."

Back in school, I recall a classmate telling me that her mother had seen me in the parking lot the day before and identified me as "the boy who caused his mother to kill herself."

To this day, even casual social questions about my family summon an ongoing debate in me over how much I should tell. I could be evasive, but somehow I resent this feeling that I should hide part of my past. Then, too, I loved my mother and was proud of her and to refrain from talking about her seems like an act of betrayal. But explaining to a stranger, or even a friend, that my mother died of suicide has its social consequences—the very least of them is an embarrassing silence.

For me, the one most enduring part of this legacy stems from a single question: Why? I doubt that I will ever fully understand why my mother chose to kill herself. I ask the question more from concern for my future than curiosity about my past. Simply, I wonder whether I carry a seed of her despair.

I chose to write my story because I hoped that by talking with others about my mother, I might learn more about her and how she influenced my life. It seemed like a long shot but it worked.

I came across a short note she wrote my father the night she died. The tone of the note, sad and self-critical, spoke clearly. Through the police, I learned that my mother had switched off the ignition before she died. They inferred she had changed her mind about dying but was too overcome by the fumes to recover.

I have a better understanding now of how tortured my mother really was and how difficult it must have been for her to leave us. After seventeen years, the sting of my mother's death is still sharp. But because of what I know now, it hurts a little less.   *G.M.*

My Sis

We were pulling our Ford Clubwagon into the farm lane when we noticed the long black hearse parked by a shed. We knew that this time, her fourth suicide attempt, my only sister, my best friend, was dead. The newspaper reported that her body was recovered from a farm pond—her death was ruled a suicide.

At her funeral I played the organ—it was the last gift I thought I could give her. The Father said it was the hardest funeral he'd officiated in all the years of his priesthood. A loving and creative lector suggested that the Prayers of the Faithful be a prayer from her husband, from each of her eight children, her brother and sister:

Lector: Lord, we know you hear the heart's cry. Hear now
            the cries of the hearts of her family.
My prayer: That as a family and a community we may all be
            one, Father, as you and the Son are one.
My brother's prayer: I thank you, Father, that you gave my sis
            to me. She was the best in the world. I ask that she
            may truly know that I felt that way.

I always put my sis on a pedestal as being the strong one. She started out her married life with a hot plate in a second-story apartment with no running water. She gave birth to ten children, eight of whom survived infancy. When one of the babies died, she had to return a stroller to the store where my brother and I had purchased it. Another time she had to give written permission for possible leg amputation following a farm accident.

I was at her side almost every day because I was a nursing student at the time. She didn't know how she'd have made it if I hadn't been there, so we cared for one another. When my first-born son lived and hers didn't, I felt guilty because mine lived. I always thought if something happened to me she'd be the one I'd trust to help with our two brain-injured sons who came along later.

Before her suicide, she had undergone almost four months of treatment at a psychiatric unit with the usual locked doors, drug and talk therapy, and shock treatments. Why, oh why, hadn't I forced her or at least been much more persuasive in getting her to a psychotherapist eighteen months earlier? I've told the psycho-therapist I'm with now that if only my sis had been sitting here with him about two years ago, she might be alive today.

I didn't realize until I read through my daily diary that hints had been there all along:

"She thought of ending it all."

"Doesn't know if she can take depression any more."

"She looks awful—so worried about her."

I knew mornings were her worst time of day; I gave her money for long-distance calls or told her to call me anytime, collect.

It has been six months since her death. I still can't look at her picture. I've had four months of psychotherapy and get angry at myself because I'm not getting better faster. Why not? Everyone's life has tragedy.

I try to keep busy. Shortly after her death I asked my brother for just one favor and that was to fly me out west in his airplane to see mom's relatives who were unable to come to the funeral. Their hugs, conversation, and promises of prayer were so welcome.

I went on an unscheduled retreat and had an appointment with a nun who has a healing ministry—visited a counselor priest in Davenport—listened to *Healing the Family Tree* tapes—read several of C. S. Lewis' books. My days off from work have to be structured to the hour. Organ playing is therapeutic. My parish priest is not afraid to give me a hug. My husband, children, several cousins, and one niece in particular have been so supportive. A few select friends have given me an invitation to call or talk anytime.

Like so many other survivors, I questioned the possibility of genetic influence. In a way, I hoped it was true, as that would relieve some of the guilt.

I believe my sister killed herself because she thought death was preferable to going back to the psych ward.

God? He's been very close, and very far. Since my sister's death, I can't seem to find Him, and just go through the motions. When she first started needing help, I'd yell at God for answers, then turn on a TV program and it would be pertaining to the question I had, or a friend would share some confidential information of her life. That provided answers to questions. I had always felt close to God and felt He did communicate with me—not so since her death. I don't know anymore how God communicates with people.

Me? I've had much psychotherapy because of depression. I've only found two ways to beat depression: try to help others (I get that through my profession); keep my mind busy (that may be my only salvation now). It has worked in the past, but I'm older. Maybe one course at a time and try for a Master's. Just can't bear to look down the corridor of years without you, Sis. Thirty-five plus years of breakfast together almost every Sunday between masses—a time to sum up the week and support each other. Thank God, I had you for fifty-eight years.   *Verabeth Bricker, Victor, Iowa*

Gary

I still can't write about Gary's death. It's been eight years. If I delve into this, I'll have to spend a few days away from work. I still get crying jags and it takes too much out of me to go into this in depth. I feel like someone came up to me, tore out my heart, walked away with it, and I'm still just standing here.

The "loss" and "missing" are just as bad as seven years ago. The "time that heals" only means I don't think about my son as much as I did those first years. I understand why he left us. He never knew how much he was loved. So sad. I feel like we always walk in the shadows. "A merry heart doeth good like a medicine: but a broken spirit drieth the bones" (Proverbs 17:22). My spirit inside is broken but I put on my "merry mask" to get through these days. It's all I can do.   *S.D.*

Other Voices

My father killed himself two years ago. My mom and I have good days, but the pain is always there. She cries so much. I try not to say anything to her about it, because I don't want to make her cry more. But I hurt, too. It's sure hard to know what to do.   *Mike*

I lost my oldest sister to suicide two years ago. I thought I'd forget, but it hurts more as time goes by. I wish she could have known how much I loved her. I wish I had told her. Maybe she wouldn't have done it.   *Nicky*

When my daughter killed herself, I took it in stride. Six months later, I could take it in stride. One year later, I still took it in stride. Now, two years later, I can't take it.   *Frank*

She was my childhood playmate, my best friend. I knew she was sensitive...she talked a lot about death. She said no one would care or miss her, except me. Her parents always laughed at her when she said she was going to do it. They would say, "Go ahead," or, "You're a coward. You won't do it." But she did. It was I who knew something was wrong. I knocked, and there was no answer, so I broke into her apartment and found her. Now her parents say it was my fault because I was a bad influence. I miss her so much and wish her family and I could be friends. I might find something of her that way and I could tell them such neat things about her. Why don't they want to know?   *Ginny*

The last thing my daughter-in-law did in her life was to tell me that she was going to kill herself. The last thing I did in her life was to let her. I didn't believe her. How can I forget that?   *Helen*

After two years of agonizing over my husband's suicide, I still have only negative thoughts. Because he was a prominent citizen, we kept the circumstances of his death secret. Now I have no one to whom I can honestly expose my feelings. My four children cut me off completely when I try to talk about their father. We used to be so close, but now I feel that they are estranged and alone. I need their support and love more now than I ever have or will. They are breaking my heart. I don't want to go on without my husband and children. I think he may have been right in what he did. Is my solution to be the same? Suicide?   *Iva*
(Note: shortly after writing this note, Iva, age 80, killed herself.)

It's been three years since my wife killed herself. She was schizophrenic. My friends have been very supportive as I try to raise our three little girls by myself. My wife's relatives are a different matter. They tried to convince the girls that it was all my fault. When I was hospitalized several months after her death, they tried to gain custody of my children. At first, I made sure my kids visited my wife's relatives but now I'm afraid to let them contact their grandparents, aunts and uncles. They don't understand and get upset with me. They miss their grandparents. What am I to do? Why does this hell have to be?   *John*

My twin brother killed himself four years ago. None of us have been the same since. The devastation we experienced has been unbelievable. My mother and father were very proud and social. Now mom stays home and dad is always gone. They don't talk to each other. She talks to me, though, and I try to tell her to seek help, but she says she'll be O.K. I don't think so. I worry about her, but

I don't know what to do. I don't like to say it but I think my parents are ruining my life. *Kate*

My husband shot himself in front of us while I held our three-year-old in my arms. My son has nightmares and wakes up screaming. I'm afraid it will affect his entire life. My husband meant to hurt me, but he has hurt our child more. Sometimes I hate him. *Lynn*

I knew for a long time before my husband's suicide that he would some day do it. He was a brilliant professional man, but often lost work and his feeling of self-respect because of frequent debilitating depressions followed by long periods of heavy medication. Neither of us believes in life after death, salvation, sin, or that sort of thing, so I do not worry about forgiveness or being reunited. He did what he had to do. It's over, it's all blackness; he's gone, it's not my fault, and that's it. *S.D.*

After my husband killed himself, my mother was always watching me. I thought she was worried about me and that pleased me, because my parents had been very rejecting and emotionally abusive when I was little. Even as a grown woman, I could never please them. Then one day I overheard her tell my brother that she thought that I was "going to do it too, very soon." There was no mistaking the excitement in her voice. She was hoping I would! That's when I made up my mind to live no matter what. *Marilyn*

94

Not So Unusual Experiences

Dreams and visions—hearing the voices of the deceased, or feeling or seeing their presence—are things some survivors dread, others hope for. Many people yearn to talk about such experiences, but feel uncomfortable about it. In the Ray of Hope support groups we have found it can be comforting and healing when one is able to share such incidents. Who can tell if these things really occur or if they are only in the mind of the bereaved?

Maybe it doesn't matter. Perhaps the most important benefit for the survivors is that often their questions about a suicided person's state of grace or spiritual existence are answered. These experiences can also be an important step in helping to resolve feelings of guilt. Survivors of suicide sometimes worry that their actions or words may have influenced the deceased person's decision to kill himself or herself. They also ponder whether death brought the deceased person his or her desired relief from pain, fear, or hopelessness. "If only I knew that ____ is at peace now," countless people have said. Dreams and visions may help provide answers and peace of mind. In the following stories, survivors share their not-so-unusual experiences.

Help Me Come Back

My son, Kurt, was dead. The police, an ambulance, and the coroner were coming. It was one month after the best vacation we'd ever had, just two weeks after his fourteenth birthday. He lay in his room with a bullet wound in his head. As I ran outside to move our pickup and make room for the ambulance, I "heard" Kurt crying and "saw" him repeatedly trying to grasp me and hold on to me while he was running alongside me. "Mom, I'm sorry, I didn't mean to," I heard or felt him say. "I want to come back. Please help me come back." Half-thinking, half-speaking, I replied, "You can't, Kurt. It's been too long. Your body is too broken. You will have to go. I love you." Then he disappeared.

Periodically, until the funeral and even a few times afterward, we could sense Kurt's presence—a form near us but seldom trying to communicate. Finally, I had a dream in which I saw him wave at me before he faded away with a group of my dead relatives. After that, I didn't feel or sense his presence in this particular way again.

95

In other dreams, he assured me it was fun where he was and asked me to please not grieve so much so he could move on in peace.

R.S.

Comforted

Our daughter Janice killed herself November 1, 1984. Tormented by schizophrenia, her mood swings were difficult for all of us, but she always knew we loved her. I missed her desperately and prayed that she was free of pain at last. The following Christmas, I moved her photograph from its usual place so that we could still see it after putting up the tree. During the night, something awakened me. I got up and wandered through the house. When I went into the living room, a single beam of moonlight was coming through a windowpane in the front door. It shone directly on Janice's picture, which glowed like a neon sign. I knew Janice was there and that she was telling me she was all right. I was comforted.

Marie Stallman

The Visit

It was a beautiful day in September 1978, the first day of school. My sister had gone shopping and had asked me to go next door to her house to meet her five-year-old daughter (my niece) when she came home from school. As my niece skipped up the walk ahead of me I saw a man in the house open the door for her and let her in. I thought I was crazy because it was my brother-in-law (her father) who had been dead for four months.

I hesitated, then quickly followed her. Since the door was open, I could hear a conversation going on upstairs.

"Who are you talking to?" I called to her.

"My daddy!" came her happy voice.

My heart started to race. "What are you talking about?"

"School."

My heart was pounding so hard that I couldn't move. Trying to keep a calm voice, I said, "When you are finished, please meet me at my house."

"O.K., but first Daddy is going to read me a story."

I wondered if I should intrude, then decided against it and returned home. A half-hour later, my niece came in to tell me she was going to play with her friends. I asked her if she had enjoyed the story. She smiled, said" yes" and ran off to play.

I felt very uncomfortable. It was strange seeing a person open the door who had been dead for four months, but I did. My niece confirmed it.

Months later, I mentioned the story to my other sister. She looked at me and then told me that she had also seen my brother-in-law but hadn't told anyone because she didn't think anyone would believe her.

Eight years later, when my niece was thirteen, the children in the family were asking whether spirits existed, etc. I told them I believed they did. One niece said, "I don't know if I believe that." I told them about the time I saw my brother-in-law open the door and asked my other niece, "Do you remember when your father opened the door, talked to you and read you a story?"

"Yes."

"Well, he was a spirit," I explained.

"But that was my father!"

"He had died four months before."

She looked at me and became very quiet. I wondered if she would ever tell of that event again.

I believe there is another level after death. Children come in contact with it. Be open to the stories they share. Most of them will tell you of these happenings if you give them the chance. You may receive the gift of sharing in their experience.   *JoAnn Mecca*

Permission to Let Go

Several weeks after my wife killed herself, I could feel a heavy, sad presence from time to time. The circumstances of her suicide indicated that she had tried to reach the phone to call for help at the last minute. I thought about that a lot. Sometimes, it helped to know that she had not wanted to leave me. But at other times, when I missed her so desperately, I felt as if some cruel trick had been played on both of us—causing us pain and anguish. Often, I would cry out, "Why didn't you try harder to save yourself? It's wrong for you to have died that way!"

One night, I awoke to see a glowing light in my bedroom. In this light, I could clearly see the outline of my wife's head and shoulders. I could sense her intense desire to "break through," as if she were struggling to be alive again. At first, I was frightened, but I wanted to help her feel better and began talking to her. I told her

97

to stop being so sad. I guess I gave us both permission to let go. I never felt that sad, anxious presence again.   *L.W.*

Doing What He Must Do

My husband had walked out on an earlier marriage leaving behind three small children. During the year after he left, one child died in its crib and another was killed in an accident. He became increasingly tormented with guilt over this in the months before his suicide. "I know God has forgiven me," he would way, "but how can those babies know how sorry I am I wasn't there for them?"

After he took his life, I was deeply troubled about his soul. I believed that suicide is against God's divine will, but I knew my husband had trusted in God. I read the Bible and talked with many people, but the doubt and questions persisted. Finally, I told God, "You're going to have to answer this one for me."

That night, I seemed to be awakened by a tall figure at the foot of my bed, wearing a flowing white robe with wide purple trim on the hood, sleeves and hem. I couldn't see the face but I knew it was female. At first I was frightened, but I was immediately enveloped in a warmth and love too encompassing to explain. Knowing that I was calmed, she raised her arm and pointed toward the wall across the room. I didn't want to look away from her but she insisted so gently that I complied. I saw a beautiful rolling meadow, bathed in golden sunlight, covered with tiny bright flowers. I saw my husband walking toward me, up over a small hill. Each of his hands held onto the hand of a small child dancing along beside him. He smiled and somehow conveyed to me that he was happy and doing what he must do. Then my room was dark again and the figures were gone.   *C.M.*

Part II
Growing Through Grief

Dear Survivor: A Letter to You

Dear Survivor:

It is said that death is a part of life, that it is the other side of birth. I believe that death can also give meaning to life, a meaning that may escape you now while your grief is fresh and raw, but which may someday bring a special quality of peace to your spirit.

As terrible as your loss seems now, you will survive it even though that may now seem unbelievable. Once that happens, you will have touched upon a new and incredible inner strength.

But for now, you may be a mixture of thoughts and feelings. Despair, longing, anger, guilt, frustration, questions, and even understanding, tumble over each other, striving for but not quite reaching comprehensible sense and shape. You seek relief—you need to heal. It is a journey and you must work at it.

And so—*cry*. The pain is real but the tears are healing. Often we must struggle through an emotion to find the relief beyond.

And so—*talk*. Talk to each other about your loss and pain. Don't hide or deny real feelings. Tell others that you need them. Talk, for the more you deny something or address it in silence, the more destructive power it can claim over you.

And so—*search*. Over and over, you will ask "Why?" It is a question you *must* ask. Although you may never learn "why," realize that it is still important to wrestle with the "why" question for a time. Eventually, you will be content to give up the search. When you can willingly let go of the need to question "Why?" it will lose its hold over you. But it will take time.

And so—*speak*. Speak as often and freely of your lost loved one as you need to. He or she will always be a part of you. Not to speak of the deceased denies his or her existence—to speak of the deceased affirms his or her life. Believe that in time, the pain of loss fades and is replaced by precious memories to be shared.

And so—*grieve*. This time of sorrow can be used to draw a family together—or pull it apart. You may be one who needs to feel and express guilt so that eventually you will gain a more balanced view of your actual degree of responsibility. You may need to give yourself permission to feel and express anger even though you think it is inappropriate.

And so—*grow*. We know we cannot control all that happens to us, but we can control how we choose to respond. We can choose to be destroyed by an experience or we can choose to overcome and survive it. When we choose to grieve constructively and creatively, we come to value life with a new awareness.

And so—*become*. Become the most you can become. Enter into a new dimension of self-identity and self-dependence as you come to love others more fully and unconditionally. In letting go of love, we give it the freedom to return to us. Become all that your loved one's death has freed you to become.

And so—*accept*. Accept that in some strange way, his or her death may enable you to reach out with a new understanding, offering a new dimension of love to others.

I believe in a loving God who is with us, offering strength, guidance and solace as we struggle with our anguish. I believe that as we regain balance and meaning in our shattered lives, we can come to see that death can indeed bring a new meaning to life. This is my prayer for you.

Eleanora "Betsy" Ross © 1983

100

After-Suicide Grief

"As soon as a suicide occurs, the surviving group has lost an inalienable right to live an unstigmatized life."
                                                    Dr. Edwin Shneidman

Several years ago, my father was hospitalized with a heart attack. After each of us had been in to see him, my family gathered in the hallway outside his room. A nurse then ushered us into a small comfortable waiting room and the doctor arrived a few minutes later. He knelt beside my mother, took her hand in his, and gently told her that her husband, and our father, was gone. He answered our questions, and then discreetly left the room.

We were given time to cry and hold each other before we were allowed to see my father again. A curtain separated the cubicle from the rest of the unit. Bustling staff members were out of sight, and the equipment had been removed. A spiritual quality filled the quiet room. No longer the mask of pain we'd seen earlier, my father's face was relaxed, serene, and peaceful. We could touch or kiss him—again in respectful privacy.

At home, neighbors greeted us with condolences, food, and offers of assistance. Someone called the pastor for us. We were allowed to grieve. This cushion of family and community protection and understanding softened our dreadful shock, pain and sadness. Throughout those days, everyone knew what to do as though we had rehearsed the scene. Together, we made funeral arrangements. Each of us contributed, each had a part. Knowing our role was comforting.

* * *

At about the same time, in another state, a widow (Mrs. A.) tried to open her front door after returning from a bridge game. She had left the door unlocked because her recently divorced son was now living with her, and was working around the house that day. When she entered the dim hallway, she discovered that the huge sliding doors to the living room were closed. She had always left them open so the sunlight from the bay windows could also light up the hall and stairway. Puzzled, Mrs. A. moved through the equally dim parlor to the dining room, opening yet another set of doors that should not have been closed. Finally, she stood before the door of the sun porch which her son was remodeling into a den.

101

Suddenly, she knew what she would find.

A double-barreled shotgun lay by his body. Blood and pieces of hair and flesh covered the sun-splashed walls. One eye hung next to what had been her son's ear. She screamed. And screamed.

Later, police cars and flashing lights drew attention to her home. A policeman asked personal questions. She wasn't sure he believed her. Reporters arrived and took photos of her son's uncovered, disfigured body. Strangers and neighbors were standing on the flower beds in order to peer through the sun-porch windows. Others walked in the front door and wandered through her home. Long after her son's body was gone, a crowd lingered outside, whispering and pointing.

Having run out of screams, Mrs. A. simply sat and wondered why all the doors had been closed.

Relatives asked one another: "What do we do now? How do we handle this?"

"I don't know," each answered after a while.

"I guess it's best to leave her alone and not bother her," someone finally observed, breaking the embarrassed silence. Two women headed for the sun porch to clean it up.

"Better make arrangements," said one of the men, picking up the phone. "Let's get this over with as quickly and quietly as possible."

* * *

A mother, Mrs. B., and her three young children, chatting and laughing about the movie they had just seen so "Daddy can have some peace and quiet" had just returned home.

"Mom, come quick!" yelled her ten-year-old son.

Dropping her purse, she ran. Her son was staring into the laundry room. She stopped short at the door. The other children gathered around her. Stupefied, they gazed up at the body hanging from the ceiling.

"Mom, what are you going to do?" a child asked.

Mrs. B. stood rooted to the spot. The baby was crawling at her feet. She couldn't think.

Finally, she stammered, "I don't know. We can't do anything right now. Daddy's dead. I guess we might as well go to bed. I'll think of what to do later."

Dazed and numb with shock, she put the children to bed, put

on her nightgown and lay down. After a moment, she got up. She went back to the utility room door and stood there until dawn before walking to the phone.

For weeks, Mrs. B. sat in a hospital room, seldom moving, silent. Relatives cared for the children. When she finally returned home, her neighbors shunned the woman who had gone to bed when her husband killed himself. Except for one. One neighbor asked her if it was true that a man has an orgasm when he hangs himself. Mrs. B. and her children moved away.

* * *

With the "normal" or "natural" death of my father, our family was given gentle answers in response to our questions; Mrs. A. and Mrs. B. were subjected to personal and/or embarrassing questions. We were given community support; they were isolated. The hospital staff respected our privacy to be alone together and also in the room with my father; Mrs. B.'s privacy was rudely invaded. Our family was given respect and reassurance; Mrs. A. and Mrs. B. were the objects of gossip or openly ignored. People were not at a loss with words to comfort my family; there was nothing to say to Mrs. A. and Mrs. B. There was concern for our comfort as the bereaved family; the focus of attention for Mrs. A. and Mrs. B. was the act of suicide. Our roles as grievers were defined—the roles for Mrs. A. and Mrs. B. were not. Our family was brought together; their families were pulled apart.

* * *

Death by suicide is like no other form of death. From the beginning, survivors may be suspected of foul play while authorities determine whether the death was a suicide, an accident, or murder. Policemen, coroners, news media, and insurance investigators haunt the family members with questions and inferences. The family's privacy is invaded and violated rather than respected and protected. Curiosity and speculation replace sympathy and understanding.

In the case of a non-suicide death, people know how to respond and react. After-suicide survivors have no guidelines for dealing with the nature of this death. Unable to give in to the natural and accepted reactions of shock and loss, they may form defenses in those first few hours that adversely affect their entire grief and resolution process.

In addition, survivors are often considered in some way responsible for the suicide. Death by suicide is more than a loss by death. It is usually seen as a personal, deliberate rejection of life and of other people, including the family. Because the stigma of suicide compounds feelings of loss, relatives of suicide victims, more than any other bereaved group, may require professional help.[5]

The shock of finding a suicided body is not the same as discovering natural death. "It is too true that most survivors of suicide share the trauma of a death that is both a shock and shocking . . . whereby family [members] find themselves confronted by a body, possibly disfigured, without the support of hospital personnel . . . In all these aspects, a death by suicide is a unique situation for survivors that is qualitatively different from the one usually experienced . . . after death. It can be characterized as an emergency situation whose timing is unexpected by those most deeply affected."[6] "This," says Adina Wrobleski, "is the real world of suicide."[7]

In order to understand the unique characteristics of grief after suicide, let's take a brief look at the usual and healthy grief process following the death of a loved one. The first reaction to death is shock and disbelief. As awareness of the loss increases, pining and sorrow set in. Some symptoms of grief are: sleeplessness, confusion, forgetfulness and/or uncontrollable crying. Intense grief can be physically painful.

It is normal to search for the deceased, to affirm his/her absence, or to be preoccupied with photos, belongings and memories. To some degree, survivors may identify with the deceased by taking on traits of the lost one—for example, by continuing his/her work.

The bereaved may feel bitter, angry, and cheated. They worry about the future and wonder how to bear life without this loved one. They may feel regret or guilt over things said or unsaid, done or undone. They may feel anger at being left alone. For a while, they may withdraw socially because they feel different or burdensome.

Months after the death, the bereaved slowly begin to function normally again. The length of this grief process depends greatly upon the success of the survivors' grief work. In the last stage of the grief-recovery process, the bereaved again begin to focus on the future. They make plans and can enjoy life, even though the sadness and the sense of loss return from time to time.

We all know that death from natural causes is traumatizing for survivors. However, professionals have long realized the unique dilemma of suicide survivors—that of dealing with death and that of dealing with suicide. In recent works, suicidologists have distinguished between the two processes in a way that can be defined and described. As a result, treatment can be prescribed.

Associated with suicide, in addition to the usual grieving process, is the experience of Post-Traumatic Stress Disorder. Symptoms of Post-Traumatic Stress Disorder are described at length in the *Diagnostic and Statistical Manual of the American Psychiatric Association.*[8] (Lukas and Seiden discuss post-traumatic stress as it relates to suicide survivors in their book *Silent Grief,* 1987.)

This disorder, resulting from a severe traumatic experience, is not new although we've only begun to discover how widespread it is. It was known as shell shock during World War I and battle fatigue in World War II. Since the Vietnam war, the Post-Traumatic Stress Disorder has been studied in depth.

Post-traumatic stress can occur in relation to a variety of tragedies and/or stressful situations such as rape, fire, abduction of a child, loss of youth or health, witnessing the death of someone else or encountering a life-threatening situation. Some of the key words or phrases in relation to these events are: sudden, violent, severe, unknown threat, death and/or life-threatening, psychologically damaging, and helplessness.

The model for the trauma presented by Thomas P. Scarano lists five stress response stages following the event itself: outcry, denial, the intrusive stage, working through, and completion.[9]

During the *outcry stage* survivors feel overwhelmed and exhausted. Their concept of time may slow down or speed up. Excessive crying or screaming is common during panic attacks. At the extreme the person may become catatonic—the system simply shuts down.

In the *denial stage,* the person uses any means he or she can to avoid dealing with the event, such as refusing to discuss or think about it, avoiding any situation or activity that would remind them of the event, depression, excessive sleeping or excessive "busyness." Some people may develop phobias, experience feelings of impending death, or may lose interest in their families, in their sex lives, and even in life itself.

The *intrusive stage* is signified by *survivor guilt*—preoccupation with what one should or shouldn't have done, accompanied by outbursts of anger and feelings of guilt because they are still alive. There may be *flashbacks* (reliving the event) so intense that the person returns to the *denial stage* or simply blacks out the event, unable to recall what happened. These "uncalled-upon images" may invade both sleep and consciousness.

There may be constant rumination in an attempt to understand and integrate one's own role and actions in relation to the event. Without proper "working through," persons in this stage may develop maladaptive symptoms such as psychosomatic problems, physical breakdown of the body, isolating oneself, behaving oddly, and not relating to other people. Without treatment, these symptoms may become excessive, prolonged, and intense.

Counseling for persons suffering Post-Traumatic Stress Disorder should include adaptive actions which retain the person's sense of self-worth without stripping away realistic defense mechanisms. A primary goal is to promote new growth and maturation.

I believe the experience of after-suicide survivors compares in many ways with the combat soldier who must always be aware of and on guard against a surprise attack by an unseen enemy. He must always be prepared to protect himself and his buddies from sudden death.

In a similar way, many survivors have lived for months or years with the dreadful suspense of finding the body of the suicidal person or of actually seeing the suicide happen. Coupled with that may have been the fear and anxiety for one's own life or of others, such as children. Like the combat soldier, they have been prepared to act on an emergency at a moment's notice. The majority of their time and energy has been concentrated on the survival of themselves or someone else. This "state of alertness" has interfered with and overridden all the normal actions of living. Like the veteran, they are already battle weary.

When the suicide actually occurs, the survivor may witness a sudden violent death much as a soldier may see his buddy destroyed in front of his eyes. And it happens despite all the precautions so carefully taken by the survivor. Wham. Survivor's guilt. Blaming one's self for being left alive and for failing to save the other. Questioning one's motives, abilities, responsibility and involvement. Flashbacks, reliving, etc. Just as the event itself was sudden and violent, so do the states of outcry, denial, intrusion, and working through have sudden violent elements.

In the following list of characteristics unique to suicide survivors, you will recognize some as symptoms of grief, some as symptoms of post-traumatic stress and some as a combination of symptoms of both processes.

These eleven points are compiled from a combination of my own studies and observations and from an article by Albert C. Cain, "Survivors of Suicide: Current Findings and Future Directions." [10] These points are also simply a description of the possible destructive aspects of after-suicide grief. Solutions, suggestions and guidelines for resolving these issues and for helping one another recover are found throughout the following chapters.

1. *Shock and Denial*: Suicide survivors experience shock not only because the death has occurred, but because it is unnatural and unexpected. We expect people to die from old age, illness, accidents, even acts of war, but not by their own hand. "She should not have died that way!" is the cry afterward. At first, survivors may try to deal with this shock by denial and repression. Some of the ways in which people react are confused memory, anxiety, feelings of dread and horror, contradictions, fantasy, and even deliberate lies. Some survivors refuse to discuss the death at all, or may engage in half-truths about the event. Others refuse to believe a suicide has occurred, insisting that it was an accident, or accusing the police of hiding facts.

In *Living Through Personal Crisis*, Ann Kaiser Stearns states: "The person who resists grieving successfully wards off intense pain. Still, a nagging ache will likely take its place. Denied feelings of grief will be expressed in hidden ways. A low-grade crisis can then endure for many years: moodiness, irritability, restlessness, nervousness, abuse of alcohol or other drugs, conflicts in relations with others, physical ailments, accident proneness, reckless spending, or general dissatisfaction and disappointment with life. Grief doesn't go away just because it is ignored." [11]

2. *Search for Meaning*: Survivors experience a desperate need to find a reason for the death. If it was caused by illness or accident, even though the death may have been untimely or tragic, we know the cause. But with suicide—even when a note is found—it is difficult to pinpoint the reason. There is always a nagging question about the degree of one's own involvement.

Some people shut out all talk or analysis of the event, while others replay the event over and over, searching for an answer to the question "Why?" Dr. Cain points out that many survivors struggle alone over the perplexity of it and "the fit of the experience itself into the larger order of life."[12] This floundering search is an important part in coming to an understanding of the experience before one can properly begin to cope with the loss and progress through the grief work. Survivors need to remove the aura of shame and restore a sense of dignity to the deceased's memory as well as repair their own shattered self-esteem. Unless they find an answer to the question "Why?" mourning may be incomplete.

3. *Incomplete Mourning*: Compound this search for meaning with denial, guilt, shame, anger, concealment, evasion, withdrawal of social and family support, subtle accusations, stigma and taboo, lack of reassurance, and the absence of a chance to share one's grief with others—and resolution can be severely crippled if not altogether destroyed. Survivors may become subject to the destructive effects and results of unresolved mourning often characterized by prolonged depression and self-destruction.[13]

4. *Depression and Self-Destruction*: In his work with survivors, Dr. Cain found these forces characterized by self-hatred, apathy, withdrawal, sadness, despair, rage, and a myriad of self-neglectful behaviors. This self-destructiveness stems from unmet yearnings and unresolved grief. Implied disapproval and lack of empathy may "drag survivors deeper into a depression from which some may never recover, or into a pattern of continued self-destructive acts including suicidal behavior."[14]

5. *Memories*: Many survivors are haunted by vivid recollections of finding the body or of scenes of violence mingled with confusion and/or conflict prior to the death. Perhaps they had spent agonizing hours of waiting in a hospital emergency room on the chance the victim might be saved. Many resent what they perceive as intimidating, cold or accusing attitudes of investigating officers and medical or emergency teams. These memories are relived and replayed in the survivors' conscious and unconscious mind.

6. *Increased Anger*: Survivors struggle with anger in at least three ways. 1. They are angry with themselves for not having prevented the death and thereby having played a part in bringing

about their own misery. 2. They are angry at the suicide victim for deliberately leaving them alone and burdening them with feelings of guilt, isolation, and desertion. 3. They are angry at others because of the social branding and sometimes outright ostracism. With non-suicide deaths, this anger may be directed toward God or circumstances. With suicide, it is also directed toward the victims and oneself.[15] *The non-suicide survivor feels angry over the death. The suicide survivor feels angry at being made to look responsible for the death.* Survivors feel angry for not being given a chance to intervene, for being forced to face both old and new problems alone, and for having to change and rebuild life styles. There is no socially acceptable way to express this very intense anger. Although it is real and justified, it just hangs there.

7. *Identification with the Suicide Victim*: Survivors go through a time of identifying themselves with the victim. They may believe that they know "exactly" what the deceased felt or thought just prior to death. This identification may go as far as imitation of the act. Some feel they can atone for their neglect of the victim by copying the suicidal behavior. This identification may be greatly intensified if there were conflicts or disturbed relationships prior to the death, or if the survivors depended upon the deceased for their own sense of identity.

8. *Importance of Anniversaries*: Suicide family survivors place great emphasis on suicide death anniversaries. They either dread or anticipate the date as a day of mourning. Especially crucial are anniversaries for each of the first six months, one year, eighteen months, and for some, the second year. Studies have shown that people strongly identifying with the deceased may choose an anniversary for their own death.

9. *Withdrawal from Social Life*: Mingled with doubt and distrust is a need to be with people. There is a hunger to be welcomed— included—but conversation and activities simply take too much energy. Fearful of closeness, survivors withdraw, playing out "object separation, i.e., the repetitive need to re-enact separations; to drive loved ones away by replaying the experiences of estrangement and reunion."[16] The resulting withdrawal of others completes the isolation and repeats the act of loss, reinforcing a feeling of worthlessness or of being unsure of oneself or others.[17] Many

survivors lose emotional and social support when it is most needed. Continued isolation (even implicit accusation) is common. Widows, for example, often refuse to remarry, feeling they are somehow permanently scarred.

10. *Profound Sense of Shame*: Survivors may feel emotionally naked. They are unable to make excuses because "someone preferred death to living with me." Some may feel that others are making the same judgment about them, and often, they are. This may leave the survivors with a badly damaged self-concept. An acute sense of worthlessness often compounds the feeling of abandonment since the other person *chose* to leave.

11. *Guilt*: Again, blame enters the picture. Survivors search for something or someone to blame. The victim? Friends? Family? One another? Themselves? Health or finances? Conflicting thoughts whirl in their heads. "Why didn't I know?" "I did know." "I could have prevented it, but I didn't. Why?" The feeling that others should acknowledge and share in the blame may occur within some families as members attempt to select "who was the most at fault" in order to pass on the burden of blame. Some people, knowing they were not at fault despite accusation, nevertheless feel guilty because they don't feel guilty.

At the news of the suicide, some people feel great relief that the stress and anxiety of the previous weeks, months, or years has ended. This may be true, for example, if the husband abused his wife, or if he threatened suicide so many times that his family is glad the ordeal is over. But their relief in turn intensifies their guilt feelings and they tend to strongly deny both their relief and any expectation about the death.

More often, however, parents, children and spouse feel directly responsible. Guilt then, may compound itself, and often, what are actually feelings of regret *or* of shame, may be interpreted as guilt. In normal death, guilt tends to diminish with time as survivors reassure themselves that they did all they could. "With suicide, guilt increases with time."[18]

It has been said that we are a death-denying society, and I agree. I believe we are preoccupied with the grisly morbidity of death. We sensationalize the experience of death. We romanticize and glorify the idea of death—but we deny the reality of death.

110

Helping Yourself Survive

"Everybody has his own path. There are a thousand paths to discovering yourself, to becoming. Every one of you will find your own way. Don't let anyone impose theirs on you."

Leo Buscaglia

Learn as much as possible about the causes of suicide. Libraries, crisis centers, mental health centers and funeral directors can provide you with the necessary resources. You'll discover that most suicide victims would have preferred to live, but at the same time they thought they could not, so their confusion resulted in suicide. Death may promise peace or appear to be the solution to a problem. Some professionals believe that suicide is not a response to a life beset with problems and failures, but is a response to life itself. They point out that many suicidal persons have been great achievers. Information like this will help you better understand what happened and why.

Inform yourself about what you may expect to experience during your grief-recovery process. This book will get you started. The appendix lists many good books on grief.

This chapter contains helpful practical suggestions from survivors themselves. Sources are acknowledged at the end of Part III.

Realize that it may take a long time to recover. Although you will never forget, nor ever again be the same person, you can still find life meaningful. Your need to search for meaning is not only justified but necessary. When you replay the events mentally and verbally, they should begin to make sense. This is not a morbid dwelling on grisly details but an action which examines and interprets the situation, thereby giving insight.

Claim your right to grieve. Experiencing the pain of grief is somewhat akin to childbirth labor—you know you must suffer through the pain in order to gain relief and obtain the joy beyond. With each grieving episode, the pain becomes less intense, of shorter duration, and less frequent. To lose your right to grieve is to suffer yet another loss.

Some people feel a need to display photos of the deceased or to sit quietly in the deceased's room. You may feel drawn to revisit favorite vacation spots, restaurants, etc. You are searching for that person, trying to recapture a sense of his presence. Searching for the deceased is normal—it affirms his/her physical absence. Once your need to search is satisfied, you may discover you still have a relationship with the deceased, although on a different level. Like C.S. Lewis in *A Grief Observed*, in releasing grief, you may somehow find your loved one.

Do not be afraid to express grief and emotions. Grief *is* emotional. It is the natural reaction to a significant loss. Find a time and place where you can cry. It also helps to talk about the loss, recall it, and perhaps write about it. Believe that in due time, the painful "reliving" will give way to a satisfying "recalling." One survivor described it as my "happy-sad memories."

You may want to plan a "cry day." Pull the shades, lock the door, unplug the phone, and cry or yell to your heart's content. Don't fool yourself into thinking that you should not cry. Modern medical science holds that tears are a law of nature. To suppress them can bring on headaches, asthma attacks, and a variety of medical conditions. Writer Morton M. Hunt says "Weeping comes as a part of the reversal of conditions of alarm, shock and anger. Tears do not mark a breakdown or low point but a *transition* to warmth, hope and health."[19]

We were discussing the value of tears at a particularly tense and sad support group meeting when Beth, who had been crying all evening, said between sniffs, "I wasn't expecting to be doing this. Usually, I refuse to have a good cry without my Puffs." At the next meeting, I put out a box of her favorite tissues.

Tell people when you need to talk or cry. Ask them to be understanding, to mention your loved one's name, to recall events and his/her characteristics. Let people know that you need time to grieve, and their supportive comfort while you do so.

Unfortunately, society has provided us with few guidelines for dealing with after-suicide bereavement. Even though you are the one in need, you may have to teach others how to help you and what to say. If you sense someone is uncomfortable with you, ask, "You don't know how to deal with me, do you?" I believe it is a sign of strength to ask for help when you need it. There is value in being able to receive as well as give.

Be careful when choosing confidantes. Some people cannot relate to your grief, some do not know how to listen, others don't want to. Be aware of those who appear to sympathize but who are actually feeding a morbid curiosity of their own. They only want to hear the bloody details.

You may encounter people who try to feed on your pain. When Bill died, there was a person in my life who *wanted* to see me suffer. Knowing that, I would not cry in front of her.

Susan had a similar experience. "While I was complaining about how my father's suicide had hurt me, I had this great friend who supported me. But when I forgave my father and began to laugh and to look at the future again, she got real mad at me. She liked me better when I was miserable." Susan's complaining had fed her friend's neurosis. When she began healing, her friend felt betrayed. Susan had mistaken her friend's expressions of her own anger as empathy for her (Susan) experience.

Survivors are especially vulnerable when the pain is fresh. Although your need to talk is acute, trust your instincts. Don't hesitate to challenge someone who invades your privacy. Counter it with a remark like, "May I ask *you* personal questions as well?" or, "I resent it when you say that to me." As Bill would have advised, "Choose someone you can ride the river with."

Watch out for the hope mongers. They will have all the answers without hearing what you really say. Don't exhaust yourself trying to point out or explain a reality they'll never comprehend. I once drew a picture of my favorite hope monger on a cardboard box, covered it with printed "Well now's," "Well, you know's," and "Yes, but's" and kicked it to kingdom come in my garage. You can always make something work *for* you.

We can't live without hope, but it has its place or we lose it. Hope is not the same thing as dogged-blind-denial or pie-in-the-sky naivete, but rather, is based on a balanced view of realistic expectations and common sense.

Beware of doctors who are quick to label your grief as *chronic* depression. While depression is a part of grief, depression and grief are not the same. True, some normal grief symptoms, such as confusion, fatigue, loss of appetite, loss of motivation, and sadness, may resemble symptoms of chronic depression or other conditions. However, normal grief is not an illness which automatically requires medication. Remember that grief work may be expected to deplete your mind and body of energy, perhaps for several months. Better vitamins than drug dependency.

Rather than scolding yourself for being depressed, think of depression as a turning point where your body sort of goes into neutral so that your mind and emotions can make important decisions. It's during depression that you decide either to give up or to survive while your body gathers the strength to carry out your decision. Depression can have some positive benefits. It makes you rest and gives you time to think about the good times as well as the bad. It can be a time to heal—to grow. Remember that many of the most creative people in the world's history have struggled through terrible depressions only to create or contribute something quite valuable as a result. Don't let depression make you depressed.

It has been said that every symptom serves a purpose, whether it is shock, anger, depression, guilt, confusion, fatigue, searching, identification, or even denial. These symptoms are a part of accepting, understanding, and rebuilding. Shock, for example, allows part of the body to continue to function while protecting the part (mind or emotions) that is stunned. Expressing anger can relieve emotions which, if pent up, could harm one's health.

One of the unintended side effects of prolonged grief can be that it gives the bereaved person control over others. One mother still sobs uncontrollably, eleven years later, whenever her son's name is mentioned, or when she sees some object that belonged to him. (She keeps many of his things within sight.) If his name is not mentioned, she takes to her bed. It is understood by the family that no one ever says or does anything contrary to her wishes for fear of "setting her off." She uses her unresolved grief as a controlling force and resists any professional treatment because she is afraid of losing this power. Don't allow yourself to become so dependent on grief that you are afraid to lose it.

Anger usually surfaces when shock wears off and acceptance begins. This anger is natural and justified. The person *did* leave you with old and new burdens to handle alone. It happened and you are angry about it. But take care not to lash out at innocent people or the family pet. Anger becomes dangerous when we let it take control of our thoughts and actions.

There is a difference between being angry and expressing anger. Find a way to express anger constructively. Yell at society, ignorance, and apathy all you want. One mother stomped on her son's grave. It didn't hurt him a bit but it sure helped her.

Another survivor bought a doll to represent her suicided sister and tore it limb from limb, while crying and begging forgiveness.

114

This symbolic action released a great amount of tension for her.

It's not uncommon to feel anger—even rage—at odd times. Addie told of how she first expressed rage at her husband. When she came into the kitchen he was sitting in a chair with his back to her. When she walked around in front of him she could see that he had killed himself. "I stood there and looked at him and got so mad that he could do this to us. So I slugged him. Just slugged him as hard as I could. I hit him so hard he fell off the chair." Can you imagine trying to explain that to the police?

Not all survivors feel anger. One mother said, "How can I be angry? He didn't kill himself to spite me. He felt hopeless and believed he was doing the only thing he could. Since he couldn't make it in life, he could make it in death."

Understand your guilt feelings. Do not be afraid to face them. Admit and explore them in order to resolve them. Just as you cannot cement over a volcano and expect it to stop boiling, you cannot make guilt disappear by denying it. It continues to churn inside and retards healing. Do not be afraid to say, "I feel so guilty," even though you know it isn't your fault. It is not the validity of guilt which is important at this time but how you feel and your ability to express yourself freely without feeling threatened. The more you confront guilt, the less its hold over you.

Some people hold onto guilt because it serves a purpose. Unconsciously, they may be trying to gain control over their circumstances. "I couldn't prevent the suicide but I can control how I feel, and by golly, I'm going to feel guilty." Others use guilt as an excuse for not changing or for not doing something about their situation. A perpetually guilt-ridden person can ward off any accusation or expectations from others. Guilt can also be a way of gaining approval. "See how good I am. I'm feeling guilty." Do not allow guilt to become a habit.

Most people are willing to let go of guilt once they have suffered enough. But why wait years for that to happen? Face your guilt feelings, painful as they may be, early in your grieving process. Perhaps they are valid to some extent. If so, admit them to God or to others, if it helps you. Don't underestimate the therapeutic power of simple confession of wrongdoing, mistakes or misjudgments. Simply state the facts without justifying or blaming yourself or others. This takes courage. It is risky but you can change yourself, others, and your relationships with others.

115

Use guilt as a turning point for growth.

On the other hand, if you know you need not feel guilty, do not allow others to assume or convince you that you should. Our society often sends double messages. You will hear some people say, "You shouldn't feel guilty," while others will assume, "You sure must feel guilty." Do not pay a lot of attention to either comment.

Remember that feeling guilty or feeling that you let someone down indicates that you felt a responsibility for that person and that's good. There has to have been a personal commitment (love) and an ability to feel compassion or you wouldn't experience guilt. You don't feel guilty over the suicide of someone you don't love, do you? You may feel sad about it, but not guilty. Find comfort in the fact that you loved him or her. In some families that love isn't there.

Consider very carefully the difference between guilt and shame. Shaming is a process that starts early in childhood. We believe parents when they express disapproval of us and internalize that shame until we become our own parent, shaming and punishing ourselves. If shame is there, eating away at your soul, you will react much more acutely to guilt feelings—you may even confuse the two. If your parents have shamed you, and you then shame yourself, and then someone close to you suicides, you're in deep trouble. The message, "Shame on you—you made me kill myself," will be taken literally by you, and you're now fighting both shame and guilt. That's heavy—and you may need therapy to help separate and settle the two issues. *Guilt results from something we have done. Shame arises from what we think we are.*

I believe that some people who are so terribly devastated after a suicide are those who already live in a world of internalized or externalized shame. James Bradshaw, in *Bradshaw On: The Family,* explores at length the subject of shame and how to become released from it. If you think that shame is a factor in your grief process you might want to buy some good books on both guilt and shame.

Guilt is easier to resolve—usually we can make restitution. But shame involves deep spiritual and/or emotional healing to be resolved. Use this grief experience as an opportunity to clear up both issues. Think about the difference between guilt and regret. You have some claim to guilt if you took a certain deliberate action even though you were aware of possible adverse consequences. Regret means feeling bad about a situation over which you had no direct control.

116

Use actions rather than thinking to resolve some of your feelings. Visit places you enjoyed together or do things you had planned to do together. John bought a camper for a trip that he and his wife had planned for years. Before they could leave, Emma became terminally ill and took her own life rather than endure severe pain. Several months after her death, John took the trip just as they had planned, alone. He visited the places they both had wanted to see and "talked to her" as he drove just as if she were sitting beside him. "I did it for both of us," he said. "Maybe it doesn't make sense to anyone else but I feel like we had our trip together." John took care of unfinished business rather than punish himself with regrets and remorse.

Keep a journal, write poetry, or write letters to your loved one. Edith could manage her busy days but not that special time each evening when she and her husband had shared a private cup of coffee and conversation. "I tried to do something else during that hour but I was always drawn back to our special time, thinking about things I wanted to discuss with Ken. Finally, I decided to keep that hour as it had been, rather than to avoid it. So, I settled down as usual with my cup and talked to the chair where Ken always sat. I answered myself the way I thought he would have." This ritual helped Edith to let go of Ken and to accept his absence.

An American Indian ritual applies this principle. Suppose the father died. The first day following his death, the table is set as if he were there. His plate is filled with food, his chair pulled out and no one sits in it. Family conversation excludes the deceased but everything else is the same. At the following meal, his chair is pushed up to the table so that "no one can sit in it." Then his plate is left empty. Gradually, utensils are removed. And so it goes, until, within a few days, someone else uses his chair, eats from his plate, and joins in the conversation.

This process, it is believed, gradually allows both the deceased spirit and the survivors to accept reality. The spirit can come to realize that it is no longer a part of its old world and is free to move on into another realm. The family is given time and actions which help them adjust to the change.

Make use of rituals on anniversaries. Although you may dread anniversaries, your apprehension may be worse than the actual day. You may want to plan a family gathering or a memorial service, or set aside the day to look at photos and mementos.

Invitations can be a problem. You want to accept them but then you change your mind, are too tired, or forget them altogether. Forestall hurt feelings by explaining this to people at the time. Ask them to call you just prior to the engagement and to not take it personally if you change your mind.

Many of the following suggestions have been offered by survivors at Ray of Hope support group meetings:

1. Learn about the grief process in order to better understand yourself and your moods, but do not gauge your feelings by what others say. While grief patterns have similarities, individual patterns may vary.

2. Join a group of survivors. They understand and will listen. To avoid prolonged grief, the sooner you join the better. Those who join early are less likely to still be grieving years later.

3. See a professional counselor if you think it will help. But remember, there is a difference between grief guidance, counseling and psychiatry (which focuses on diagnosis and medication for genetic disorders). Maybe all you need is grief guidance.

4. Be with people if you want to. Spend time alone when you want.

5. Don't tell people you are all right if you aren't. You can be honest without going into details. Resist pressure to wear a smile until you feel like it. There's nothing wrong with an honest frown.

6. Don't automatically assume that everyone is blaming you.

7. Talk to your loved one through imaginary conversations. Recall special things, explain how you feel now, and explore your future. Say good-bye even if you have to say it more than once.

8. Don't clear out your loved one's things too soon. You may feel quite differently about them a year or five years from now.

9. Change things if you want to—your hairstyle, the furniture, or your wardrobe. But don't be in a hurry to make major decisions about moving, changing jobs, etc. If you consider moving, make sure you will still have a support system in the new community or the move itself will just become another stress factor.

10. Your body, as well as your emotions, is recovering from the blow. Take care of your health. It takes energy to grieve and to heal.

Your resistance is low and you are susceptible to illness during bereavement, so exercise properly and eat nutritious food, even though you may not feel like it. Get plenty of rest.

11.	Use the time of renewal to get in touch with yourself. Discover your strengths. It helps overcome the fear of being alone.

12.	If you have been widowed, make the most of being independent. Making decisions alone may not be easy or enjoyable, but they have to be made and you are not answerable to anyone but yourself for them. There is great satisfaction in knowing you can do it.

13.	Take time to do things you *like* to do and *want* to do, with no excuses.

14.	Think in terms of what "I will do," "can do,"or, "want to do," not what "*I should do.*" Should do's can wear you out. When they come from others, ignore them.

15.	Start living in the present by referring to your belongings as "mine" rather than ours/his/hers. (Of course, some things will always be "ours" and/or "his.")

16.	Consult your lawyer, banker and other professionals on legal and financial matters. Don't rely on family and friends too much, even if it is easier.

17.	You are quite vulnerable during grief or depression. Do not let an unscrupulous church or charity representative take unfair advantage of your time, guilt or finances.

18.	Give thanks each day for your health and well-being, your family and friends. Be thankful for the precious memories you and others share of your loved one.

19.	Find a church where you feel comfortable. Many congregations now sponsor grief groups and singles groups for all ages.

20.	Search the Scriptures for verses offering comfort and permission to grieve. The Bible is full of examples of people who overcame tremendous losses.

21.	Forgive. Forgive yourself, the deceased, others. Never underestimate the power of forgiveness.

22. Do examine carefully the things you think and say to yourself. You may have learned things during childhood that are not true,

but are influencing the way you think and act now. You may still be reacting to a critical parent or stressful event. Sometimes we think and act according to what we've been told by someone rather than what we've learned for ourselves. Sort out your beliefs and feelings and question their validity. In their book *Telling Yourself the Truth*, William Backus and Marie Chapian call this process "Misbelief Therapy."[20]

23. Read a book about rational verses irrational thinking.

24. Make some lists:
> How do I belittle myself?
> What do I like about myself?
> What have I accomplished?
> Things I enjoy—and don't enjoy.
> The most important things in my life. The least important?
> What do I need but am not getting?
> Compliments and positive strokes I have received.
> What causes me stress?
> What relieves my stress?

25. Question what you do and how you feel:
> What is this grief/depression doing *to* or *for* me?
> Do I deserve punishment? Why? Why not?
> Am I making amends? How? Do I need to?
> What are the payoffs for depression or grief?
> What are the payoffs for letting go of depression or grief?
> If I were not depressed, what would I be doing?
> What are my expectations for myself?
> What has this done *to* or *for* my sense of self-worth and self-esteem?
> What really matters? Does not matter?
> What is my belief system? Do I limit or handicap myself?

26. Don't be too hard on yourself. Expect a certain amount of physical distress, daydreaming and panic over an uncertain future.

27. Don't be too hard on others. Don't expect others to fill all your needs.

28. Don't make it difficult for those who sincerely want to help you. Some people can still understand the *feeling* of loss and grief even if not *your* actual experience.

29. Remember that people who love you don't want you to hurt.

30. Pay attention to your gut instinct.

31. If you know you can't do something, don't try. If you don't want to do it, don't apologize.

32. Remember that if there had been no love, there would be no guilt.

33. Remember that to say "I am responsible for my actions" is not the same as to say "I am to blame." Taking responsibility is to empower yourself. Wallowing in blame or shame is emotionally crippling.

34. Do seek out counselors with knowledge of both grief guidance and the post-traumatic stress syndrome.

35. Be aware that sometimes the burden of grief itself is more miserable than the loss itself.

36. Learn to recognize defense mechanisms so that you can tell when you are using them, such as excuses, rationalizations, projection, denial, withdrawal, overactivity. Listen carefully to yourself to see if you are being realistic. Examine your own attitudes and actions objectively.

37. Expect to remember conversations and situations where you think you could have said or done something differently. Consider instead that actually the suicided person may have lived longer because of your love and concern.

38. Allow yourself to be concerned with but not obsessed about the "right" or "wrong" of the event. You need to be able to say that something was right or wrong, but do not become preoccupied with blaming people. You will hurt yourself and others even more. Assure yourself, "I may be changed but I am not destroyed." Direct your energies toward learning, growing, and finding a new and richer meaning in the lives of others and yourself. Refuse to let that death be for nothing.

Helping Survivors Survive

"In order to meet the need, we must first understand,
In order to understand, we must become informed,
In order to become informed, we must care,
And caring is what it is all about."

Helping survivors survive is no easy task. Often, without intending to, we react against the confused person rather than the crisis situation, thereby making matters worse.

Many people have contacted me for suggestions on how to help a survivor they are concerned about. Family and friends also struggle with questions, frustrations, and feelings of helplessness. "What shall I do or not do?" they ask. "What can I say to help ease the pain for this person I love?"

The next two chapters attempt to help you with this problem. Most of the suggestions come from survivors themselves. "Begin," they say, "by being sincere." Next, learn what you can about the causes of suicide and the grief process of survivors.

Survivors have a strong need to search for meaning. They are trying to understand something they can't understand. Recognize and understand that their search is justified and necessary. This need must be satisfied before they can fully accept the loss and get down to the business of grief work.

Help them accomplish this by being willing to listen to their story over and over. The most sincere compliment we can give anyone is to pay attention. Take time to be sensitive to the inner need. It makes no difference how often they tell the story or how much it varies. It is in the involvement of replaying of events—struggling to understand and accept within one's own frame of reference—that the survivor finds a fixed sense of what happened.

Not only are survivors working to rebuild their own self-image; they also need to develop a positive image of the suicide victim. They need to believe that their loved one made a rational decision. This process may take many months, but it is an important part of the recovery and it has a maturing effect on the thinking person.

Suicide survivors carry a triple burden—accepting a loss by death, believing the death was self-inflicted, and their struggle to reshape a new life style. Research on suicide survivors indicates

122

that they suffer intense psychological and physical reactions during grief. Suicide deaths usually are more sudden, have a greater impact on survivors, and allow no time for preparatory grief. Anger at the suicided person and fear of following in his/her footsteps can produce a bondage with the deceased which is frightening. Survivors need to rely on family and community and may feel abandoned if that need fails to be met.

When social response to survivors of suicide is influenced by stigma, survivors tend to withdraw. Make a special effort to encourage others in the family and community to offer comfort and support. This will allow survivors to use others as support for building a new life style. It will also help them to discover, develop, and reinforce coping strengths they already possess.

Shock, denial, and sorrow may last longer following a death by suicide. Let survivors recover at their own pace, whether it takes two years, four years, or more. Each person's timing is different. Each must follow his/her own inner messages. Don't tell people how you would grieve if it were you. They know how and when they need to grieve. Be patient. It's their grief. Take care not to imply that someone is mentally or emotionally unstable just because she/he is grieving.

Searching for the deceased is normal. This searching (and/or denial) process may be seen when survivors place photos about, treasure certain items, leave the room untouched, or keep personal belongings and clothing. That is all right. These things should not be disposed of too quickly. Many a treasured memento was once a painful reminder. It may be better to put some things away at first and then, months later, sort through them and make decisions. It takes time to completely comprehend and accept a loved one's physical absence. Advise patience and be patient yourself.

Expressions of denial, anger, and guilt may be much stronger in survivors of suicide. Let them talk freely about their anger and guilt. Don't argue about who *is* or *isn't* really guilty or how much guilt one *should* or *shouldn't* feel. It is important to consider only, "How guilty do you *feel* you are? Let's talk about it. Tell me how you feel." Survivors know how they feel. Perhaps it is out of proportion, but they must see that for themselves rather than be told. Most people will begin to sort things into a different perspective after they have had a chance to bring them out in the open and examine them through discussion with concerned others.

Depressed persons often sleep a lot and that sleep can be a form of practicing for death or a restoration for life. Don't tell a survivor to "snap out of it" when they are obviously depressed. Depression can be frightening to both the depressed person and anyone else involved. But consider the possibility that depression can be a time of *transition* as well. With that thought in mind, we can grow or be productive during transition.

Most important, give survivors permission to feel bad. They should not be made to feel guilty for feeling bad. Responses which insist that they should "do something," or which refuse to acknowledge their feelings, may be perceived as an attack on one's courage to say, "I feel bad." That can be emotionally paralyzing. For example, Suzanne was describing the frustration she encountered during a suicidal depression following her friend's suicide. "My family just wouldn't hear what I was saying. When I told my sister that I was so weak I couldn't even put toothpaste on my brush, she said, 'Oh yes, you can.' Every time they said I could when I knew I couldn't, they doubled my burden. You know, it's like they just put another bullet in my gun. I had reached for rescue and my rescuers became my persecutors."

It is very easy to unknowingly invalidate or squelch someone's efforts even though your intentions are the very best. For example:

If they say	You don't say
"I can't handle this."	"Oh yes, you can."
"I'm falling apart."	"Oh no, you're not."
"I feel so guilty."	"No, you're not."
"I feel like killing myself too."	"No, you don't."

Usually, these responses are meant to discourage negative thinking. But what if it's not negative thinking? What if it is a realistic expression? Perhaps it is your response that is inadvertently negative in the sense that you have invalidated the other person's feelings and squelched a courageous attempt at honest expression. Instead say, "Explain what you mean."

These responses pop up a lot when the subject is guilt. It is a touchy subject most of us want to avoid. But listen carefully. Perhaps that person is not just wanting to wallow in guilt. Maybe he/she is trying to say something more but doesn't know how. Consider the possibility that the person has become aware of the

124

impact of his/her actions and influence upon others. Perhaps that person is facing what it is like to be wholly responsible for the influence of his/her actions upon someone else, and is *owning* that responsibility. This is a frightening but exciting step toward maturity. It takes a lot of courage to say, "I am responsible for this or that action"—especially after a suicide. Respect that courage and give it permission to emerge.

On the other hand, remember that some people think that asking for help or advice indicates a weakness on their part. They may indirectly seek your advice, then seem to resent it when you respond. In this case, you are in trouble no matter what you say. Try to avoid giving advice when it isn't directly asked for. Instead, you might ask, "Would you like to hear what I think or what so-and-so did in a similar situation?"

Don't say, "Call me if you need help," and let it go at that. They won't call you. Instead, do something specific. Ask if you can baby-sit the kids for a while. Go fix breakfast, make beds, take out the garbage, mow the yard, walk the dog, help answer mail, pull weeds, wash the car. The list is endless.

I once showed up on a friend's doorstep with cleaning supplies in hand and announced, "I am a gift from heaven. I do windows and toilets." She burst into laughter and said, "Would you believe it, that's just the two things I have been worrying about and can't get done." One survivor said, "I can't cry on the shoulder of a phone." Better to just *be there* to offer a hug or a shoulder.

Don't be hurt or put off if your invitations appear to be met with evasions or lack of enthusiasm. Since Bill's death, I've been told by various people that for the first couple of years, I never followed through on invitations I had accepted. Apparently I was so preoccupied at the time that I probably couldn't move from my chair or I simply forgot. But I do remember the times my friend Joyce came in and said, "We are going shopping (or to a movie) and we want you to come along. I'm here to help you get ready." Usually, with that sort of urging, I'd go and enjoy myself.

Death anniversaries are very important to suicide survivors. Contact survivors each month on the date of death for at least six months, and again on the first and second year's anniversaries. Do not hesitate to mention to bereaved persons that you know the anniversary is approaching. They will be grateful that you didn't forget. Remember the deceased's birthday, mention his/her name

125

from time to time, and recall little things. It may provoke tears but they will be thankful, healing tears.

Do not be afraid to ask survivors if they have suicidal thoughts. They may welcome the opportunity to discuss the topic and will appreciate your concern. You won't be "putting something into someone's head" if it wasn't there already. If a person is thinking about suicide, you can guide him/her to professional care and perhaps save a life. When someone confides in you, "I feel like killing myself," curb the impulse to sound off on *your* feelings about the act of suicide. They are telling you more than that. They are telling you that they also are experiencing fear and fatigue, and a lack of achievement, pride, and dignity. They are saying ten things at once.

If a survivor is very disturbed, professional help should be sought. But aside from that, the best you can offer is empathetic understanding, acceptance, patience, and a listening ear. Allow survivors to open their hearts. Don't be threatened by emotion. People don't want advice as much as they need a nonjudgmental, nonpatronizing atmosphere.

There are times, however, when listening may not be enough, as with delayed or unresolved grief. The following symptoms, according to the *American Psychiatric Association Diagnostic Manual,* indicate a need for professional help if one or more of them is noted daily for two or more weeks.[21]

1. Changes in appetite with marked weight gain or loss.
2. Insomnia or excessive sleeping.
3. Marked overactivity or extreme lethargy.
4. Prolonged feelings of worthlessness and/or guilt.
5. Suicidal feelings and threats.

I would also suggest that *extreme* isolation or the *extreme* inability to be alone is cause for alarm.

Helping a survivor of suicide can be perplexing, requiring much tact and patience. But if you succeed, consider yourself eligible for sainthood. See more suggestions in the chapters *Widowed by Suicide, Helping Yourself Survive* and *A Time to Listen: A Time to Talk.*

A Time to Talk: A Time to Listen

*"Listening is then a great act of love at that moment,
for it makes the other person more whole."*

Dr. Abraham Schmit

*Far too often, we are more worried about our ability to say the right thing than we are about giving an understanding ear to a mourner. We think we must offer advice or philosophical thoughts to the bereaved when a hug, a handshake, a deep look into the eyes, our presence, or making contact is what counts most. But we can't avoid talking altogether, so what can we say?

Dr. Abraham Schmit, author of *The Art of Listening With Love*, says that listening with love can transform people and relationships. "This kind of listening frees the speaker to search deeper and deeper for a fuller understanding and admiration of himself."[22] He means, listen to *their words* rather than *your thoughts*.

Most of the material in this chapter is taken from an ongoing Ray of Hope study of after-suicide bereavement. The questionnaire asks survivors to list (1) the things that were said and done which caused them the greatest stress, and (2) to suggest things a concerned helper *can* do and say. Included are additional comments some of the survivors made about the points they listed.

Take time to examine your motives when you offer your help. If they are less than pure, your offer of help will generate more resentment than gratitude in the long run. Motives that are actually self-serving or self-centered can sneak up on us. Be especially aware of the following pitfalls and examine your motives by asking yourself these questions:

* Do I resent his/her plea for attention? Why? Is my own need for attention so great that I am jealous of someone else who needs it?
* Am I more concerned with seeing this person's pain relieved, or am I making this conversation a power struggle because I need to be in control?
* In blaming him/her am I projecting my own feelings of guilt because I can't face them myself?
* Am I judging or labeling the person rather than understanding his/her reactions as part of the grief process?
* Am I saying this because I think it's the right thing to say or is it what I truly think?

127

DON'T

* Condemn   * Patronize–"Well, now. . ."
* Judge   * Argue
* Blame   * Advise
* Criticize   * Ignore
* Laugh or jest   * Put off

* Compare—such as, "So-and-so didn't carry on like you do."
* Overtalk—know when enough is enough.
* Put down—such as, "That's nothing. It happened to others."
* Overspout platitudes—that's as helpful as a box of rocks.
* Compete—you can't help me if you are more interested in proving you have suffered more.
* Heap on guilt—I feel guilty enough. Don't add to my burden.
* Try to convince me that my loved one "had a choice." (I may not believe that and I don't want to argue about it right now.)
* Moralize—such as, "Think of what you are doing to your family." (I *am* thinking about what I'm doing to my family. Are they thinking about what they are doing to me?)
* Pressure—such as, "Now, put a smile on your face." (You are asking me to pretend for your benefit. There is nothing wrong with an honest frown. Don't ask me to lie about how I feel.)
* Make assumptions. Check things out with me.
* Remind me of obligations to others. That may be part of the problem which has triggered my depression. I am aware of my inadequacies in meeting my responsibilities. Harping on it will only increase my sense of helplessness and make me resent you.
* Dare or encourage me if I threaten suicide, on the mistaken notion that you will bluff me out of it. What I hear is that you just don't understand or are deliberately insensitive to what is really a desperate cry for help.
* Label me. That reveals more about you than it does about my actions. It tells me that you judge people without getting to know the circumstances.
* Preach. Some people may respond to spiritual guidance but don't shove it down my throat! Nor do I appreciate a sermon on the evils of suicide.
* Get defensive. We're talking about why my loved one took his or her own life, not your reasons why you wouldn't do it.
* Don't complain about your spouse, parent or children to me

when I've just lost my spouse, parent or child.

DO:
* Really care enough to listen. You can't fake caring and concern.
* Tell me you care and are available should I need you. Then *be* available.
* Respect my privacy if I decline an intense conversation. Sometimes, it's too exhausting to talk. Sometimes, I want to avoid the embarrassment of losing control in front of others.
* Be aware of how you discuss your own family in my presence.
* Write a line or two in the card you send.
* Come to my home with a hug for me and my children.
* Be trustworthy. Don't offer to listen if you aren't going to. And ask yourself why you want to listen. Don't use my misery to satisfy your own morbid curiosity. I will sense that something is wrong and may later regret or resent having confided in you. Then, both of us will have lost.
* Give me and my loved one the benefit of the doubt.

BE CAUTIOUS ABOUT SAYING:
* "Don't worry, you can have more children." (Insensitive.)
* "Maybe you'll get married again." (Also insensitive.)
* "You just have to forget he/she ever existed." (That's ridiculous.)
* "He/she died over a year ago. You should be over it by now." (Better update your information about the grieving process.)
* "Anyone who commits suicide is weak." (Actually, it may take a lot of courage and strength to kill oneself.)
* "Life goes on." (Maybe so, but mine doesn't feel like it right now and I don't care.)
* "He or she had a choice." (Intellectually I can say that but inside it's not like that. There were indications after the fact and I have to deal with them.)
* "Well, it was God's will, you know." (How can that sort of pain and desperation be God's will?)
* "People who kill themselves are insane," or "They were crazy, you know." (Actually, less than 5% of suicides are mentally ill.)
* "They are in hell now—all people who commit suicide are demon-possessed." (How do you know? Do you have inside information?   Also, this was a terrible thing to say to me. It added to my hurt.)

* "I know how you feel." (Oh no, you don't know how I feel. You only think you know how you would feel.)
* "Oh my, you must feel so guilty!" (Please don't *automatically* assume that I should *automatically* feel guilty.)
* "You're strong, you'll be just fine." (Are you really telling me that you won't be here to help me?)
* "You've got to get on with your life." (What are you talking about? This *is* my life.)
* "You'll get over it." (No, I don't know that I'll get over it and neither do you. In fact, at this point, I don't want to get over it.)
* "It will take time but you'll be all right." (I know it will take a long time but I don't want to think ahead like that because it discounts what I am going through now.)
* "So-and-so wouldn't want you to carry on like that." (Why not? And how do you know? Wasn't "so-and-so" worth it? My grief is acknowledgment of his/her worth and he/she deserves my grief.)
* "Grief will make you a better person." (You don't say! Well, maybe God should make someone else die and then I can be an even better person.)
* (To others) "Well, I'd really like to help____, but I'm afraid that he/she won't listen to what I say." (Make sure that isn't a cop-out for indifference or an unconscious attempt on your part to impress others with your concern.)
* (To others) "She/he keeps trying to bring up the subject but I don't want her/him to get upset, so I ignore it." (That doesn't make sense. Maybe it's you who is afraid of being upset.)
* "Don't think about it." (I have to think about it. It happened.)
* "Don't talk about it." (Why not? Don't ask me to pretend nothing is wrong when it is. That's asking me to lie.)
* "You *have* to talk about it." (No I don't. There are times when it is just too overwhelming to talk. Sometimes, it isn't any of your business.)
* "Be brave! Don't cry!" (Why not? Tears are a natural expression of grief, loneliness and longing, a tribute to the one I miss. There is nothing shameful or unacceptable in my tears, or, do you mean that my tears bother *you*?)
* "Well, now, time heals all things, you know." (That may be true but it doesn't make me stop hurting now.)
* "Snap out of it." (I want to but I can't.) (Massive stress has

weakened the body. Give it time to repair itself. This comment can also be insensitive.)

DO SAY
* "I can't begin to imagine how you feel, but I'm here."
* "I remember 'this' or 'that' about _____." (Single out some special interest or an attractive personality trait of the deceased and comment on it.)
* "I don't have an answer."
* "You have a right to feel as you do."
* "Although you feel alone now, there are some of us who have been where you are. When you are ready, we may be of help."
* "There is no right or wrong way to grieve. Take your time."
* "You may not believe it now, but time will help in some ways."
* "Life can be unfair; this is unfair."
* "You're on my mind. I know you're surviving but how *are* you?"
* "I'm glad you are showing your anger with me because it lets me know how you really feel—maybe now we can talk."
* "You may not get over the death but you will get through grief."
* "Tell me how you feel," or, "What do you think about____."
* "I don't know what to say to you. Help me."
* "I feel so helpless. Do you?"
* "I have so many questions. Do you?"
* "Would you rather not talk about it?", or, "Do you want to talk about it?"
* "I wish I knew what you are thinking."
* "It's okay if you are at a loss for words when you are with me."
* "Of course you don't always know what to say. I know that."
* "It isn't easy, is it?"
* "How do you plan to deal with this?"
* "You must be very confused. Do you want to talk about it?"
* "I'm confused. May I talk about it?"
* "If you care to tell me what you want or need, we can work together to find some answers."
* "I just can't find the words. I'll write to you." (Then do it.)

Suggestions from a Support Group
(Contributed by the Omaha-Council Bluffs Ray of Hope Chapter.)

"Give us approval for trying to resolve our feelings rather than

131

encouraging us to deny what we feel is or was our responsibility. This is growth—let us do it."   *Pam*

"Just let me be where I am. I can only be into today."   *Kate*

"Sometimes when people ask me how I'm doing, I'll say, 'I'm not doing well at all.' You'd be surprised how many will answer, 'Oh that's good.'"   *Roberta*

"It's never too late to send a card. It's been three months and I still look for them in the mailbox."   *Mike*

"When I got cards on the anniversary of my son's death day, I did not feel as if I were going through it all alone."   *Marty*

"So many people knew but never responded when my husband killed himself. I want to ask them did he mean so little that you can't even call or come over? Doesn't he deserve our grief?" *Barb*

"It's very painful when your own people fail to offer support, or condemn you for objecting to rejection."   *Jean*

"You know what was really great? We looked out one morning and the neighbor was mowing our lawn."   *David*

"Some people helped me that way too. Like little elves, they knew what to do and did it."   *Pam*

"It helped me when people let go and cried. I felt in touch with those people."   *John*

"People encouraged me to move—or come and visit them or to get out of the house. But I don't want to go away. There's a lot of me in that house. I want to be where I am."   *Bert*

"I don't want to see myself as a victim but in reality I am a victim. Part of this grief process is that of having been victimized." *Kate*

"I don't like it when people always ask me how my mom is doing. I say, 'She's OK,' but I want to say, 'Her life stinks—what did you expect?' or 'She's home alone, why don't *you* call *her*?' I guess they think they're doing their duty by asking us kids. But actually that's a way of avoiding her."   *David*

"I want to be normal again. But I know it will be a new normal. I see a different me taking shape."   *Jana*

"I want to be different—not necessarily better."   *Joe*

"For a while I was so angry over her suicide that I wanted to kill someone—maybe even myself. Some days, I'd go around just looking for someone to fight with. At first, I didn't want to think or hear that anything positive would come of this. But as time passes, and I mellow, I do find myself finding things that are positive. Maybe that's not so bad."   *Jim*

"If you really want to know how to help us survivors, then why don't you (my friend or family member) go to a support group and learn what to say—how to help."   *Lisa*

"Don't shut out friends that were close to the person who suicided. I could tell the family of my friend such neat things about him if they would listen. Maybe it wouldn't hurt as much as they are afraid it would."   *Joe*

"It's too bad that we are the victims and still have to educate the public."   *Marty*

"My husband died. I disappeared. I am a suicide-survivor victim."
Barb

"I feel like I goofed—big time. Like someone put something over on me and all the world sees it. I am embarrassed and humiliated."
Jim

"People notice us in a different way. We feel as if we are the object of something—but what? We can only guess."   *Bill*

"Don't call me co-dependent. It's not true. Co-dependent people stay with the situation and take the abuse or just complain. They don't put the troubled person in hospitals or go to counselors or just leave. I tried all those things. I'm not co-dependent."   *Kate*

"We know that we have no control over the situation when someone dies a 'natural' death, and that helps in dealing with it. With suicide, however, survivors realize (or believe) that we *did* have some control but messed up. The result is a personal affront. We feel as if we have been deceived—betrayed—duped. It's like running through the world naked. It makes news." *The Group*

"People are often quick to imply that if we had forced psychiatric care or hospitalization on our loved one that we'd have prevented the suicide. But what would you do? You take your child, or anyone you love, whose psyche is sick, and frighten them with incarceration, or remove them from the familiarity of home and family, isolate them, give them drugs, tie them up, befuddle their brain with shock treatments and what can you expect? You've got to look at it from both sides." *The Group*

"Include us, please. Don't say, 'I'll see you at the meeting,' or 'Are you going to church?' or 'Are you getting out enough?' or 'You should try that new restaurant in town.' Instead say, 'Join us,' or 'We'll pick you up.' Widows much more than widowers, complain of being left out of social functions. Men are invited out, taken care of. Women seem to be expected to find their own way although they should be no more of a fifth wheel than is a man. One widow says, 'A friend of mine got divorced and we had a freedom party for her. She received gifts of sexy underwear and promises of being introduced to this or that eligible man. I've been widowed eight years and I've never received that kind of support. Don't get me wrong. I'm all for her starting a new life. She's my friend and I want good things for my friends. But, I want good things for me too. I want that kind of support for me too." *Wives of suicided spouses*

Suggestions from Support Group Leaders

"First of all, remember to give your leaders a pat on the head from time to time. We all need that, like a good old loyal dog."
Pam Tanous

"Remember that the focus for the survivor changes from dealing with the *shock* of the loved one's death to the *shock* of dealing with one's own life." *Pam Tanous*

"With survivors of suicide it is often not the crisis which exists in reality that should concern us. Rather, it is the crisis which their mind perceives as reality that's important." *Mike Millea*

"Grief is not a mental disorder. Survivors are not "sick" but they do need attention and understanding just as do those who are suicidal. In both cases, that cry for help is also a cry for life."
Roberta Blaesi

"This condition wreaks havoc with the survivor's sense of self-worth. The survivor needs to be seen, heard, recognized, validated. That form of nourishment is needed as much as food."   *Dee Wicks*

"Survivors of suicide suffer from an assault to their self-image. That's not the same as having low self-esteem. Low self-esteem is basic—it goes way back—but this blow to the self-image is situational. In order to help, you need to be sensitive to the whole pattern."   *Elaine Petersen*

"Grief is characterized by its intensity and focus. Its persistence sets these survivors apart. I don't see how they can endure without people who love them."   *Jana Knudsen*

"It helps survivors to understand that their grieving depression is different from clinical depression. The survivors' depression is situational—*they know the reason why*. Clinical depression affects a lot of people who attempt or complete suicide, but they don't understand their depression."   *Mike Millea*

"Grieving people have so much to give—they are so sensitive to life and death."   *Rev. George Barger*

Many survivors are suffering from Post Traumatic Shock Syndrome in the sense that they have already battled for years with the fear and stress of suicide threats and/or attempts in the home. Some are exhausted from the "need to be there all the time just so something wouldn't happen." Others lived under constant threats from the suicidal person that he or she would withhold love and affection if the family didn't behave just as he or she expected. The entire scene can be a form of blackmail where the survivor experiences years of guilt for not meeting the needs of the suicidal person long before that person completes suicide. The survivor then feels, "I knew the worst would happen. I tried to prevent it and I failed. At the same time I'm glad its over." This severe before *and* after stress can cripple a survivor emotionally without proper love and guidance.

Tips for Listening

It's very difficult to be objective in a conversation involving a person with whom you are emotionally involved. Some listening techniques used by counselors, however, can also be useful in non-professional situations. For example:

* Listen intently. Hearing is passive; listening is responsive.
* Don't insist that the speaker get all the details exact. That doesn't matter so much at this point. It's the feelings that matter, right or wrong. Settle the feelings first. Facts can be dealt with later. Even then different people will see the event different ways.
* Suspend your own feelings. Don't make prejudgments which can shut out new messages.
* Ask yourself, "What is this person really telling me?" Avoid jumping to conclusions.
* Let them know when you don't understand. Repeat what they have said, using feeling words to describe emotions and interpreting what you hear. Double check.
* Let them know when you do understand.
* Focus on main issues and avoid being sidetracked by details.
* Say, "I think I'm hearing you say thus and thus. Am I right?" Practice this until you can reflect back on what has been shared with you. Confirm what has actually been said.
* Don't be surprised if you get an "I don't know," in answer to your questions. Often, they don't know. That's part of the problem.
* Make sure you are both speaking on the same level. It's pretty hard to "talk turkey" with someone who isn't also talking turkey.
* Realize that no matter how tactful you try to be, someone may not see it that way.

Understand that it is difficult for some people to share deep feelings. They may fear being hurt, rejected, or ridiculed. Some people have never experienced unconditional love from others and do not know how to accept it. They believe that talking will not help, that they are always misunderstood or tuned out by others, so why try. Some people may believe they have no worthwhile ideas to offer and so withhold comments and personal feelings.

Some people are just very shy, others very private.

Be patient and understanding with these people. Their suffering may be compounded by their inability to communicate. You may have to take the lead more than once. If you feel you must say something, point out that, although tragic, suicide is not something shameful to be hidden away. Dealing with it openly can help restore the shattered lives of the survivors.

Bear in mind that a broken heart or broken spirit is not that different from a broken leg. We give a broken leg time to heal. We treat it gently; we withhold expectations and demands that it perform before it is able to. We'd never say to the person who is lying on the street with a broken leg, "Well, if you won't help yourself, we can't help you, either," or, "He just wants attention, so ignore him." That's like claiming that a crying baby just wants food so ignore it, or that sick people just want medication, so ignore them.

It's all justified attention, whether it's food for the baby, medication for the ill, or warm, loving care and patience for the broken in heart or spirit. Often, it is the sharing of the grief reaction itself that helps bring out an acceptable understanding and emotional healing. By our presence, we affirm that the mourner is not alone. Just as joy shared is joy increased, grief shared is grief diminished.

Widowed by Suicide

*"It's as if there is something mysterious about us
that not even our best friends will tell us."*
A Surviving Widow

It has been said that when your parent dies, you lose your past; when your child dies, you lose your future; and when your mate dies, you lose your present. I believe that when any loved one dies, you lose something of all three.

When a husband dies, the wife also loses her companion, lover, peer, confidant, friend, and in many cases, part of her financial support. One wife summed it up by saying, "He was the person with whom I shared my hopes, dreams, fears, and concerns. I expected us to grow old together. My husband was my past, present, and future."

When a husband dies by suicide, his widow may feel that she is different from other widows. Her husband died deliberately, not by natural causes such as an accident or illness. She may feel deserted or abandoned by him. Some widows have called this the ultimate rejection. I've even heard it described as psychological rape. "He took something from me against my will," or, "He destroyed my ability to trust."

During the first Ray of Hope support group meeting in 1977, those of us who had been widowed by suicide were drawn together. All survivors of suicide share many similar feelings, but there are differences depending on whether the survivor is a parent, child, sibling, friend, lover, co-worker, peer or spouse. Those of us who had been widowed by suicide wanted special meetings to meet our particular needs.

For example, one widow said, "I felt so sorry for a friend of mine when her son suicided, but now that I'm widowed, I envy her because she at least had her husband to share her grief with—I'm all alone and feel so overwhelmed."

"Overwhelmed" is a word often used by women who have been widowed by suicide. They suddenly find themselves responsible for everything—parenting, running the home, running a business or earning the family income—in addition to grief. "I couldn't take time to grieve for over a year," says Pat. "I had to take care of his business, his employees, all his problems he left behind." Some wives lose the sole source of family income and may even be deprived of her husbands death benefits. The suicide of a husband/father can affect the standard of living in a way that does not occur when the suicide is that of a different family member.

In suicide situations, I have discovered that attitudes toward surviving wives are often different from attitudes toward surviving husbands. Frequently, the wife is blamed no matter what the case. For example, if a husband kills himself, it's the wife's fault. If a wife kills herself, it's also her fault.

A woman who completes suicide is often described as unstable, unable to cope, or "the nervous type." The implication is that she has a character defect and that her problems stem from her own internal weakness. In other words, she killed herself not so much because circumstances drove her to it, but because as a woman, she was too weak to handle them. A man in her situation, it is implied, would not have succumbed.

On the other hand, society tends to justify the husband's action by attributing it to external causes. Comments such as, "He was under a lot of pressure, you know," or, "He wasn't himself," or, "With his family and his business falling apart, how could he help it?", indicate that people tend to blame external forces, and not the man himself. This tendency to justify the man's action prevails despite the popular idea that to die by suicide indicates weakness or mental illness, and despite statistics which show that twice as many men as women kill themselves.

Surviving wives tend to assume greater responsibility for their influence over others than do surviving husbands. Widows also believe more often than do widowers that parents, in-laws, and even their children hold them responsible for the suicide. Sadly, their perception may be right. Many times, a mother would report that one of her children told her, "It's your fault that Dad killed himself." In some cases, these children had defended their mother against the man's abuse, then changed their attitude after his death, leaving their mother hurt and puzzled.

When older children change attitudes after their father's death, they may not necessarily mean to hurt their mother. Perhaps they feel guilty over their own negative thoughts or interactions with their father before his suicide. Maybe they were afraid or ashamed of him. Now, they are trying to compensate in order to make themselves feel better. Seventeen-year-old Doug, said, "I didn't know my dad was so unhappy. I thought he was mean on purpose and I hated him sometimes. Now I'm sorry and I can't tell him. By defending him when someone criticizes him, I feel like I'm making up for it. I can't tell Mom that because she thinks I'm blaming her if I defend him."

Most of the surviving husbands I talked with have stated that children and other members of their own family (not necessarily the case with *in-law* family members) were supportive of them rather than critical. Children and other people may, in fact, have hostile feelings toward the surviving man, but are less willing to confront men than they are women about those feelings. Society in general, appears to be intimidated about confronting a man about his attitude or behavior, but is most aggressive when confronting a woman under the same circumstances. Comments from male support group members ranged from, "Sure, people feel sorry for me. Why shouldn't they?" to, "I'll always love her but I just want to put this behind me and get on with my life."

Actually, women want that too, but they seem to approach it differently. Generally, women want to learn how to handle their grief, while men want to get rid of it. G.M.'s father (see *Legacy* in Part I of this book) moved away after his wife's suicide, remarried quickly and never mentioned her name after that. How easy it is to run from the phantoms we fear or to pretend they don't exist.

Society's tendency to blame the woman also affects her view of herself. Surviving women talk more about feeling guilty than do men. "I should have known." "It was my fault." "I wish I could make it up." People seem to *expect* the woman to have guilt feelings.

Marie, who struggled for years with intense guilt feelings, had worked her way through them at the first support group meetings she attended. Elated, she looked forward to sharing her new freedom with family and friends. Several weeks later, she returned to a meeting, shaking her head. "I can't believe it," she said. "Some people are actually upset because I changed so much. They want me to feel guilty. Now, I feel guilty because I don't feel guilty."

The widow's self-image also may adversely affect her ability to recover from grief. Traditionally a woman's identity is centered around family and marriage; a man's is not. Studies indicate that more women kill themselves following the loss of relationships, while more men complete suicide following a business or career crises. Because of this, a wife's suicide may not be a personal blow to the husband's self-esteem in quite the same way as his suicide is to hers. This is not to imply that he does not miss her or struggle with feelings of responsibility. However, his ability to recoup faster and to go on with his life may be enhanced because he has not lost his image as a man, and because he encounters a more supportive society among his peers and family.

When the surviving wife is blamed for her husband's death, it obviously affects her relationship with others and especially with men. Jean, a member of the support group, discovered that some men were actually afraid of her. When she explained her husband's death to an acquaintance, he responded with, "What's the matter with you? Weren't you good enough to keep him alive?"

"How could he say that?" she cried. "I know many widows and widowers whose spouses died of lung cancer from smoking or from a car accident and no one accuses them of failing to keep their husband or wife alive."

"I've thought about this," continued Jean, "and I believe the reason why some men feel threatened by a woman whose husband killed himself is because he sees her emotional strength as dangerous, especially if the man is afraid of being in touch with himself. He fears that she might see through him too much and expose all his secrets or weaknesses. The strong or insightful woman is avoided because she will not be easily controlled or fooled by a man who is unsure of himself and needs to feel in control." Jan, another group member, agreed, but added, "It's really sad because with my new insight into myself and others, I am less judgmental and more loving. I'd be a better wife now, not a dangerous one. A mature man would welcome my depth of understanding."

Many of the women agree that men tend to shy away from intimate relationships after learning how their husbands died. "I have good relationships for a while," says Lynn. "Men tell me that I have helped them. But they date—and marry—someone else.

One man listened attentively to my story, gently probing for details, then said, 'I'm staying away from you. You're lethal.' Would he have said that to me if my husband had died in any other way?" she asked. "I think not."

Both men and women express concern about telling people that their spouses killed themselves. Jim, a widower, says, "Sometimes, after I explain how she died, people just look at me and I think I can hear them think, 'You are stupid. Your wife killed herself.'

141

Judging from comments that have been made to me, I realize that people have assumptions which reflect back onto me. It's as if they think I am a weirdo—that I can't carry on a relationship. The whole thing is so unfair because my marriage was a lifetime commitment to me."

As a result, many widows and widowers of suicide either evade the truth or lie about how their spouse died. "When I'm truthful about his suicide," says Nell, "men scrutinize me, then they don't come around. So, when I meet someone new, I say he died suddenly, or unexpectedly, or of heart failure. The issue with me is that he died. When I mention suicide, their reaction changes and the issue becomes *how* he died."

There seems to be general agreement among all of us, both widows and widowers alike, that the blow to our self-esteem and the time involved in adjustment definitely affects our attitudes toward intimate relationships and alters the way we look at life. According to comments at Ray of Hope support group meetings, wives or women seem to have to work harder, or at least differently, than do men or husbands in order to free themselves from pain, trauma, and social stigma. (This does not imply that men grieve less intensely or recover better than women.)

As *widows*, we discovered that we usually waited longer than men before attempting to rebuild a social life with the opposite sex. Two to four years is not unusual for women to wait, while many men start dating within a few months. Widows also feel over-whelmed when they are faced with the deceased's business affairs. "I'm just too busy to have time for a social life," say many women.

As *women*, most of us fell into one of four categories: those who withdrew from all close relationships, those who avoided relationships with men, those who married soon after their husband's death, and those who had relationships but refused to remarry. Many of the women in the last two groups described their new relationships as destructive, but hesitated to end them.

One young woman said, "I don't fit into any of those categories. I went with every man I could, as soon as I could. I was intimate with over fifty of them in two years. Steve's suicide was such a rejection of me that it just about killed my image of myself as a desirable woman. Maybe I thought I was showing him (or myself) that someone wanted me after all."

Comments from some of the women in long-standing but

destructive relationships were:
* "Now, I doubt my ability to be a good wife or mother."
* "I'd rather have a little happiness with a lot of pain than no happiness with no pain."
* "People think I'm the merry widow. It's my front—a facade. Inside, I'm afraid to let anyone know how much I hurt. When people say or assume things that hurt me, I just laugh it off. That's my way of protecting myself."
* "I'm really hard on this guy. I push him around. I think that if he leaves me, then I'll know it was because of me that Larry killed himself. Maybe I'm testing to see if I really am a dangerous person—you know, if I pushed Larry into it. If this guy stays with me, then I guess I'm O.K."
* "I think I take abuse from him (my present relationship) because I'm trying to make up for what I didn't do for Jim."
* "Maybe no one will want to marry me now. Maybe this relationship, bad as it is, is all I'll ever have. I don't want to take a chance on being alone again."
* "The effect of my husband's suicide on me is permanent. Relationships all seem to fall apart. I feel rejected over something and withdraw. For some reason, I now tend to choose relationships with no future or commitment."

Some women choose to be alone. "I will never allow myself to go through anything like this again," they say, or, "I will never again love someone so much that I could be hurt this much," or "I've had so much hurt, why invite more?"

Many of the women shared the underlying attitude that they would avoid the pain of another loss of this kind at any cost. For some of the women, the answer meant withdrawing or isolating themselves from close family members as well.

Lola, for example, lost her husband, son, and a daughter within ten years. A surviving daughter and son try to stay in touch. "I want to respond to them but I can't," says Lola tearfully. "I can't take the chance. Being close means that I'll love them too much—I'll want too much from my daughter or son, and should I lose one of them also, I'll hurt too much—more than I can handle."

Another common attitude is, "I no longer have the patience or tolerance for nonsense—for people who play games—so I just stay away from people I choose not to deal with."

Karen Kenyon, author of *Sunshower*, (Richard Marek Publishers, 1981), the story of her own journey through this special kind of grief, wrote to me, "What a hold the person who takes his or her life seems to have on us! I wonder how much energy we should still give to the subject. The ironic part is that the topic keeps calling me. Not that I bring it up, but the world calls on me, and so the door is opened, and since I know I can contribute I sometimes take up the task again, but there should be a time to say no."

I think some people hang onto the past because they are still trying to feel protected—and to belong—in the old way. They think it's all they've got. But it isn't. Virginia Graham says something in her book about widowhood that helped my decision to make a major break with unhealthy ties recently. She wrote, "Maybe what you miss most is the burden of your marriage, not the joy. Maybe you're only mourning the loss of predictability."[23] Her comment can apply to any sort of burdensome relationship and helped me to see that I was grieving over what was familiar to me, but not good for me. What freedom that realization brought about.

I believe those of us who are widowed by suicide sometimes think we have to become strong to offset the hurt. The more sensitive we are the more we feel the hurt. People who are less feeling appear to be stronger because they don't care. They can throw something off and go on—but the caring suffer more and may appear weaker when they are actually stronger. Perhaps it's this strength that separates survivors—especially the women—from other people. It's so misleading because other people then think that we are so strong we don't need anyone else—but we do. Having a strong character doesn't mean we are not vulnerable to pain and loneliness.

Not all survivors' stories are war stories. In many cases, family ties are strengthened after a time, as happened with my oldest son, Daryl, and myself. Sometimes, family members need to process their grief with others outside the family before they can reunite with their family. This is an important point to consider by anyone who is puzzled or worried about the distancing of one or more family members. Give each other and yourself permission to take some distance if you need to. It may not be a personal thing and not everyone will understand the need for distance, but some people have to do it because it feels right at the time.

While these attitudes of both the woman who is widowed by

suicide and of society toward her are mutually debilitating, I believe they can be overcome. The wife of a suicided spouse should take care not to project her fears of rejection, judgment or abandonment onto other men, thereby ruining her chance to love or be loved again. Many a woman does heal from these terrible wounds to her psyche and goes on to take part in close loving relationships and remarriage. As her feelings about herself as a worthwhile person develop and radiate outward, the world around her relaxes and responds in kind. But she needs patience, assistance and understanding to get there.

For suggestions on how to cope with grief, see the chapters on *Helping Yourself Survive, Helping Survivors Survive*, and *A Time to Talk: A Time to Listen*.

What to Tell The Children

"Together, parent and child, you will try to build the temple of tomorrow's dream upon the grave of yesterday's bitterness."
Rabbi Earl Grollman

Children, like adults, need to grieve and deal with their feelings. Losing a family member through death is traumatic enough. Losing a parent or sibling by suicide compounds the agony. Since children may cry one minute and laugh or play the next, their suffering isn't always obvious. But it would be wrong to assume that they aren't deeply affected. Because they are too young to have developed coping mechanisms, children desperately need the help of caring adults to go from denial through the pain and despair of depression to acceptance and hope. Yet, their special needs are often not recognized by caregivers or family members, and are therefore missed.

Studies show that nine out of ten suicides occur in or near the home. Except for spouses, children are the second largest group of persons to witness a suicide or discover the body. Think about the effect that has on a mind. Even if children did not witness the death or discover the body, they may have arrived soon afterward. During the commotion with police, ambulance, etc., they often are overlooked, pushed aside or removed from the scene.

In some cases, a child has been directly involved—asked to help in the act. For example, a child may have been instructed to push away a stool or help steady the gun. A mother who took an overdose of sleeping pills, told her six-year-old daughter, "When Daddy calls, tell him that Mommy is asleep and won't wake up." Now a woman in her twenties, the daughter still struggles with self-blame and anger at both parents. She has vowed that she will never have children of her own.

She is struggling with what suicidologists refer to as having inherited a legacy of suicide. Another example is that of a young widow who tearfully reported that her seven-year-old son asked, "Mom, how will I grow up to be a man now that Daddy is gone?" She answered, "Oh, you'll be a man—a fine one—just like your daddy was." He responded, "Does that mean I'll shoot myself too?"

A teen-ager, whose father suicided after killing another person, says, "I feel tainted—as if I have inherited bad blood." An inher-

146

itance is something handed down; a legacy is something that can be inherited. (I am NOT saying here that suicide is genetically inherited, but that the idea can be seductive.) Many authorities cite the alarming statistic that survivors have a 300% increased risk of suicide. We should never underestimate the power of that legacy.

Children of a suicided parent show a higher rate of psychiatric disturbance than those who have lost a parent through other forms of death. Studies show that some adults who lost a parent by suicide during childhood seldom experience a day in which they don't recall the parent's death or fantasize their own suicide. Some fear that they are destined to die by their own hand.[24]

Many suicidologists believe that boys who have lost a father by suicide are especially at risk to self-destructive behavior and possible suicide themselves. While the loss of either parent is traumatic to a child, the loss of a father prior to adolescence (whether through death, divorce, or emotional estrangement) has been shown to be especially stressful to boys.

The period after a suicide is a crucial time for avoiding a serious disintegration of the parent/child relationship and for creating a special bond through love and sharing. Most professionals believe children should be told the truth about suicide under the following conditions: (1) they should be told while the parent or family is in counseling or therapy, (2) the information should be given to the child gently and perhaps gradually, (3) counseling should be continued after the children have been told. However, the subject cannot always be confined to the counselor's office, it can come up anytime. When it does, some of the following suggestions may be helpful.

Invite children to share feelings by saying something such as, "My heart aches sometimes. Does yours?" Or, "I miss Daddy's smile so much. What do you miss the most? When do you think about him? What do you remember?"

Encourage questions about death. If you don't have an answer, don't hesitate to admit, "I don't know," but be willing to say, "Let's talk about it," or, "What do you think?" Listen carefully to the child's questions. Don't answer more than is asked. Keep in mind, however, that children may have difficulty verbalizing their thoughts and feelings. For example, they may ask, "Do you still love me, Mommy?" when they really want to know, "Will you leave me like Daddy did?" Questions about heaven and death may really mean, "What's going to happen to me?" or, "Who will take care of me?" Constantly reassure them of your love and continued presence.

While talking is important, don't overtalk. Actions speak louder than words. By your actions, you are telling the child how you are handling yourself and what you expect from the child.

For this reason, don't be afraid to cry or show grief in front of your children. Rev. John H. Hewett says in *After Suicide*, "You will teach your child about suicide, whether you plan to or not. They will watch you and notice your responses. They learn from you how they should act in the aftermath. So, decide now to be a good teacher."[25] A child imitates the parent's behavior. When a parent acts as if nothing has happened, the child will model this behavior with the same kind of pretense. As a result, the child feels insecure.[26]

If you avoid expressing grief or talking about the deceased, you are also sending a message which says you don't care about that person and don't miss him or her. Children may misinterpret sadness, depression or preoccupation as personal rejection ("Mom (or Dad) doesn't care about me") or as blame ("They blame me for my sister's death"). A child may suspect that you wish he or she had died instead of the other person. A child may feel that if you don't miss his brother or sister, you wouldn't miss him or her either if they were dead. In a child's mind, that may mean that you don't really love any of them. Not knowing how to express this fear, your child may become withdrawn, rebellious, angry, or resentful. This misinterpretation is not limited to small children. Adolescents, teenagers, and even adult children may share this feeling.

You might say to a small child, "Sometimes, I miss Daddy so much that it makes me tired and all I want to do is sleep. Sometimes I don't hear you when you talk. That doesn't mean I don't love you. Let me know how you feel and let's be patient with each other."

If, on the other hand, you actually are rejecting or blaming the offspring or sibling, don't try to fool him or her. Hiding the truth of your feelings won't work. Children know when you aren't honest. They know when they are being resented. You have a lot of power in your hands when you reject or blame the child. Power that can destroy the child, the family, or yourself if you aren't careful. This situation may require professional help for both or all of you.

Regardless of the child's age, be honest and consistent about what happened. Misrepresentations and changing versions will create suspicion and confusion which lead to distrust and resentment. Even young children may know more about death than you realize. Tell the truth in simple words without dwelling on the gory details. It is especially dangerous to lie to a child who was present or nearby during the event. Avoid saying, "Oh, you saw that on TV," or "You must have been dreaming." The child may not argue but may come to distrust both himself and you.

Euphemisms, half-truths, and evasions tend to increase anxieties and add confusion. The child already has enough self-doubt, anger, guilt, and fear. If you pretend that Grandpa has gone on a long trip, the child becomes confused and may refuse to trust you. Respect a child's emotions and intelligence.

Depending on age, children may not have learned yet how to express emotional pain in words. Watch your child at play. His or her "acting out in play" will tell you far better than the child can explain how he/she is handling the situation.[27] Look for nonverbal clues such as a return to infantile behavior, thumb-sucking, bed-wetting, nightmares, or a fear of going to sleep. Other clues are fighting, temper tantrums, poor grades, excessive crying, or even relief—especially if the child had been afraid of the deceased person. Older children may constantly chatter, be full of nervous energy, or develop stomach aches or flu-like symptoms. Some children may assume the responsibilities of the deceased family member by trying to become, for example, the "man of the family." Others may try to become artistic or athletic in an attempt to follow in the footsteps of a deceased sibling. They may also withdraw or become rebellious.[28] Be patient with all these behaviors rather than to punish; assure the child that although this behavior is of concern to both of you that it will pass.

Offer the child acceptable ways to vent their anger and energy through physical activity—permission to yell and scream sometimes, a punching bag to hit or hammer and nails to pound.

One of the most common feelings which has to be dealt with is guilt. For example, if a child has wished a parent or sibling dead during a disagreement and that person later dies, the child may feel directly responsible, believing that their thoughts were powerful enough to kill. "I hoped Daddy would die and he did." Because such "wishes" are more likely to occur in families characterized by

149

conflict and quarreling, the children may already feel guilty about a lot of other things. They may blame themselves for being a burden to their parents, for causing strife in the family, or simply for being "bad." If they knew about an earlier suicide attempt or threat by a family member but kept it secret, they may blame themselves for not preventing the death. If they wished "he'd do it and get it over with," they may later be consumed with shame and self-blame.

Other emotions to recognize are anger and feelings of rejection. Children may feel angry at a dead sibling or parent for leaving them or for inflicting grief, anguish, and shame on the family. At the same time, since they may feel the need to be loyal to the deceased, they are torn inside. Helpless and despairing about their inability to change the situation, they may lash out against anyone for any real or imagined shortcoming.

For this reason, be careful not to point a finger at anyone. A child who has witnessed marital arguments may blame the surviving parent for influencing the other parent or for not preventing the death. They *need* to know that other factors were at work. Creating divided loyalties or instilling anger will only harm the child.

Avoid "blaming" God. Don't tell the child that God needed her daddy in heaven or took her brother to be with Him. She will believe that God is responsible for the death of her parent or sibling and will find it impossible to believe in a loving heavenly Father. [29]

A third common emotion is fear. Young children may suddenly fear being alone or may panic in normal situations. They fear change and separation because they don't know how to handle it.

I believe that even small children feel an innate need to protect their parents and much of their behavior stems from this. For example, an older child may hesitate to discuss the subject because he/she doesn't want Mother to cry. When she does, the child feels guilty and helpless because of failing to keep Mother happy. In frustration, the child may lash out in anger at either the parent, someone, or something else.

Sometimes a child will attack someone he/she perceives to be an offender and cry, "Don't hurt my Mommy." A child may try to protect the remaining parent at any cost. After all, it's dreadful to realize that you are tiny, dependent, and may lose the other parent as well. If the suicided parent cried often (or yelled, for example) prior to the suicide, then crying or yelling is a bad sign in the child's eyes. Some children may decide to protect the remaining parent by staying glued to Mom or Dad's side. You can't fault a child for wanting to protect you, but you can talk with him or her about it.

Most important is a loving attitude by the surviving parent and other family members. Handle the child's feelings delicately. Forcing a child to repress honest fears about loss can prevent him or her from learning to adapt to the changes that loss brings and may create a potentially explosive situation. Encouraging a child to express thoughts, feelings, and fear will ease their sense of helplessness and responsibility.

Some ways children can express themselves other than through conversation is through the creative activity of art or poetry. Encourage them to draw pictures, keep a journal, write a poem or story. Many professionals emphasize the value of family memorial services at home, church or grave site. *Together*, make plans and carry them out; to donate flowers, plant a tree, or share pictures and stories about the deceased. Anniversaries such as birth dates and death dates are a good time for these events.

Some communities have support groups, camps or special activities for children after the death of a parent, relative, friend or sibling. Read books about loss and grief and don't forget the funeral director as a resource for printed material, films, and videos. Let children see you confront your grief and share in your efforts to resolve it.

Give children the affirmation of life they so desperately need to dispel their own morbid thoughts and death wishes before they get out of hand. This is postvention in the truest sense—preventing a suicide a generation in advance.

What About God?

*"For he shall give his angels charge over thee, to keep thee in all thy
ways. They shall bear thee up in their hands, lest thou
dash thy foot against a stone."*

Psalm 91:11, 12

The subjects of God, salvation and forgiveness are very important to many survivors who have contacted Ray of Hope. They ask:
"Is suicide an unforgivable sin?" "Where is my loved one now?" "Is
she or he doomed to eternal damnation?" Sometimes they question, "Is something wrong with my faith if I give in to my grief?"

Some people seem to think it is wrong for a Christian to grieve
for any length of time. At a prayer meeting, a young widow was
trying to explain her feelings. Amy was at the stage where longing
and pining can cause symptoms that are more physical than
emotional. Her entire body ached. One well-intentioned member,
in an effort to help her, quoted one Bible passage after another.

Not being widowed herself, she had completely missed Amy's
point and insisted that Amy should have more faith, read more
Scripture. "But I do," Amy wailed, "and I still hurt." Of course, she
hurt—and she would continue to hurt until the stage had run its
course. The implication that she was unfaithful to God because she
felt grief only compounded her pain with new guilt and fears.
Sometimes, a physical need must be met before one can be spiritu-
ally responsive. When Amy was ready, her faith was the source of
strength she'd always known it was. Having faith means being
open to the healing of grief—not the absence of grief.

The Bible is filled with stories of people who mourned. Scripture
gives us explicit permission to grieve, and provides promises of
healing, examples of how to mourn, and suggestions for using the
experience to help ourselves and others. For example:

God uses sorrow: John 16:33, 2 Corinthians 7:9-11.
Rejoice in sorrow: Psalm 31:24, Psalm 126:5-6, Rev. 21:4,
    Rom. 12:15.
David mourned Jonathan: 2 Samuel 1:17-27.
Jesus grieved: Matthew 26:36-46, John 11:32-38.
Jesus overcame the temptation to despair: Hebrews 5:7.
Resolving anger: Matthew 5:23-25, 18: 15-17, Ephesians 4:26.

152

Resolving anxiety: Matthew 6:34, Philippians 4: 6-9, 1 Peter 5:7.
Resolving guilt: Psalms 103, 1 John 1:9, Jer. 3:13.
Resolving loneliness: Isaiah 40:31, Philippians 4:13.

After suicide, some survivors begin to question their belief that nothing exists after death. This idea no longer supplies the comfort they seek. They want more, a spiritual concept that allows them to co-exist with that person after all. A future beyond becomes meaningful. But what if that future is one of lost souls and condemnation?

Several suicides are recorded in the Bible but none of these cases mention eternal damnation.[30] Judeo-Christian history contains a long record of martyrdom which is considered a form of suicide. Jewish tradition includes a belief that since man is created in God's image, then suicide is destroying God's image. Those of the Jewish faith consider this a sacrilege, but not a condemnation of someone who was in great physical or mental anguish. Even Judas was not condemned for suicide, but for betraying Christ.

One may argue that the commandment, "Thou shalt not kill" (Exodus 20:13), applies to suicide as well as murder or homicide. But this may not be entirely scriptural. The Hebrew word used for 'kill' (*ratsach*) means to violently slay or murder with force and premeditation. It is not used in connection with suicide accounts in the Old Testament, which seems to reinforce a distinction between suicide and murder. With suicide, death is considered to be the desire of the dying persons rather than a "wanton uncontrolled attack upon the life of another." [31]

Perhaps God looks more at the *intent* of the suicide victim. Consider the circumstances of a young Christian woman who killed herself to avoid being raped and killed by a group of soldiers during the takeover of her country. It would seem that the soldiers' intent was to experience a thrill through the act of rape and killing. The girl's intent was to seek relief by killing herself. For survivors who are concerned with questions of sin and salvation, a look at the victim's intent can be very comforting. For those who are concerned with pronouncing judgment, a look at the intent may be quite revealing.

The Bible is ambivalent about suicide and perhaps that is for the best. If suicide were definitely condoned as an acceptable way of coping with stress, many lives might be needlessly destroyed. On the other hand, if suicide were explicitly condemned, it would conflict with the biblical image of a just and compassionate God.

If suicide is generally viewed as behavior which influences the time and method of one's own death, then all forms of self-destructive behavior fall into that category. If self-destructive actions were unforgivable, a large number of mankind could be automatically condemned. Where would that leave hope? I believe the very silence of Scripture concerning suicide allows for hope—both for the victim and for the survivor.

A Minister's View of Suicide

Condensed from a sermon, Suicide: An Unpardonable Sin? *by Rev. Wasena F. Wright, Jr., at the Mount Vernon United Methodist Church in Danville, Virginia, July 19, 1981.*

Wherever or however suicide occurs, it is tragic. It brings great sadness and confusion into the lives of all those involved in the life that is gone. The church ought to assure loved ones that there is a loving Father who cares and understands.

But from what I have observed on these tragic occasions, the church has often been more judgmental and more despairing than hopeful. I don't mean this as a condemnation of the church; the reason is probably that we are not sure what the church believes about suicide. We are aware of the usually unspoken, unofficial, "underground" doctrine of many churches—that one who completes suicide is lost forever. We have heard suicide called an unpardonable sin. But most church members are confused about the matter. And those of us who are supposed to be leaders in the church are not doing much to help our people understand the issue. I have not found a single sermon on the subject of suicide. I'm sure sermons on suicide have been preached, but they are not easy to come by. So I have been trying to reach some conclusions of my own about the subject. Let me share some of the results with you.
I. First, let's look at the Scriptures.

1 Samuel 31 is the story of Saul leading his army to defeat in battle against the Philistines. Saul himself was not afraid of being killed by the Philistines, but of being captured and taken back as a prisoner to be an object of mockery and shame. Saul took his own sword and fell on it, taking his own life. When his aide saw what Saul had done, he fell upon his sword and died, also.

In Judges 16 comes the account of Samson and Delilah. You may recall how Delilah was able to learn that the secret of Samson's strength was in his hair. As he slept, Delilah had a man shave his head, and the Philistines were able to capture him. They blinded him, bound him, made sport of him and humiliated him. They gathered to make sacrifices to their god for delivering Samson to them, and at the height of their celebration they brought out Samson to humiliate him further. They tied him between two pillars which supported the temple. Samson prayed to God for strength that he might take revenge on the Philistines for taking his eyesight. With a surge of strength, he pushed on the pillars, shouting, "Let me die with the Philistines!" The temple fell with devastating results, killing Samson and thousands of the enemies of Israel, assumed to be enemies of Israel's God.

I never thought of Samson's death as suicide until I read an article by Tina Richards in the March-April 1981 issue of *Your Church* magazine. Mrs. Richards, a church employee and free-lance writer, writes out of her own experiences in dealing with her husband's suicide, and she shows some interesting insights.

She points out that Samson was not "ill." He knew exactly what he was doing, and even asked God for the strength to do it—and God gave him the strength. He took his own life, yet in Hebrews 11:32-34 we are given names of great men whose faith enabled them to accomplish greater things, and Samson's name is included.

Other cases of suicide recorded in the Scriptures include the suicide of Judas in the New Testament. Suicides happen at all times and at all places—including Biblical times and places—and yet the subject is never directly addressed in the Scriptures. There is no explicit condemnation of suicide in the Bible. Suicides occurred in the time of Jesus, but He never spoke out against suicide. And Christians have not always condemned suicide.

II. Let's examine the church's attitude toward suicide in history.

The early Christians' attitude toward suicide was one of acceptance, particularly when persecution made life unbearable for them. The Apostles did not condemn the practice, which apparently was rather common. In fact, several motives for suicide were regarded very favorably. The suicides of the martyrs were not considered displeasing to God. Saint Cyprian declared that the Christians were invincible because they did not fear death and did not defend themselves against attacks. Tertullian, addressing Christians in prison awaiting martyrdom, encouraged them to go to death unafraid, citing some celebrated ancient suicides and reminding them that the joy that awaited them would enable them to endure the torture.

Religious fervor has led many persons to put an end to their lives so that they might sooner enjoy the bliss of paradise. Throughout history there have been accounts of mass suicides, including that which occurred at the fortress of Masada, where 960 Jewish occupants formed and executed a suicide pact as the Romans were storming the fortress. Another more recent example is the tragic mass suicides among the nearly one thousand followers of the fanatic religious leader Jim Jones, at Jonestown.

If there is no explicit condemnation of suicide in the Scriptures, how did we get the common church position that suicide is a sin?

Saint Augustine was the first to denounce suicide as a sin. Unquestionably he shaped the later attitude of the church toward suicide. In *The City of God* he discusses the question at great length. He concludes that suicide is never justifiable. He bases his opinion on the fact that suicide eliminates the possibility of repentance and is a form of homicide and therefore a violation of the sixth Commandment. It is interesting that for the first 400-500 years of the Christian Church the sixth Commandment, "Thou shalt not kill," was interpreted that one should not take the life of another.

Saint Augustine found himself in a dilemma regarding some of the suicides that had already been canonized by the Church. The Church had made saints of some who had committed suicide, so Augustine admitted certain exceptions. He said that some, Saint Pelagia, for example, had received divine revelation which released them from rules applying to others.

In the fifth century, the Church concurred with Saint Augustine, and suicide was specifically condemned by ecclesiastical law. By the time of Thomas Aquinas, suicide was considered not only a sin, but a crime. In his *Summa Theologica*, Aquinas formulated the attitude that the Roman Catholic Church still holds regarding suicide. This argument against suicide is deeply rooted in fundamental Christian doctrines, such as the sacredness of human life, the duty of absolute submission to God's will, and the extreme importance attached to the moment of death. Aquinas stressed the argument of Augustine that the person who deliberately takes away the life which the Creator gave him displays the utmost disregard for the will and authority of his Master, and, worst of all, that he does so in the very last moment of life when his doom is sealed forever. This Aquinas regarded as "the most dangerous" thing of all because no time is left to expiate it by repentance. The Roman Catholic Church has never wavered from this pronouncement, and her power was so great that Christian Europe legalized her teachings. Those teachings, of course, were ingrained in those who later came to this country, and this is how the prevalent Christian feeling about self-destruction originated.

The eighteenth-century philosopher David Hume, in his famous "Essay on Suicide," examines all the arguments against suicide. He says, "If suicide is criminal, then it must be a transgression of our duty either to God, our neighbor, or ourselves." He concludes that a person who retires from life does no harm to society—he only ceases to do good, which, if it is an injury, is of the lowest kind. Hume insists correctly that there is not a single line of Scripture which prohibits suicide. Instead of interpreting the commandment "Thou shalt not kill" as a divine prohibition against suicide, he holds that it evidently meant to exclude only the killing of others, over whose life we have no authority.

Also in the eighteenth century, the French author and philosopher Voltaire, though opposed on principle to the philosophy of despair, admitted that despair may be absolute and inescapable. In such cases, suicide may be defined as an act of necessity.

Rousseau writes (in *La Nouvelle Heloise*) that when life becomes a burden to its possessor and is a benefit to no one, the sufferer has a natural right to cut it short.

III. Conclusion: How then shall we view suicide?

Is suicide a sin? If I must give an answer, my answer is yes. I agree with Augustine that God is Creator, the Giver of life. I believe human life is sacred because it does come from God. I believe we are given the gift of life for a purpose. We have our contribution to make to life. God knows and we do not when the purpose is fulfilled. It is wrong to take away the life God has given, whether it be one's own life or the life of another. So suicide is, for me, a sin.

But is suicide an unpardonable or unforgivable sin? Here I must answer with a resounding no! Suicide destroys the body, which ought to be a temple, but can scarcely blaspheme the Spirit.

If suicide is a sin, then let us remember that we are all sinners in one way or another. But we have a God who offers us forgiveness; a God who loved us enough to come to us in person and lay down His life for the forgiveness of our sins. Think about it; "He laid down His life" for us. In John 10:17-18, Jesus says:

> For this reason the Father loves me, because I lay down my life, that I may take it again. No one takes it from me, but I lay it down of my own accord. I have power to lay it down, and I have power to take it again; this charge I have received from my Father.

If Jesus gave His life voluntarily that we might have life, could His death be suicide? If He laid down His life, if no one took it from Him, could that be seen as suicide for the benefit of others? Then there must be the possibility of an act that is technically suicide but not a sin. Are there, as Augustine supposed, "exceptions"?

The real tragedy of suicide is not whether or not one repents. The real tragedy is that a person gets boxed in and feels such despair that he or she can find no way out. Paul Tillich, in Vol. II of his *Systematic Theology*, writes:

> In despair, not in death, man has come to the end of his possibilities. . . .The pain of despair is the agony of being responsible for the loss of the meaning of one's existence and of being unable to recover it. One is shut up in one's self and in conflict with one's self. It is out of this situation that the question arises whether suicide may be a way of getting rid of one's self. . . .There is a suicidal tendency in life generally, the longing for rest without conflict.

Tillich says in another place, "Suicide actualizes an impulse latent in all life." In this he is in agreement with psychiatrists who say that almost everyone, at one time or another, has thought of suicide, though few actually commit it.

Arnold Bernstein, a psychoanalyst, who frequently deals with suicidal people, wrote an article entitled *"My Own Suicide."* In this article he says that there are situations in life which could possibly make him commit suicide. He said:

> I long ago surrendered that arrogance of believing that I am better than persons less fortunate than me. . . . We are all so much more fragile than we know, and our strength can dissolve into weakness with a turn of the wheel of fortune. . .because what we feel and do can hardly be understood apart from our past and present life circumstances. . . .We must all bear in mind, "There, but for the grace of God, go I."

God knows our weaknesses. We are all so fragile, and we are hurt and inflict hurt so easily. We all need to be more loving and understanding where this kind of tragedy has occurred.

Most Christians believe that the decision to end human life is something that should be left up to God. Nevertheless, we must not become judgmental and arrogant at this point. Saint Paul, in his letter to the Romans, calls us to have faith that nothing can separate us from the love of God in Christ Jesus. Listen to him:

What then shall we say to this? If God is for us, who is against us? Who shall separate us from the love of Christ? Shall tribulation, or distress, or persecution, or famine, or nakedness, or peril, or sword? No, in all these things we are more than conquerors through Him who loved us. For I am sure that neither death, nor life, nor angels, nor powers, nor height, nor depth, nor anything else in all creation, will be able to separate us from the love of God in Jesus Christ our Lord. (Romans 8:37-39)

As I read over this list, I believe that death by suicide does not have the power to separate us from the love of God. The God I know and worship loves and cares for everyone. He cares for the one who commits suicide and loves the person with a love that exceeds any form of earthly love. And I believe that in judging that person He will take into account more than the manner of death.

Suicide is a reality. Many of us know someone who has completed suicide, or someone who has attempted it. It is important that we consider the subject, because the way we view suicide will determine how we are able to relate to the family of the suicide victim or to one who has attempted suicide. We, as the people of God, need to be able to bring comfort and understanding to those who try to handle the emotionally shattering experience of suicide. It is not up to us to pass judgment. We leave that to a loving Father.

The Scripture from 1 John says ". . . and the blood of Jesus His Son cleanses us from all sin." This assures us that no sin can place us outside the love of God as revealed in Christ Jesus our Lord, and I submit to you that suicide does not have that power either.

Dr. Wright, a native Virginian, is a graduate of Ferram College, Randolph-Macon College and Union Theological Seminary in Virginia. He received his Doctor of Ministry Degree from St. Mary's Seminary & University, School of Theology, in Baltimore, Maryland. He is a member of the American Association of Suicidology and he has organized a Suicide Survivor Support Group at Mount Vernon United Methodist Church in Danville, Virginia. Copies of Dr. Wright's sermon in booklet form may be ordered from Annandale United Methodist Church, 6935 Columbia Pike, Annandale, VA 22003.

In the Aftermath: The Funeral and Investigation

"The visitation is the social release of the body.
The funeral is the spiritual release of the body.
The burial is the physical release of the body."
                                        Ed Vining, Past President
                          Illinois Funeral Directors Association

"Funeral directors are in a distinctively unique position regarding suicide survivors. They are virtually the only professionals to come into contact with nearly all suicide survivors. Their influence on the suicide survivor's grief resolution process can be invaluable, and unequaled by any psychologist, physician, counselor, clergyman or other caregiver."[32] They are in a position to counteract three important issues which contribute directly to survivor stigma and to delayed or unresolved grief. Counteracting those issues is easy once the funeral director and family are aware of them.

First, suicide is the only form of death in which we argue over the right or wrong of it. It is the only form of death where we come into contact with moral and value judgments concerning both the deceased and the survivors; and where the survivors' own moral and value judgments influence decisions concerning the funeral. The debate begins immediately.

Should the service be public or private? Or none at all? Do we hold it in the funeral home rather than church or synagogue, and why? Who officiates, the clergy or a friend (just in case suicide is a sin)? Do we keep the details from grandparents and/or children? How? What do we tell the newspapers to print and what do we say to insurance people?

What do we tell visitors in case they ask personal questions? What if he or she was mentally ill? Can suicide be inherited? Whose fault was it? Was it mine? Should we see the body before it is prepared for visitation?

The basic concern is not so much that someone died but that he or she died by suicide. We need to ask if some of the issues would be so important if the person had died in any other way.

The funeral director can discourage the family from rushing through the service too quickly. Sometimes, decisions for a quick

161

or closed funeral are based on shame, fear and humiliation. Be sure these feelings don't overshadow judgment when making plans. A private or quiet service can do the very thing survivors want to avoid—invite questions and draw attention to the mode of death. The more you hide, the more suspicious it looks. Funeral directors should take care to explain the importance of the funeral ritual.

The second factor is that of acceptance of not only death, but death by suicide: intentional, deliberate, self-inflicted. Listen to people carefully; are they saying, "I can't believe he's dead," or "I can't believe he killed himself." There is a big difference there. Self-inflicted death is not the same as death by natural causes and its very nature makes it difficult to believe and accept.

These survivors often need to accept the fact of suicide before they can even begin to deal with grieving over the reality of death. This is a double blow; not just death, but suicide.

An opportunity to see the body before it is prepared can help a family to come to terms with self-inflicted death—"He really did do it himself." The idea of seeing a bullet wound may be unthinkable at first, but weeks or months later, when one still questions if it actually was suicide as opposed to an accident, murder, or natural death, they may regret not having seen for themselves. Time alone with the body also helps to overcome shock.

Kay, a young woman who attended Ray of Hope meetings, had been away at college when her teenage sister shot herself. Everyone but Kay participated in rushing the girl to the emergency room, and was there when she died. When Kay arrived home her sister was ready for visitation. "I envied their being there when she did it—seeing all the blood and gore. They can accept that she shot herself. I can't. When I saw her she looked asleep." Kay also mourned another loss. She explained how the experience created a sort of bond among the rest of the family. They shared a common experience. She did not; she was left out.[33]

When Iris Bolton's son shot himself, Iris insisted on spending time alone with him before he was sent to the funeral home. She needed to see and touch her son in death just as she had at his birth. It was an important part of closure in their mother-son relationship. Seeing was believing.[34]

Funeral director Bruce Conley says, "It is the simple permission to hold the lifeless body of a loved one, to speak the unspeakable words of anguish . . . to share the guilt of a loved one's parting note—the simple permission to do these things and more, which bring a comfort that nothing else can give. So simple yet so profound in the midst of the crisis."[35]

The funeral director can advise the family members to at least seriously consider seeing the body before preparation. He can explain what they might expect to see, answer questions about autopsies, preparation for burial and the like. He can point out that it might aid them with acceptance of the idea of self-inflicted death, thus eliminating some of the future denial and searching, and then give them time alone to make their decision. Some people definitely *know* that they do not want or need in any way to take part in this and that should be respected. However, the offer and explanation should still be presented by the funeral director to all the family. Sometimes, not knowing can be as bad as knowing.

On the other hand, those who witnessed the death or found the body may already have all the visual proof they need. We tend to remember what we have last seen, so in some cases, viewing the body in the casket may help to soften the impact of an ugly memory.

Third, death by suicide seems to infer a weakness or failure on the part of someone; the family, the suicide victim, or both. Much of the survivors' grief work consists of repairing these damaged images. They work to repair the self-image of the suicided person to show that his or her actions were justified in some way. They also work to rebuild their own shattered sense of self-worth as a valuable and competent parent or spouse.

This is a large part of the suicide survivor's grief work and the funeral director can do a great deal to start that rebuilding process as soon as possible. Remember that suicide survivors tend to be apologetic or defensive when they should be proud of their loved one. The goal is to replace the curiosity and embarrassment of visitors with memories of the person as they were at their best.

Bruce Conley suggests that funeral directors encourage the family to arrange a sharing table the night before visitation. Ask each family member to bring something uniquely precious to themselves—a photo, a personal article or a memento. Perhaps someone has written a poem or a moving tribute. Encourage the family to share, not only the sorrow of death, but memories of living.[36]

Something a little different than a sharing table is an appreciation table. I attended the funeral of a fourteen-year-old boy whose thirteen-year-old sister tended a display of her brother's prized possessions and achievements. She showed visitors his artwork, poetry, model airplanes, and 4-H awards. His favorite toys were there; his baby shoes; his first book; school pictures and papers arranged to show his progress and accomplishments as he grew up.

This was the family's way of saying, "Our brother/son was a valuable, worthy, talented person and we are proud of him." People left that service with impressions of Chris as a person rather than "that boy who killed himself."

The funeral director should suggest in advance "that family members write personal letters to the deceased, expressing those unspoken thoughts and feelings that death prevented them from saying while the person was alive. The letters may be sealed and privately placed in the casket by family members—each in his own way, place and time."[37] Others may want to place a personal item, or other token of affection or of good-bye in the casket as well.

Usually, death brings families together. Unfortunately, suicide tends to pull them apart. The funeral director can use the actions of sharing and participation to unite that family from the beginning.

The Suicide Prevention Center, Inc., in Dayton, Ohio, offers these suggestions for funeral directors:

1. Offer printed copies or recordings of the service.
2. Offer printed material and other resources concerning suicide. At some later time the family may benefit by seeing some videotapes or movies which explain the reasons for suicide, especially that of a teenager or young adult.
3. Have information available about sources of legal and financial aid in the community, especially for the wife and family of a suicided husband.
4. Offer information about support groups, grief groups, counselors and therapists who are knowledgeable about death by suicide.
5. Utilize trained members of survivor support groups and/or other suicide support agencies in your area to circulate freely among those present at the visitation to provide one-to-one assistance.[38]

In addition, the funeral director should be aware of the unique aspects of after-suicide grief and be willing to spend some extra time discussing that with the family or call in a survivor who is willing to counsel about funeral plans and after-suicide bereavement. Many funeral homes now have grief counselors to help their clients understand the dynamics of their grief.

Funeral director Ed Vining cautions that involvement of the funeral director is proper up to a point. He says that too much involvement makes the funeral director primarily a caregiver, while with no involvement, the funeral is just a business transaction.[39] However, armed with adequate information and sensitivity, the funeral director is in a position to assist greatly in reducing the stress and damaging repercussions of this tragedy. With effective intervention, some issues do not grow into big issues.

The Investigation

All too soon, the shock of the suicide wears off and survivors begin to ask questions—questions they were unable to formulate or confront immediately following the death, such as, "How do the police know it was self-inflicted?" "Why won't they tell me how they know that it was not an accident or murder?"

These questions may have been there in the mind immediately following the death, but all natural responses and spontaneous grief in the case of suicide must be put on hold during the investigation. And that's what is so dangerous for the survivors.

"Within seventy-two hours after suicide a sense of shame and guilt is already established in the survivor," says Karen Letofsky, "and this sense of guilt increases."[40] With death by suicide, we are denied the immediate response of comfort and permission to cry or grieve, as these feelings and sympathy from others must be pushed into the background while dealing with investigative personnel. "Only after the investigation is complete will these personnel extend support to the bereaved and by then it could be too late."[41]

William Anderson, coroner in McLean County, Illinois, says, "I'm often confronted by survivors who have many of the questions and statements used in the booklet, *After Suicide: A Unique Grief Process*; memories, guilt, shame, anger, incomplete mourning, the lengthy search for meaning, depression, denial and repression reactions. I would sum it up with the following: suicide survivors do not understand what we do as coroners.

"A complete autopsy is used to eliminate rather than prove a point, i.e., did or did not have cancer, did or did not die from gunshot wound, did or did not die from brain tumor—did or did not have blood or urine alcohol, did or did not have carbon monoxide, did or did not have drug overdose and/or therapeutic levels of prescribed drugs, did or did not find bullet or bullets in body and did or did not have other trauma. The scene of investigation is usually conducted with a police agency, i.e., position of body, measurements, position of the weapon, etc.

"The families usually demand right *now* to see the suicide note and they have a right to. Suicide is a horse manure death for everyone to work on—family, fire department, coroner, police, news media, etc. We often are not prepared to handle the surviving family members and it is frustrating to us to not have the answers.

"I believe the coroner must in some way detach himself from that frustration so that he or she can conduct an independent, unbiased, and in the end result, a proper (homicide, accident, suicide, natural or undetermined) verdict as a proper "cause" of death (autopsy). At the same time, this should be done with a sense of compassion and diplomacy in regard to the surviving family members, and to their right to know what the police and coroner's investigation has shown in their family member's death."[42]

One of the most involved and perhaps most misunderstood duties of the coroner or medical examiner is that of determining if the death is accidental, suicide, homicide or of natural causes.

Although exact duties may vary from state to state, a general outline of their duties is as follows. They:

"1. Investigate:
   a. The manner of death (homicide, suicide, undetermined, accident or natural).
   b. The cause of death (through the use of autopsy, psychological autopsy, medical records).
2. Identify: a. The body. b. The evidence. c. The facts.
3. Notify the next of kin.
4. Estimate the time of death.
5. Assimilate this information into investigative reports and autopsy reports.
6. Conduct inquests into manner and cause of death.

7. Serve as coordinator between the decedent's relatives, law enforcement agencies, public health agencies, hospitals, public institutions and political bodies of government."[43]

"The position, condition, and location of the body itself is frequently highly significant. The items on or about the body, the condition of clothing, direction and nature of fluid drainage are important."[44] "These things tell us if the person died here or somewhere else. Was there a fight or struggle? Did someone alter the scene or change the condition of the body after death?"[45]

What types of deaths are investigated?

"1. Sudden or violent death (whether apparently suicidal, homicidal, or accidental), including but not limited to deaths apparently caused or contributed to by thermal, traumatic, chemical, electrical, or radiational injury, or complication of any of them, by drowning or suffocation, anesthetic deaths or therapeutic misadventures.
2. Maternal or fetal death due to criminal abortion, or any death due to a sex crime or crime against nature.
3. Death where addiction to alcohol or to any drug may have been a contributory cause.
4. Death where the circumstances are suspicious, obscure or mysterious, or where (in written opinion of the attending physician) the cause of death is not determined.
5. Death without medical attendance by a licensed physician."[46]

The coroner or medical examiner looks for such things as:

"1. Wounds: Bullet, blunt instrument, stabbing, cutting, etc.
2. Burns: Thermal, chemical, electrical.
3. Crushing injuries: Injuries from machinery—moving or stationary. Vehicular (includes automobile, streetcar, bus, train, motorcycle, bicycle, etc.).
4. Injuries from an explosion.
5. Poisons taken orally, by injection, inhalation or absorption from body surfaces."[47]

167

He also looks for evidence such as any instrument or object that can be associated with the death. He takes measurements between the body, walls, windows, doors and other fixed objects and of any distances between where the body was found and where the wound and injury took place. He looks at auto skid marks, takes fingerprints and obtains blood-alcohol analysis.

Witnesses and family members are asked for names, address, phone numbers, where they were at the time of death, what they saw or found, and any other pertinent information, such as, the deceased's vital statistics and medical history.

If they are conducting a psychological investigation, they may also ask questions about the victim's past reactions to stress and to family crisis. They will examine past behavior by asking family and friends if the victim suffered any recent loss or change in home, job, finances, or relationships. They may inquire about mood change, changes in activity, or talk about suicide or about going away.

"Cumulatively, these things tell if this is a genuine suicide or perhaps something else—a murder made to look like a suicide or an accident masquerading as a purposeful act."[48]

Some tips for the coroner and medical examiner suggested by the Dayton, Ohio Suicide Prevention Center, Inc., are:

1. Remember that anger of suicide survivors may not necessarily be directed at anyone in particular although it may appear that way. Actually their anger is directed at everyone and anyone.
2. Keep the privacy of the family in mind when notifying them. Some survivors have felt that they were the last to know of the death as other people were told by the coroner's office when they were trying to locate the family for notification. It is better to just indicate to others that an emergency has occurred.
3. Notifying family members of a death over the phone is a cold and isolating experience for them; better to be there in person.
4. It is important not to leave the survivors alone after notification. When you leave, try to arrange for a family member, friend, neighbor, clergy member, etc., to stay with the person.
5. Include family members in decisions that are being made. When all the decisions which involve them are made for them, they are likely to feel powerless, and helpless.

6. In determining that death was a suicide, one will have to interview people closest to the deceased person, family, friends, and co-workers. All of these people, with various levels of intensity, will be grieving and upset by the death. The most intense feelings will generally be among family members. The way in which the coroner's office deals with these people is important for their self-esteem and learning to cope with death. In being sensitive to the feelings of family members it is good to keep these things in mind.[49]

We cannot underestimate the value of proper education for first responders, the clergy, funeral directors, and other health professionals, and how that information, in turn, contributes to understanding support for suicide survivors.

The Value of Support Groups

"Though we meet as strangers, by our love we will be known."
Iris Bolton

People who come to suicide-survivor support group meetings are fighters. They are saying, "I don't want this to destroy me."

In times of crisis or stress, the help and support of other people is invaluable. Historically, persons in need have been offered assistance by family members, friends, neighbors, and church and community groups. Today, however, hundreds or thousands of miles may separate family members. Many communities are so transitory that people hardly put down roots and get to know each other before they move on. Therefore, distance and other limitations (demanding schedules, family activities, etc.) often keep even the most sympathetic friends or family members from helping one another. Support groups partially fill this gap.

The objective of these support groups is to offer a variety of ways to help with grief work. (See appendix for information on obtaining a list of group locations.)

1. *Meeting other survivors.* Support groups provide a chance to share with others who have had a similar experience. You can express yourself without having to provide background information in order to explain or justify your position. That's a relief!

2. *Acceptance.* Some survivors fear rejection if they share their true feelings with friends and family. In the group, you can loudly express anger, wallow in guilt, and say what you want. Members of the group understand and can offer support and empathy better than friends and family members who may want to help but feel uncomfortable trying to do so.

3. *Someone listens.* You can talk freely in an accepting atmosphere about your thoughts and experiences no matter how frightening or offensive they may seem. You may discover you are not so different—not "going crazy" after all.

A newcomer to one of our meetings watched in open-mouthed silence as another member grasped for words, repeated herself, lost her train of thought, spilled her coffee, and tearfully apologized for her confusion. Finally, the new member said, "This sounds awful but it sure helps me to see you like that. The other day, I took the butter from the refrigerator, put it into the microwave, then put my purse into the refrigerator. Then I sat on the floor and cried because I thought I was going crazy." Her story sparked a valuable and funny discussion on how disorganized thinking is a part of grief.

4. *Someone cares.* As members begin to feel a responsibility for one another, someone may confront you in a way that no family member would dare try. This interaction can force you to take responsibility for your own decisions and actions. It can help you keep from giving in to the temptation to withdraw behind excuses and cop-outs. You may become angry at a fellow member who "calls" you on something but you'll probably learn to accept credit for failures *and* successes more realistically.

The group can also guide you through potentially explosive situations. For example, survivors often identify themselves with the deceased in an extreme way. They put themselves so much into their shoes, so to speak, that the thoughts of the victim become their own. This kind of thinking can be dangerous because the reasons for committing suicide may suddenly appear quite logical and even appealing. When members see this taking place, they may allow you to identify up to a point because they know you need to do so, but they will pull you back before you get lost in it. They are well aware of the danger points now and will take no chances.

5. *Getting in touch with yourself.* Isolation and emotional stress can distort your thinking in many harmful ways. One mother was blaming herself because her daughter often cried and became depressed after discussing her grandfather's suicide. In reality, the mother was handling the situation well. At a meeting, the daughter told us, "I get mad at Mom sometimes when she talks about Grandpa. But if she didn't, I'd never work it out."

A father in the group insisted that he was not angry at his suicided son nor did he blame anyone. It was obvious, however, that he was seething with anger and he soon transferred his anger to the group. Undaunted, one woman demanded, "Then, just who the hell are you so mad at?" When he hedged, someone else repeated the question. Then, gently and without condemnation, the group helped him to put his feelings into perspective. It was a breakthrough for a proud man. He didn't have to lose face and he benefited greatly from sharing his feelings.

6. *Finding role-models.* Lack of a role model contributes to your uncertainty and sense of isolation. Sometimes you just don't know how to act. Within the group, you meet others who have developed

workable problem-solving strategies and are willing to share ideas. Although group members cannot make decisions for you, they will suggest alternatives and will be interested in the outcome.

7. *Rebuild self-esteem.* The group helps you to enhance your self-esteem in at least two basic ways. Genuine acceptance of you and your problems helps give you a sense of worth. As you participate in the group and help others, you feel needed. This sense of making a positive difference in someone else's life is especially important if you feel rejected by the one who suicided.

8. *Supplement therapy.* If you are already in some form of therapy, the group can be a valuable addition to your treatment. If you have never considered therapy, the group can make you aware of other mental health resources.

9. *The family.* In a group you can move back and see your family system from a distance. You can see yourself and how you interact with your family without the defensiveness that often arises within the family group itself.

10. *Information resources.* Most groups offer printed information on aspects of grieving, living alone, coping with children, etc. Some have a selection of cassettes, pamphlets and book lists.

11. *Reintegration into society.* Grief and stigma associated with suicide can cause survivors to withdraw, believing they are a burden on society. Although in some cases additional professional help may be needed to return an individual to the mainstream of life, the group helps them re-establish social interactions.

12. *Meeting survivors socially.* Many groups schedule social activities, especially during difficult periods such as holidays when members are most likely to feel lonely. Often close relationships develop within the group and members contact each other outside the meetings for support, talking, listening, and friendship.

13. *The most important thing for leaders to remember is that this may be more of a crisis situation than a chronic condition (like drug abuse). Many people may only come to one, two or a few meetings. That's all right. They may know how to handle grief; they just need help with the crisis and you probably met that need—don't get discouraged.*

14. *Reaching out to others.* Many survivors feel a great desire to pass along their release and renewed interest in life. Chances are your heart will reach out to others in a new, sharper dimension. There are numerous ways to help, but you already have what can help the most—your experience and your healing. Share it.

Part III
About Suicide

How Not To Drown

Imagine you're standing on a river bank and just within arm's reach, a wader steps into a deep dark hole and begins to sink into the water. He thrashes about and calls for help. What do you do?

Would you look down and say, "So you think you're drowning, do you? Well, don't look at me—you have to learn to help yourself sometime," or, "Well, if that's what you want to do, go ahead. Drown."

Would you say, "Oh, you're drowning, are you? Well, you probably brought it on yourself. You asked for it," or, would you casually remark to others, "So-and-so is over there drowning but he just wants attention, so ignore him."

Would you say any of the above or would you reach out a hand to pull that person to safety, offer comfort and call for assistance? Indeed, you would give that person the attention he or she needs in order to survive.

The person who has fallen into a deep dark hole of despair and confusion leading to suicide, or a deep dark hole of sorrow and confusion following a suicide, is in just as much danger of drowning in unresolved emotion. Yet, it's so easy to ignore these outstretched hands and cries for help, or to complicate things by responding with a thoughtless or insensitive remark.

That drowning person doesn't want a list of instructions on how not to drown. He or she simply wants to be saved as do the suicidal. The survivor wants to be comforted. All want love and acceptance.

174

The Crystal Orb

"That question, 'Why did they do it?' seems to elude all of us in the final analysis. We tell ourselves that the real answer died with the victim. But, I wonder, did it really?"

A survivor

Consider a single crystal orb. A multifaceted shimmering crystal orb suspended on a delicate thread hanging in a window. The bright sunlight glitters on the many angles of the crystal, reflecting in countless rainbow colors, covering the walls and ceiling of the room. Occasionally, something—a slight change in air currents, perhaps—nudges the nearly invisible thread, causing the crystal to spin, or sway, ever so slightly. You do not really see the crystal react but you know that it has, because you notice the brilliant rainbow reflection on the wall beginning to move; floating back and forth, twirling around, bouncing up and down—sometimes disappearing and then reappearing where you least expect it—changing hues as it moves across different surfaces of wood, fabric, glass or wicker. This dance of colors and their effect can range from delightful and soothing to beautifully mesmerizing to near psychedelic hysteria.

As you watch and study the crystal, you do know that the sunlight from above has touched the light deep within the crystal, and the colors are a reflection of what is around. But you do not know which outside color is reflecting back inside to create more color. How do you know which surface of light or color is reflecting off which other surface of light or color? We don't. The brilliance of the facets may blind those of us who are looking but cannot see.

Isn't our human emotional makeup a lot like that? Constantly changing. Constantly being affected by the slightest change in the world around us, and at the same time, constantly changing in a way that affects the world around us, until we can't pinpoint exactly what started it all, or where, or why. The private emotional drama of the person who considers and acts upon suicide must be even more so affected by unseen and unaccountable changes both within and without.

Just as you and I cannot discover the source or trace the exact sequence of the crystal reflections, how can the suicidal person explain the multi-facets of his or her emotional makeup as it affects a decision? Rather, pondering on it may contribute to the confusion and anxiety. How easy it is to judge ourselves and others by reflected colors and not by the light within.

A friend told me about an ancestor who went into the woods and shot herself. The story was that she did it because she could not have a new dress. She was thirty-one. It was 1933. Do you think she really killed herself only because she could not have the dress? I don't.

We can speculate. We can imagine her feelings of frustration and hopelessness perhaps. But many women did not get a new dress during those years and they didn't shoot themselves. I doubt that the woman could have explained exactly why she chose suicide at that age or that moment in time.

I believe it is that way for the majority of suicides. Regardless of what seems like the motivating factor or practical aspects, no one can pinpoint or trace or explain all the reflections upon reflections which bring the person to that point. Perhaps, least of all, that person herself or himself who is at both the center and the edge of the crystal. Perhaps that is why most suicides leave no note, or if they do, it often does not answer any questions. For those who are gone and those who are left, it is like trying to determine the beginning or ending reflection of the swinging, shimmering crystal orb. No one knows. Not even the crystal.

Reflections About Suicide

"There is such an incredible loneliness there; a separation from life that begins long before the dying begins."

The primary purpose of this book is to help answer the questions that survivors ask themselves, others, and God in the months and years following the suicide. The one big question asked by all is, "Why do people kill themselves?"

Obviously, those who could best answer the "why" question are not here to do so. We can, however, study the setting and events leading up to both attempted and completed suicides. We can listen to the people who are thinking and feeling suicidal. We can use attempted suicides, completed suicides and the survivors' grief to gain some sort of answer to the why, and also to reach out and help all those touched by suicide.

If the first part of this book indicates that I am sympathetic with the plight of survivors, this part will appear to say the opposite; that my sympathies are with the suicided. Both are true. While I don't pretend to have all the solutions for both those who suicide and those who grieve, I do want to share my thoughts and observations about (1) *why* people kill themselves, and (2) *who* kills themselves.

Frankly, I think there are as many reasons for suicide as there are people who do it. But, reasons there are. Have you ever heard a child say, "When I grow up, I'm going to kill myself"? Something has to happen along the way to bring that about. What? I agree with the reasons for suicide cited by suicidologists, such as hopelessness, helplessness, isolation, loneliness, substance abuse, peer pressure, divorce, unrealistic expectations, loss of identity or self-esteem, loss of control, and affective illnesses (panic disorders). Some suicides, such as autoerotic asphyxia, are purely accidental. In addition, age, gender, ethnic background, social traumas, and health and financial status are listed as contributing influences. I believe all these factors are valid, but I think there is yet more to consider.

Suicidologists cite a number of common denominators when listing factors that influence the decision to suicide. While two of those denominators are feelings of *low self-esteem* and feelings of *helplessness*, I'm not so sure they are as "common" as we often think.

Consider those who have rebelled against a situation of conflict or abuse and have fought for the chance to develop their own individuality. An example might be the teenager who suicides because he believes he can't measure up to expectations and is not aware of alternatives to his dilemma. Suppose family conflict and arguments took place prior to the suicide. Would you say that his suicide was (1) part of his rebellion or retaliation to an injustice or a situation over which he had no control, or, (2) an act of giving up because of helplessness and low self-esteem? Maybe it was both, but you've got to have some pride and self-esteem in order to rebel or fight. Sometimes people with low self-esteem don't fight. They give in rather than give up. Another example of suicide as an expression of fighting back or of rebellion may be that of a person or group of people who choose to kill themselves rather than submit to torture or a perceived enemy. We're helpless when we don't have a choice, not when we do.

Another example is that of people who actually have very high self-esteem, but who find that things over which they have no control interfere with life. These are the ones who say, "I've had it. I won't live this way." That's not indicative of low self-esteem or helplessness. In both examples, I believe the people are saying, "I don't hate myself. I only hate what has happened."

Another common denominator is *isolation*. A. Alvarez, in *The Savage God: A Study of Suicide*, discusses the relationship between society and suicide as it relates to isolation and explains how society (the family and the community) ignores or rejects certain individuals for whatever reason (illness, race, old age, poverty, under-achievement, for being less than the accepted norm, and so forth) until the persons quit trying to help themselves and begin to withdraw. The more they withdraw, the more they are left alone, often becoming an object of disapproval.[50] These people are stunned—unable to stop the circle of mutual rejection as it closes in on them and wipes out alternatives, choices and escape.

Consider the devastation which can arise from this sort of alienation. The words, *loneliness* and *isolation*, as we commonly perceive them, are simply not strong enough to convey the depth of despair brought about by the feeling or knowledge of being ostracized, ignored or disapproved of by all of society.

This loneliness can be enhanced—not alleviated—by family gatherings, the social fellowship of summertime, holidays and even church groups. These people are the loners at the edge of the crowd or not present at all. In their heart they *know*, with crushing

178

reality, that they are not really an accepted part of the congenial, jovial sharing. This realization repeats itself; sometimes shattering through their consciousness like a summer thunderstorm; sometimes seeping into the soul like a Siberian chill.

Unable to tolerate the terrible ache (and here we *do* have hopelessness and low self-esteem) the person kills himself. All of society—the community, the family and the victim—have together brought about a climax of suicide. They all made choices leading to that; choices to ignore and ostracize, choices to withdraw.

An example is that of a twelve-year-old boy from Oslo, Norway who was badly scarred from measles. As the kids tormented him and his parents ignored him, he became withdrawn and sullen. Other adults began accusing him of just about anything that went amiss in the community. He hanged himself because he could no longer endure the rejection and "mobbing," a term used to describe long-lasting teasing and harassment, both in school and at home. ("Suicide Can Result from Excessive Harassment," Associated Press, January, 1983.) This is not a case of isolated individual self-killing; it is collective murder.

The first step in helping individuals and society out of this seemingly unsolvable impasse is for someone to recognize the problem and begin programs of self-acceptance and social cohesion. (For suggestions, see chapters, *Helping Yourself Survive* and *Breaking Free.*)

I also believe that some people kill themselves because of overwhelming urges which are influenced by chemical changes in their brain. Their moods can be changed by internal workings over which they have little or no control, and which are further influenced by environment. These genetic or chemical influences can also cause *clinical* depression—the kind that sticks like glue. It persists—it squeezes the juice out of life. Churchill called it the little black dog that followed him. That's different than *situational* depression which is usually brought about by some loss or series of events too overwhelming to handle.

Survivors need more information about these chemical changes and influences, whether genetic *or* drug-related, for their peace of mind. One mother said, "If the reason for my son's suicide is something that was beyond his control or my control, then that takes a lot of the burden off my shoulders. It helps to know that maybe the part of his brain that controlled his behavior just didn't

179

work any more. That's tragic—but it helps us to know that maybe he couldn't help himself."

Unfortunately, studies show that medication and counseling have not lowered the suicide rate. The AMA states that nearly 50% of suicides are "treatment suicides" (people who were in the process of getting help). That tells us that while drug therapy is valuable in relieving depression, it does not always alleviate the urge for suicide. The reasons for any suicide are multidetermined—biological, spiritual, psychological and social, therefore an understanding and treatment of the whole person is needed.

Some people may not be influenced by any of the above reasons but simply decide that now is the time to stop living. There may be no deep dark secrets, no seething caldron of anger, guilt or frustration, not even a "message to die"—just a calm, simple complacent decision of, "Oh well, this is it. The time has come."

Nowadays, some people are choosing "death with dignity" over pain, senility or poverty. Perhaps some are tired. I mean *really tired*. It *is* possible to feel just too tired to keep on living. Maybe some are just bored. In many cases, their suicide *appears* to be a well-thought-out action they wanted. However, some of those who think their decision is rational may not realize they are depressed, or are just plain fooling themselves. Most people really want to live even when they think they don't.

Much has been studied and written about the above factors and some very good books are listed in the resource guide in section IV. In *The Savage God*, Alvarez gives an excellent historical-cultural overview of how society's attitude throughout the centuries has changed and shaped our current and often conflicting views and reactions toward suicide.

However, later in this section I want to discuss two additional reasons (or factors) for suicide that come to my attention too often for me to discount. Those are: (1) I believe that many people kill themselves because they believe that is the message they have received from their own significant others. They feel victimized—pushed or driven to suicide (see the chapter *The Deadly Message*). This is not to claim that a message to die is a major or common factor in all suicides, but that it's influence is possibly often disregarded. (2) I also believe many people kill themselves because they lack a base or center in their spiritual life which produces inner resources and generates inner strength (see the chapter *A Unifying Force*).

But first, and perhaps just as important a question as why people kill themselves is the question, "*Who* kills himself or herself?" This may not be as simple to determine as we think.

Again, suicide is the only form of death in which we argue about the right or wrong of it, form personal opinions and project moral and value judgments upon both the suicided and the survivors. Yet, how can we rightfully judge these issues?

It gets complicated. To begin, some experts describe three categories of suicide: intentional, unintentional, and subintentional. With *intentional* suicide, obviously, someone fully *intends* to die and does so by choosing a sure-fire method.

With *unintentional* suicide, the persons do *not intend* to die. They want to live and resolve things. They are crying out for help and die by mistake. Something goes awry —a miscalculation of some sort.

Subintentional suicide includes those who live in such a way that their life style or actions have a direct influence on the time and way in which they die. This includes all sorts of self-abusive and self-neglectful behavior and could be just about anyone, which is the primary reason why it is so futile to label, judge and stigmatize either the suicided or the survivors. Alvarez quotes Daniel Stern, who says, "all of mankind [is] engaged in a massive conspiracy against their own lives that is their daily activity."[51]

Mrs. C. tells about her experiences in a psychiatric hospital following a drug overdose. Two days after admittance, she was asked to seat herself on a chair placed in the center of a small room, facing a table where four mental health-care professionals were waiting. They asked her questions about her background, her feelings, her current depression and her view of herself.

"I suppose there is medical support for this sort of questioning," says Mrs. C., "but I felt like my privacy was being invaded and my person exposed—like being emotionally raped. Finally, one of them asked me, 'Why did you want to hurt yourself?' That did it. I lost my temper. I sat there for a moment and looked at them. One was so obese she draped over the chair. The person beside her was chain-smoking. Another reeked of alcohol. It would have been funny if it hadn't been so sad. These people, who were abusing their own bodies, were asking me why I wanted to hurt myself.

"Then I said, 'I didn't take the pills because I wanted to hurt myself; I took them because I *didn't* want to hurt anymore. If I wanted to hurt myself, I'd do what you are doing. I'd smoke myself

181

to death, drink myself to death, or eat myself to death. Like you, I'd live on in such a way that I'd destroy my lungs or liver or heart or whatever. And like you, I'd take a long time to do it—hurting myself all the way. I took pills because I'd rather die quickly without pain than to destroy my body slowly as you are yours.'"

Shortly thereafter, Mrs. C. was dismissed from the room—and the hospital. But she had made a good point. Many people do choose to live in such a way that they hurt themselves slowly and die in agony. In a way of speaking, that is subintentional suicide. "These are the people," says Alvarez, "who do everything to destroy themselves except admit that that is what they are after. . .everything except take the final responsibility for their actions."[52]

However, society doesn't judge or condemn these people for their mode of death when they die. In fact, we praise and admire their courage for enduring pain, all the while ignoring the fact that they chose a life style leading to this death. Do you see the ridiculous contradictions in our opinions and attitudes?

It would seem that society approves and applauds when we kill ourselves slowly; passes judgment when we do it quickly. Perhaps that's the only real difference between many suicide and non-suicide deaths. One is slow and expected and called natural death. The other is quick, unexpected and is called suicide. One deliberate way of dying is socially acceptable; the other deliberate way is not.

There is yet another difference. The subintentional suicide does it in such a way that we can all become involved in their suffering. We get to hear about the pain, visit hospitals, compare surgeries, fuss over the sufferer, send cards and gifts. We can rub shoulders with blood and pain, and satisfy our nurturing instincts at the same time.

Maybe society resents the obvious suicide because he or she has deprived some of us from using a socially acceptable excuse to be symbolically involved with death and dying. When we are involved with someone who is slowly dying we can check out death for ourselves. We can look at death without trying it on. We can be voyeurs of pain and death—not experiencers. Perhaps there is something very normal, very human in us that needs to do this from time to time.

Alvarez compares the many centuries of mankind's personal involvement with gruesome torture and death (such as public executions, gladiator shows and hand-to-hand combat) with the notion that modern day's preoccupation with violence is "preternatural and is augmented by the violence served up, continually and inescapably, to entertain our leisure on film, television, in pulp fiction, even on the news."[53] He points out that the historical public was amused, excited, and delighted rather than shocked with displays of blood and gore; much as we are entertained by violence in the media, which Alvarez describes as "a kind of pornography, at once exciting and unreal."[54]

Those earlier people were involved with death in a way that satisfied both natural curiosity and the natural instincts of the darker side of the heart (whether we want to admit to them or not). In today's society, most people die only at a distance: in hospitals, in fiction, on TV, and in the news. We are separated from participation in the natural event of bloody death—*except for suicide*. With suicide, we can forget TV and jump into the fray. We publicize the death, rub the survivor's nose in it and glory in the aftermath. And therein lies the fascination—as if *suicide* were a substitute for the public execution or gladiator show. We can use the event of suicide to follow a natural inclination to examine death close up—but at what a price. No wonder survivors suffer deep scars from the resulting exploitation and humiliation.

There is yet another similarity between public execution and suicide, and that is survivors' guilt. A primary reason for abolishing public execution was the intense complications of survivors' guilt. This is why hospital visits, contact with the sick and infirm, the ritual of mourning, and active participation in funeral preparations are so important. All these activities are positive involvement which help to alleviate survivors' guilt. Even as civilized human beings we still need to participate in one another's death experience as well as life experience; but in a meaningful humane manner rather than as a proxy executioner.

In addition, those who die the "normal or natural" modes of death usually pass on with the loving, supportive care and attention of family and friends right up to the last minute. And that's the way to die, isn't it, sharing it with someone who is being there just for you, or holding your hand?

My sister-in-law, for example, was ready for death when she died of liver disease a few years ago. She was very ill and wanted to go. While she was hospitalized, there was time for the family to

183

gather, to take part in the last moments of her life, to witness this great event and passage in her life. As a result, this involvement helped to ease death for her, and made sorrow more acceptable for the family. My sister-in-law wanted death at the end but didn't choose it; some suicides choose death but may not want it.

I also believe there is a difference between *suicide* and *self-inflicted death*. Suicide is deliberate, intentional, but not, to my way of thinking, ever an accident. Self-inflicted death, however, may not be deliberate and/or intentional. One can accidentally die by self-inflicted death and not have meant to "commit" suicide at all. I can understand why some people refuse to use the word suicide. They have examined the circumstances and deep in their heart are convinced that death was not the victim's intentional deep-seated desire. They do know that it was a tragically mistaken or impulsive self-inflicted death. That's different.

In a similar train of thought, there is also a difference between wanting to *be dead* and wanting to *kill oneself*. For example, "I wish I were dead," usually means, "I wish I were free of this *situation*," and that statement is a cry for help. On the other hand, "I want to kill myself," may mean, "I wish I were free of *myself*," and in that case, is a statement of intended action. The difference is in the focus. In wanting to be dead the focus is on a *state of being* which is free of pain and violence and is directed *against a situation*. Wanting to kill oneself is focusing on an *act* of violence and is directed *against the self*. I think it must take great passion or great fury to kill oneself.

We are so quick to say that the suicided person had a choice; that they choose to die. I don't think it's that simple. I think people *decide* to kill themselves rather than *choosing* to die. Think about it. There's a difference. In order to make a choice, one must be aware of alternatives and free to choose one. If one does not know what other choices or options exist, and, as a result, believes that he or she has no other choice, then suicide is not a free choice.

In *Family Therapy for Suicidal People*, Dr. Joseph Richman writes that in order to make a truly free choice one must first have the necessities of life: home, health, happiness, acceptance, self-expression, career, and social features which provide a background for genuine choice. If someone believes that they lack one or more of these necessities, and are being pushed or driven to suicide, what then happens to free choice? [55]

I believe it's the living who put so much emphasis on the word *choice*. With the suicided the emphasis may have been *solution*. They did not view their decision as a choice but as the *solution*. Perhaps I'm not questioning the use of the word "choice" as much as the implications behind its use. For example, I don't think one can make a choice without having first been influenced.

To say, "I had no part in his or her choice," may actually be an insult to one's self, as if to say, "I am so simple, helpless and dysfunctional that I have no influence on anything." We just can't use the phrase "their choice" as a cop-out to avoid owning up to our own influence and involvement with another person's life. It's that *degree of influence* that survivors wrestle with.

I used to bristle when people argued with me that Bill had a choice. I would politely demure, "You might be right," when I wanted to retort angrily, "You don't know that. You didn't know him. How can you presume to read his mind? This 'choice' business is only your perception of reality, and maybe in your reality there *are* choices. You have to respect his sense of reality, and in his reality there was not. And in his perception of reality, yours doesn't matter. He acted on his reality, and you have no right to judge that! Just because your choice or view of reality is different doesn't mean it is the only right one."

I have mellowed since those days and am willing to concede that his decision was also, in a sense, his choice. I think my earlier defensiveness was more influenced by my perception that all this talk about choice often is a generalized answer to everything. I also saw it as a put-down of Bill's mental and emotional state—an implication that he wanted to die although I knew that he didn't. And, it was an effective way to shut me up.

The subject of suicide has been greatly rehashed, debated, condoned, and denounced. Well-informed researchers have pondered, probed and discussed the id, the ego and the super-ego; the wish to kill, the wish to be killed and the wish to die; the victim, rescuer and persecutor; projection and introjection; sadism and masochism—all as relates to suicide. (Indeed, one can become so carried away by study and research about suicide that one might be tempted to try it either for the sake of science or to escape the mountains of prose.) And yet, we still can't pick any one isolated act of suicide and satisfactorily explain all the variables. We can offer you a selection of variables to choose from; that's the only beginning we have.

Even if all we ever have to answer the "why?" are reflections and introspections, we still must continue to search for common denominators in order to establish guidelines that will help us prevent *senseless* self-destruction, however we may perceive it, choice or not.

In summary, it's pretty difficult to determine who does or does not die by what we traditionally consider or define as *suicide*. It is far more preferable, I believe, to turn one's thoughts and energy away from judging either the deceased or the survivors to healing the wounds of both the suicidal through prevention and of survivors through postvention.

Suicide may be one's choice, it may appear to be rational, it may seem to make sense, and may be done in the cleanest way possible, but there is still something sad and wrong about it. There is such an incredible loneliness there; a separation from life that begins long before the dying begins. It's so sad when someone thinks or knows that he or she must die alone like that. I believe that the passage from life to death should be a natural experience and should be shared with loved ones in attendance just as is the birth passage into life.

Perhaps the final reason why grief after suicide is so difficult to resolve is because we know that life should not have to be something from which anyone chooses to escape.

The Deadly Message

"The more one thinks they are lowly and flawed as a human being, the more one's choices diminish. One becomes bonded to violence."

Dr. John Bradshaw

"Next time, cut deeper."

"Next time, take more pills."

"Next time, take better aim."

"Why were you ever born?"

"Oh, we took family pictures while you were gone."

"All the family was together last week. We didn't call you because we didn't know if you were home."

"If it weren't for you. . ."

"I wish you were dead."

"Oh, go shoot yourself."

"We don't reject you—it's all in your head."

"Oh, we forgot about you."

"Don't listen to her. She lies."

"You make me sick."

"Oh, just stop talking about it and do it."

Idle words? Words uttered in a moment of anger or teasing and not really meant to be taken seriously? Perhaps to some of us that would seem so—but to many others the message is deadly serious. It is a message clearly telling someone to die.

We like to perceive ourselves as a society that always has the best of motives at heart and always does the best it can for one another. For the most part, I believe that as well.

But it is just not always true. Any history book, any current news media shows us differently. We do kill each other deliberately. Parents do abuse—and kill—their children. Some hate what they are doing and seek help in order to change, but there are those who seem to abuse deliberately, who know they will again, and do not appear to want to stop. The causes for that behavior are not the issue in this chapter. The issue here is the abusive use of scapegoating and victimizing as relates to the message to die.

In his book, *Family Therapy for Suicidal People*, Dr. Joseph Richman describes the process of scapegoating, the reasons for it, the ways it is acted out, and counseling techniques for healing the problem or changing the situation.

In a process Richman calls, "the 'quasi-courtroom procedure' one member of the family is subjected to a series of charges of wrong-doing without the opportunity to defend himself and with no one to support or defend him."[56] As a therapist listens to these charges, a pattern emerges; "Those who are doing the scapegoating are [actually] fighting for their lives."[57] There is a "rigid all-or-nothing quality" about scapegoating . . . where one is totally guilty . . . the others are totally blameless.[58] (Vogel and Bell (1968) have traced the steps through which a child is inducted into the scapegoating role.)

The following examples show that the "message to die" does exist in some families, and may be obeyed by the chosen family member. Names and events have been changed and altered to form a composite of cases. Any resemblance to any person or family is purely a coincidence.

MRS. J.

A mother whose twenty-year-old son had suicided reluctantly attended a support group meeting with her daughter. As she left, she said, "I don't need your meetings or your sympathy. He was my third child, and from the moment I knew I was pregnant, I knew I never wanted him. I had two more babies after him, but it didn't change things. I still didn't love him or want him. Even when he was little I'd tell him that I wished he would just go off and die. I don't understand why I felt that way because I love my other children and grandchildren. He knew how I felt. He accused me of not loving him, but I always denied it and called him a liar or a trouble-maker. And as he got older, he did get into a lot of trouble. I regret some of the things I said and did to him—it was wrong but now that he's dead, I really don't feel any grief or guilt. Just relief. We're all better off now that he's dead."

Her attitude may sound shocking but is, in actuality, all too commonplace.

JANIE

Janie, a beautiful young woman who attended support group meetings following the suicide of her brother, struggled with strong feelings of hatred toward her father, who she believed was responsible for her brother's death. The eighteen-year-old was often in tears when she discussed the situation at home, and often trembled when we spoke to her or touched her.

At the third meeting she announced, "I finally had the nerve to accuse my dad of what I think. I said to him, 'Well Dad, you finally killed one of your children.' He just looked at me, laughed, and said, 'How about that. Maybe you'll be next.'"

A couple of days later she left for college. Two weeks later she hung herself in her dorm room.

JOE

Several years ago a young man named Joe bought a revolver, wrapped it in bright paper and placed it far back under the Christmas tree. He wrote on the card, "To all of you from me." When the gift exchange was completed, Joe drew out the package, unwrapped it, placed the gun to his temple and said, "I'm giving you all what you want most for Christmas. My death." He pulled the trigger and died.

This appears to be a terrible judgment to hand down to his family—but Joe believed he had been driven to this point. And perhaps with reason. From childhood, Joe had been ridiculed and beaten by his parents, brothers and sisters. He was often left out of family meals and festivities—sent to his room or locked out of the house as one punishment or another. No matter what happened or went wrong, Joe was held responsible.

Joe's mother would sometimes call all the children but Joe to come into the house from where they were playing. After a while, wondering where they were, Joe would wander inside to find them finishing a meal. Joe's father would say, "You're late again. If you can't come to the table on time you don't eat." Joe's mother would smile sweetly and say "What's the matter Joe, honey? Aren't you hungry?" Joe wasn't hungry by this time as his stomach was a painful knot of fear, sadness, and puzzlement.

His father had a routine of favorite lines about Joe whenever he had an audience.

"Oh, he'll always be worthless."

"I don't know where he came from, someone's garbage, mor'n likely. Don't pay him any attention."

"He's sure not like one of us."

"I keep trying to lose him but when I turn around he's still there."

189

Joe knew his father was not joking. Neighbors knew the sound of blows and sight of bruises on Joe's body were no joke either. But in those days you minded your own business—not the neighbor's.

After Joe's death, the father ordered that every photo and every possession of Joe's was to be destroyed. They were. "I don't ever want to hear his name mentioned," the father said. "As far as we are all concerned, he never lived—never deserved to live. He did what he wanted to do. So be it."

In the years that followed, one member of Joe's family died in a psychiatric hospital, another became an alcoholic, one sibling ran away from home, another became involved in a series of abusive relationships, another one is in jail. Each lives privately with his or her pain and memories, but no one ever mentions Joe. Someone, however, still keeps fresh flowers on his grave.

I believe that far too many suicides occur because someone believes (either rightly or wrongly) that they have received that message to die. Tragically, many have often perceived wrongly. Also tragically, many have been right. These messages may be the kind that forbids any notion of leaving the family fold, or they may completely exclude the offender. Richman believes that many suicidal persons probably receive more death messages than they send out, and says, "Suicide is itself a communication of unresolved problems and unfinished crises in all those touched by the act, not only in the suicidal individual."[59]

He also states, "At the time of the suicidal crisis, the potentially suicidal person has become the bad object for the entire family. . . . For this to occur the guilt, shame, sense of failure, and separation anxieties are all placed upon the suicidal individual, through the process of projective identification" . . . which is accompanied by "the expressed or implied message that his or her demise is necessary, after which there would be no problems." [60]

If the person who has symbolized all the ills of the family actually dies, the family may, at first, feel that atonement has been accomplished. But they needed their scapegoat—how dare he or she do this! Too late, they realize that the suicided person represented both the good and bad of the family, so the death leaves the family feeling "as if part of themselves has died."[61] Now they are frustrated and angry. They did indeed kill part of themselves—the part they had projected onto the scapegoat.

190

Richman explains that (1) scapegoating is a means of dealing with overwhelming guilt on the part of the abusers; (2) the scapegoat is blamed for all problems, and the intensity or widespread nature of the scapegoating is an indicator of the family's desperation; (3) scapegoating is used to avoid confronting family problems or dysfunction; (4) through scapegoating, the family participates in the suicidal act, either directly or indirectly.[62]

John Bradshaw, in *Bradshaw On: The Family*, discusses the relationship between scapegoating and the closed family system. He explains how dysfunctional parents reenact their own original pain onto their children. He says that we must understand that, "every persecutor was once a victim," or in a Biblical sense, "the sins of the fathers go on and on." He adds, "The abused child in the persecutor is angry and hurt" but since he or she is forbidden to express anger toward the parent, that anger is "either projected onto others, turned against self or 'acted out.'"[63]

Bradshaw says the dysfunctional or abusing family is locked into a closed family system. "Shame governs the entire family. The rigid roles are cover-up defenses against the shame core.... All feel abandoned and alone at the deepest level. This shame is inherited generationally and is perpetuated through the rigid roles and ego defenses." Bradshaw believes that, "shame is the organizing principle in all dysfunctional families."[64]

By no means is a closed family system always or necessarily outwardly brutal. They may appear to be most loving and the closest of families. There may be a great show of concern over one another and lots of fuss over doing things together. That's wonderful if it allows for healthy rebellion and individualism. It's the family that perceives itself as *close* when it's actually *closed* that is dysfunctional.

A number of factors are common in the way the abusive or dysfunctional family communicates their deadly message to the scapegoat. For example, *common themes in tone of voice* are: scorn, impatience, disgust, sneering, patronizing, or condescending— usually accompanied by similar facial expressions.

There are also *common themes in attitude*: condemnation, judgment, vindictiveness, blaming and shaming, punishing, and self-pity on the part of the abuser.

Common expressions (see the beginning of this chapter.)

Common reactions toward the scapegoat if he or she confronts the family may be one of denial or reverse accusations, such as, "Oh, that's all in your head", "The neighbors all know we love you so why don't you?", "You ask for what you get," or "Oh, all you want is attention (or pity)."

A common self-image of those who abuse is an incredible belief in their own innocence. They never see themselves at fault, but blame others or the world. They worry a great deal about what neighbors or other people think. They are afraid someone may discover the truth, so they work hard to retain an image of their own "goodness" and the scapegoat's "badness." A typical comment in this case might be "We did everything for this kid—spoiled him/her rotten—and this is how he/she treat us—but don't tell him/her what I said because I don't want him/her to get mad at me."

Common actions are: the silent treatment or deliberately ignoring (the ultimate in rejection) the distress of the suicidal person; walking out, leaving or turning away (which is tantamount to abandonment and symbolically represents one of the most profound and despairing forms of non-verbal communication); blocking out (refusing to hear or comprehend), such as, "I don't even listen when she tries to tell me what's wrong. I just let it go in one ear and out the other"; hanging up the phone on the scapegoat and failing or "forgetting" to pass messages of need or crisis on to a possible helper, rescuer or comforter.

An example is Wanda, a woman who sought therapy to overcome strong feelings of rejection and thoughts of suicide ideation. She reported that she had several hospitalizations for cancer, and each time she had notified her parents and siblings. Each time they failed to visit, call or send a card or flowers. When Wanda confronted them later they claimed not to have known about it, or that "they forgot." They accused Wanda of being "selfish" for wanting family support. "Oh, you always want *something*," one said. "The amount of covertness, indirectness, [blaming], and covering-up found [in these families] is truly striking," claims Richman.[65] They are experts at excuses and justification (Excusi-fications).

Other scapegoating actions include: (1) anger when the scapegoat (victim) expresses his or her feelings, with comments such as, "Shame on you for talking that way" or "I never heard of such a thing"; (2) claims of illness "caused" by the scapegoat, with comments such as, "When I'm dead and gone and you see me in my casket, you'll know that you killed your mother (or father)," or (to others) "It's because of him (or her) that I am so sick all the time"; (3) creating a false image for the outside world which shows the scapegoat to be the bad person. The greater the need for a façade, the more the abusive family will create an effect of innocence and extreme insensitivity to the victim's pain or despair.[66]

Richman points out that abusing family members often appear "dominated by the theme of complete innocence and the denial of any guilt...." They feel a great "sense of rightness of their [abusive] actions."[67] That would explain why these people continue to abuse, and do not appear to regret their actions, instead of seeking ways to change their actions and attitude.

Richman says that strong denial of abuse is evidence that the abusers are desperate. In a closed family system any resistance to one's prescribed role is a threat to the dysfunctional family, especially to the member who is most insecure and fearful and has learned to control the family.[68]

He adds, "A real or supposed fragility of a central figure in the family . . . dominates the family atmosphere. The family rallies to protect the figure, but the means taken are maladaptive and the result is a further closing off of the family." [69] Richman compares this person with a "queen bee who must be protected. . . even at the sacrifice of lives."[70]

"Devious and destructive measures" are used to accomplish this and "conceal problems from the outside world," Richman says, and notes that the controlling figure may be an ill member of the family, such as an alcoholic parent, or an emotionally unstable parent or grandparent.[71] The controlling figure may present a variety of façades from that of a sweet, harmless innocent to an adult-sized screaming teenager. (See example of Fred, p.200.)

The family goes along with the controlling figure because it's easier. Resistance to the scapegoating or defense of the victim requires thought and courage. Who has the time or inclination to face the wrath of the abuser on behalf of the victim, especially if the abuser is bigger and stronger, or hands out the money, or happens to be an elderly family member who owns valuable property?

It's an old story for parents to threaten or to actually cut off someone's inheritance as a form of control or punishment. It's also possible to use family heirlooms, money or other material things as a way to sow discord among children or relatives, or to involve the scapegoat. Let's face it—greed is a solid controlling factor.

Triangling is also a factor in family scapegoating. This occurs when one member discusses the scapegoat (or suicidal person) with other family members. The victim knows the talk is going on behind his or her back and also knows that anything he or she says will be repeated and discussed with others. The victim believes he or she has no defense against being maligned by his or her own family, through labeling, innuendos and assumptions. If a myth or lie is voiced often enough it becomes a reality in the mind of the listener and can destroy relationships and reputations.

Richman calls this a two-edged double-binding. Faced with this double-bind, "the suicidal person has almost literally no one to turn to and no where to go. He or she is alienated and isolated both outside the family and within it."[72] He adds, "The person may be ostracized as a form of punishment in order to bring him (or her) back to the former role...."[73] After all, the family desperately needs the scapegoat—that's why they create the role in the first place.

Scapegoating works only with those who desperately want what the family refuses to give. It does not work when the scapegoat refuses to cooperate.

And then there's guilt. Richman says that "scapegoating is a means of dealing with overwhelming guilt."[74] If we blame the victim we can avoid facing our own guilt. Victimizers often hate and reject their victims in order to justify their abuse of the victim. This action is age-old.

The executioners of Jesus Christ had to invent a case against him in order to justify crucifying him. Adolph Hitler had to build a case against the Jews which would not only justify his obsessive hatred but would enlist others in the abuse and extermination of them. These people were compelled to hate their victims in order to abuse, and then blame the victims for deserving the abuse.

In addition, the physical presence of the victim or scapegoat reminds the parent or abuser of their unacceptable yet denied feelings toward the victim or child. The victim (or child) is, in fact, a justified and bonafide accuser of wrongdoing. The victim/child's very *presence* states, "You have mistreated me," or, "I know that you hate me," or, "I could tell the world what you are really like." The victim's presence is a reminder of the victimizer's guilt, so the victimizer or abusive parent tries to relieve their guilt by ignoring or removing the child or victim. The victimizers must rid themselves of the accuser in order to appear guiltless both to themselves and to the community.

Scapegoating is not always directed to just the suicidal person, and the family can change their focus from one person to another. In the case of spouse suicide, the surviving spouse may find that he or she is the new target. With the death of one child, another may become the object of disapproval.

For examples, one young woman, whose brother had suicided was constantly told by her mother, "You're getting to be more and more like your brother. You remind me of him all the time and get on my nerves just like he did." As time passed the young woman began thinking about her own suicide. Eventually she did it. Maybe that kind of talk contributes to the fact that suicides seem to "run in families."

Sometimes victimizing comes home to roost, and we are forced to face the results of our own actions.

Many years ago a young child died in the hospital, a victim of severe abuse. The child had been chained to a bed for most of its life, forced to drink its own urine and fed its own feces. Years later, immediate members of the family were charged with murder. Interestingly enough, other family members were charged as "accessories after the fact," because they knew about the abuse but never reported it. They were judged guilty by association and silence. Neither the law nor the Scripture allows us total separation from that of being our brother's keeper. In this case, that of withholding information (legal) and the sin of omission (scriptural).

The choice of suicide, says Richman, "is never a purely individual matter. Hopelessness. . .is intimately related to the decision to kill oneself, and hopelessness is an interpersonal family systems phenomenon. What then of the many suicides who receive the [message] that their self-inflicted death is necessary for the survival of their loved ones?" He asks, "How can they [then] choose life?"[75]

"They can," he asserts, "if they [all] recognize that the suicidal urge is the expression of a [family] problem that needs correction. Such a positive use of suicide as a signal can best be accomplished by providing . . . a loving attitude so the one in distress knows that he is wanted and accepted. Rather than becoming part of the problem, the family and society can then become part of the solution." [76]

We must never assume that abusing families are that way forever, and must never underestimate their ability to change. All

195

the strength, determination and love (yes—love) that goes into maintaining an abusive situation can go into just as energetic a building of a new family system. This happens when they find a way to get rid of the fear and clearly see the benefit of doing so. Then watch out. That's the joy of counseling for everyone.

Do you know what is the saddest thing of all about rejection and family scapegoating? It is actually self-injury. That child or victim is, by birth, a part of his or her parents. When family members reject or hurt that person they are hurting part of themselves. It's the ultimate case of "we treat others the way we feel about ourselves." Scapegoating is crazy-making at the least; it can be a game of slow insidious murder at the most.

This chapter is written to *identify and explain* scapegoating as it relates to suicide. This is not to say that scapegoating is present in all families where suicide occurs. It is not. Disappointment, rejection, loss, sorrow, and pain are a part of everyone's life. As humans we can only do our best with what we know at the time and we still make wrong decisions and mistakes. If we're lucky we learn from those mistakes. However, it is not thoughtless mistakes that mark an action as scapegoating, but *an attitude*. It is—*the predictable, relentless, ruthless consistency of rejecting actions, combined with a certain tone of voice and choice of words, followed with excuses and self-righteous justification, and a lack of concern for the victim's pain—often covered up with a pretense of love—that marks scapegoating and victimizing.*

Unfortunately, we all have this capacity to victimize others, which can develop in overt and insidious ways depending on influencing factors. But the vast majority of families where suicide or scapegoating occurs feel trapped and need help to become untrapped. That's a different situation than one of premeditated, ruthless cruelty or torture which is a deliberate, intentional, malevolent action; the sort where the person feels no guilt or conscience, but actually experiences gleeful delight when slyly planning or carrying out a trap or trick on the object of their vindictiveness. Most family and social scapegoating is reactional and not intentional, although it can appear to be. Very often life wishes as well as death wishes are present in those who are destructive, even though the death wish may be dominant at the time of abuse (or suicide) which is usually based upon a crisis.

Identifying the scapegoating and double-binding as I have in this chapter is only the first step. The main problem is to modify destructive relationships. This can be done by sorting out individual fears in order to reduce tension, and then to suggest alternatives in family behavior and interaction which leads to further healing.

We can make terrible mistakes but still come out alive and happy. We may hurt someone terribly through those actions, and although we can't change the past, we can have some positive influence and control over the present and future, provided we understand the past. That is the primary key to forgiving and forgetting.

If one feels they have been, or are, trapped in a scapegoating situation in any way, see the following chapter, *Breaking Free*, for suggestions on being set free and for healing.

Breaking Free

*"The greatest game of all and the only game worth playing
is to stay alive when others want me dead."*
Ernest Haycox from Sundown Jim

Many a scapegoat has lived out much of his or her life hanging on the family cross while hearing and believing the words, "You brought it on yourself." Authorities agree that a child's role in the family is established well before the age of three. The scapegoat can be marked while he or she is still an infant. These early messages are very difficult to overcome, especially when that message has been one of "to die" or "not to be."

But restoration and healing of the spirit *is* possible. If you want down from that cross badly enough you may have to find your own way. That first step can be a big one; it means making a decision to change your attitude and change your actions. There are a number of additional steps to choose from in your progress.

These can be any combination of the following: developing self-insight and awareness, an understanding of family interaction, joining support groups, improving communication skills, seeking family and/or individual therapy, making a spiritual connection for strength and the ability to forgive, or distancing yourself if necessary. A good beginning is to understand the basic differences between a functional and dysfunctional family system.

"Functional parents," says Bradshaw, "will also model maturity and autonomy for their children. Their strong identity leaves very little of their consciousness unresolved, repressed and unconscious. The children, therefore, do not take on their parents' unresolved unconscious conflicts. The parents are in the process of completeness. They model this process and do not need their children to complete themselves.... The children are not constantly judged and measured by their parents frustrated and anxiety-ridden projections."[77]

The family is also "a survival and growth unit," and "is the soil which provides the emotional needs of the various members. These needs include a balance between autonomy and dependency. . . ."[78] Bradshaw explains that a healthy functional family system is based on equality and that each person is whole and complete, each is independent, each is committed to each other and

198

to self-discipline, and each has access to the freedom of self-development and self-expression.[79] They fight but they fight fair.[80]

This functional family system does not fall together haphazardly or by happenstance. It develops through communication and conscious *decisions* of its members to be accountable to themselves and to one another.

The dynamics of the dysfunctional family (as relates to scapegoating) was described in the chapter, *The Deadly Message*. Dysfunctional families are created when the children of other dysfunctional families marry each other, explains Bradshaw, and that perpetuates the generational patterns of the closed family behavior given to verbal, physical or emotional abuse or neglect.[81]

Bradshaw states that, "co-dependence is the most common family illness because that is what happens to anyone in any kind of dysfunctional family. In every dysfunctional family there is a primary stressor. This could be Dad's drinking or work addiction; Mom's hysterical control of everyone's feelings; Dad or Mom's physical or verbal violence; a family member's actual sickness or hypochondrias; Dad or Mom's early death; the divorce; Dad or Mom's moral/religious righteousness; Dad or Mom's sexual abuse. Anyone who becomes controlling in the family to the point of being experienced as a threat by the other members, initiates the dysfunction. This member becomes the primary stressor. Each member of the family adapts to this stressor in an attempt to control it. Each becomes *outerdirected* and lives adapting to the stress for as long as the stress exists. *Each becomes co-dependent on the stressor.*"[82]

He adds, "Co-dependence is at the bottom a spiritual disease because (its) . . . core belief. . . is that my inner state is dependent upon what is outside of me." [83] People who are caught up in this mode of thinking spend a lot of time and energy making controlling demands on the world and the people around them.

Richman says, "When most suicidal [or dysfunctional] individuals leave home, they do not leave home; they set up the same maladapted relationships on the outside that existed within."[84]

Many individuals from closed family systems also live in a tiny closed world of their own. Since they cannot see beyond this closed world they have an exaggerated unrealistic idea of their place within the whole world, believing that others are as involved with their thoughts and actions as they are. They depend on that response from others for their own self-image and identity. Not all of these people quietly withdraw. Some live a noisy show-and-tell life style, always on stage for a wide-eyed audience. They can be quite amusing or entertaining up to a point.

An example of this is Fred, an independent businessman who keeps his small staff hopping in attendance to his personal needs, wants, and problems. They mow his lawn and clean his house when business is slow, patiently listen to long tales of woe, provide transportation when he wrecks his car, and clean up broken glass following his temper tantrums. They sympathize when he bad-mouths someone who isn't fooled by his performance, and laugh patronizingly when he makes fun of someone he thinks he has fooled. They apologize to insulted clients for his arrogance, and make excuses to clients in order to cover up his drinking problem.

The primary stressor in Fred's family was his father who tyrannized and embarrassed the family with cruelty and neglect, alcoholism and uncontrollable rages. Throughout Fred's childhood his mother was the long-suffering victim/rescuer.

Fred's sister was the family scapegoat and her child is now being trained for the role of the next generation's scapegoat. Jackie, the child, is constantly berated for "not trying," and for "being lazy." Jackie is kept in line by another of Fred's siblings whose mode of operation is to rescue the lazy Jackie by enrolling Jackie in a series of activities, accompanied with loud proclamations that Jackie "won't stay with it." Of course, Jackie doesn't "stay with it" and can then be chastised for not staying rescued and is then compared with cousins who are achievers. When this sibling is not setting Jackie up to be rescued, there is still Fred's mother, other siblings, co-workers and acquaintances to be rescued. This sibling stays pretty busy with managing other people's lives.

Meanwhile, back at the office, Fred has his own little rescue squad of employees in readiness should a crisis arise. Fred's favorite time for a crisis is early in the day so he can start drinking before noon. In the lull between crises, employees sit around and talk to Fred about how he can improve his attitude.

Fred listens attentively, agrees with their observations, basks in their undivided attention, and drowns in his own self-importance. He knows he won't change. Why should he? Everybody's happy. An ex-wife, sick of the sycophancy, took Fred's children and left years ago so Fred has created a new family. He is surrounded by hired "mommies" who give imitation love; assistants who feel important giving advice *to* him and protecting clients *from* him, and a secretary who offers her own form of after-hour comfort and gets paid before going home to hubby—although business is floundering.

Neither Fred nor his family have considered the enormous amount of time and effort that goes into perpetuation of the victimizing/rescuer dysfunctional process; nor are they aware of the ridiculous nature of Fred's "Ugh-me-God," mentality. Each time Fred blames someone else for a situation he has created he is actually giving that person his power. No wonder he drinks and rants and raves. He makes himself helpless.

Father is no longer able to intimidate Fred and take away his power so Fred gives it away through unaccountability. Fred's emotional make-up is stuck in early childhood where it was first traumatized. He has also imitated his father's method of control by "throwing his weight around" and "shooting off his mouth."

Fred could direct his abundant energy and creativeness into successful productivity if he were not still controlled by a pathological terror of not having his basic needs met for physical survival and emotional affirmation. He could direct his fine intelligence into a determined quest for maturity, honesty, accountability and self-discipline if he were not compulsively obsessed with alternately adoring himself and victimizing himself.

Fred is living a self-destructive life-style that could be termed as subintentional suicide, and is characterized by "hang-ups", such as, problem drinking, recklessness, affairs with married women, poor judgment in decisions, an obsessive need for constant attention, incredible grandiose self-absorption, and misrepresenting the truth. Fred's story illustrates the claim made by Richman and Bradshaw that dysfunctional individuals go beyond their family home to recreate the dysfunctional family system.

In a similar manner, many scapegoats do not directly obey the message to die but continue to live in other dysfunctional and self-destructive ways. They may become ill—starting in early childhood—rather than to overtly attempt suicide. Some continue to play the game of always trying to fix things and gain love. Some deny that any form of abuse even exists; always understanding, forgiving or not noticing. Some separate themselves either emotionally or through physical distance. Some disappear completely.

As stated earlier, there *are* alternatives which offer more than mere coping or surviving.

Individual therapy or counseling is valuable for helping one to locate and face the causes of dysfunction, for developing skills for dealing with oneself and others, and for achieving self-fulfillment.

Support groups of all kinds are available either as a supplement to or alternative for therapy. Bradshaw points out that support groups are like a *new* family where you can learn new and different roles. You can be accepted and gain new self-respect.[85] Pam Tanous said of her Ray of Hope support group members, "They have bloomed over the months—like a little flower garden."

Al-Anon and Alateen are excellent sources of help when the dysfunctional family or suicidal behavior is complicated by alcohol, and/or other substance abuse.

Spiritual counseling can deal with healing of memories, with inner growth, and with forgiveness: receiving forgiveness from God, forgiving others, and the most difficult of all, forgiving oneself, rather than excusing oneself.

Churches and synagogues also offer support groups, caring relationships through "extended family" programs, and a community which offers involvement and commitment that can help change inter-personal social relationships.

Family therapy which provides healing and growth for all is invaluable. Find a family therapist who will contact family members directly, rather than leaving it to the patient. Sometimes such a call may bring the entire family, or only a few, but the therapist should keep trying. Although he works with whoever comes, he should not give up contacting the family. Family therapy can provide ways to break through the rigid roles, deception and games. Some therapists use a variation of the well known AA "twelve-step program" to help families set up a healthy communication system at home. The common goal in family therapy is to confront those terrifying and unspeakable issues of guilt, condemnation, shame and fear, and move into unconditional acceptance of self and others.

"Eventually, it may be necessary to deal with the guilt," asserts Richman. "The goal of the counselor is to help the family recognize and distinguish between irrational guilt, which is punitive, destructive, blaming and preventive of maturity; and rational guilt, which is healing and leads to ultimate forgiveness, self-acceptance and maturity."[86] Good therapy helps the family "to replace devious, unclear and indirect communications with direct and honest statements."[87]

Guilt is a primary issue in effective therapy and healing and a primary reason why people refuse therapy. Refusal to confront guilt causes great difficulty for family therapy to be effective—or even occur. The family may proclaim the therapist is "against" them and "for" the victim. Out of pathological fear of exposure, relatives who are the most destructive are also the most clever at avoiding the very people who could help. Their actions mark them as the ones in greatest need and the least likely to be helped.[88]

All abusing family members need treatment, claims Bradshaw. "Even if you were not the one being abused in your family, you still carry the covert secrets of the family system."[89] Children "act out" the family secrets which can occur in future generations (such as battering, incest, etc.).

Bradshaw says, "The last [thirty-five] years have ushered in a new awareness about the impact of families on personality formation. While it's always been known that our families influence us, we're now discovering that the influence is beyond what we had imagined."[90] He continues, "If we do not know our familial history, we are likely to repeat it . . . . The source of the wounds which destroy our wholeness can be uncovered by exploring our family systems . . . . The family is the source of the wars within ourselves and to a large degree, the war with others. Wars are evil . . . . They embody lying and killing. They seem to have a power that transcends individual choice."[91]

James Lynch, *The Broken Heart*, approaches the theme of relationships by illustrating how loneliness and isolation can literally break a person's heart. He cites Dr. Harlow's infant monkeys who were isolated with terry-cloth surrogate mothers and as a result of the "overwhelming physical and emotional destructiveness of this type of early social deprivation" suffered severe depression. Even after being united with other monkeys, they lived out their lives as loners—isolated—unable to function normally.[92] A child's earliest need is for a warm loving accepting parent in order to mirror an image of affirmation and acceptance of one's self. Without that, disassociation can result.

Bradshaw describes disassociation as a "disconnection between the act of victimization and the response to being victimized."[93] That means that childhood trauma can be so unbearable

203

that the victim "actually leaves the body." They don't remember the event. They lose connection with the *memory* of what happened—but they retain the *feelings* of what happened.[94]

However, as Bradshaw points out, "these 'body memories' are what allow the healing work. . . to take place in therapy."[95] Instead of running away or denial one can choose to confront those early terrors at their source and resolve them. This requires the kind of insight and self-awareness that banishes co-dependence.

Through confrontation and communication, a person can exorcise the family demon of victimization in order to re-connect through love and understanding, in place of rejection and blame. This re-connection is necessary for wholeness and healing to be complete. It takes a great deal of courage. Someone has said that self-purification will always be a person's greatest weapon.

For some people, the answer to self-affirmation and actualization—in addition to or instead of education, counseling, therapy, and support groups—is to make a spiritual connection for strength and guidance. This may be especially valuable when the parent has deliberately withdrawn: in the form of actual physical absence, or of having been present but emotionally detached and unconcerned, or when the parent was present but manipulated the relationship by replacing love and support with patronizing indifference or outright ostracism.

When a parent is physically present but deliberately withdraws love, support and acceptance from a child, something in that child dies. There is no loneliness like the forsaken loneliness of spiritual abandonment—it is a devastating injury to the blood bond. These messages of denial of a child's "right to be," instilled early in life, produces a starvation of the soul which, in turn, plants the seeds of self-destruction.

As a comparison, consider Jesus cry of "Why have you forsaken me?" After the Spirit of God had withdrawn, Jesus was left unprotected, open to experience the agony and suffering of the world without contact with His father. In a similar manner, the child who is emotionally abandoned without the support of his or her parents, may be in a state of desolation and confusion.

There is, however, tremendous hope here for the person who is looking to religious faith as part of his or her deliverance from abuse. This is the message of the cross—that personal suffering has already been experienced for the believer.

But Jesus was a survivor. He knew the source of his strength despite the situation, and because of that, they didn't kill Him dead. I believe all survivors know that the strength for restoration and healing is there if they *want to know* that it is there.

Never underestimate forgiveness as a powerful means of release. Some therapists believe that for some people, to forgive is more than they can handle right away—that the absence of painful feelings must come first, followed by a calmness with no desire to dwell on the abuse or forgive the abuser. Then, if the person so desires, forgiveness can begin. I feel it's the other way around. Whichever way you favor, I think true resolution can occur only when both parties seek it. If you say you want resolution but are avoiding the action required, you are fooling yourself.

Sometimes, the only way to escape abuse is to completely sever ties with the family in order to avoid manipulation. But be careful. Bradshaw says, "A victim [usually] lives life as a victim . . . they continue to trust untrustworthy people and . . . end up being victimized [again or reenacting the abuse]."[96] If you carry those old love/hate feelings with you, they will carry over into your new life and relationships. Anger and hate are not really the opposite of love because they are feelings which still keep us involved. The real opposite of love/hate is indifference. Not the kind of indifference which declares, "I don't care if you live or die," but the kind which shows in actions and attitude that "I am living a fulfilled life without your approval or disapproval and want the same for you." Examples of ways to show this are through detached concern and tough love.

This is the action taken by Wanda, a "scapegoat" who wanted to break the family chain of verbal abuse and emotional neglect. Her suggestion for family counseling was met by a whirlwind of resistance and excuses. The family refused to participate but Wanda continued in therapy for herself.

"My brother's objection to therapy," Wanda says, "is that since the past is dead, I should be ashamed to bring it up now. I should forget it. I feel like he's choking me when he says that. How can I go on with the future when I haven't resolved the past?"

Wanda's brother may be using this reference to the past as a cop-out, a dodge—a way to avoid facing the results and responsibility for his own past actions or inactions and guilt feelings. It's also a way of punishing Wanda for reminding him of their neglect—a way of hushing her up. In effect, he's saying, "Don't bother us with the can of worms we gave you."

There is no way to ignore the past. The past—our history—is the sum total of what we are now. If you had no past, you wouldn't be you—you wouldn't be anyone.

That's why people are so disoriented when they lose their memory. Every present moment is an encapsulation of your past and your ancestors' past. If one of them had deviated by one notch, (claims Marcel Proust in his assertion of the relevance of the past to the present) your present would be different. William Faulkner said that the past is not only not dead, it is not even past.

Studies indicate that people plagued by unresolved past traumatic experiences may be more susceptible to colds, flu, and other major illnesses later in life. Confronting these past events realistically helps us to understand and deal with them constructively.

Wanda's family's refusal to discuss the past is a refusal to consider growth and insight for everyone concerned. Refusal to examine the past can cripple a person's confidence, making them afraid to reach out. To deny the past is to deny a valid part of our individuality.

Regardless of Wanda's tactics or the results, her intent was to promote both individual and family healing. Just wanting to reconnect (at the risk of further pain) was a tremendous step for her. However, in doing so she suffered another loss—the family did not share her desire to forgive and grow. I think that all children, young or adult, want to love their parents, but some parents just make it so difficult.

"I realize," she says, "that I can continue to love my family at the same time I hate their behavior. I can separate the two issues now, and that's a big help to me."

Therapy is paying off for Wanda. She realizes that scapegoating makes the persecutor come off as strong and the victim as weak whereas the opposite may be true. She has discovered she has the strength to separate herself from the abuse. Breaking the habit pattern takes time for both victim and the abuser. Just as scapegoating builds up step by step over time, its takes time—step by step— to overcome it. Those who abuse have a tremendous amount of pain and shame to be healed and a tremendous freedom to be experienced if they seek that healing. The freedom for all is worth it.

A Unifying Force

"It has been said that the audience we play to is the one person who does not give us a standing ovation."

Author unknown

I also believe that many people kill themselves because they sense the lack of a solid moral ethical foundation in today's society and their own life. This resulting confusion over misplaced values has instilled a fear of the unknown which many people do not know how to confront. Admittedly, many people who do not feel the need for such a foundation are not suicidal. However, most of the suicidal persons I have worked with feel this moral lack deeply because they crave these same enduring values. (Which is exactly why the suicidal person holds so much promise and is worth saving.) I see this (at least in my experience) as another basic factor which emerges as survivors try to explain the reasons for suicide.

Ralph Kinney Bennett describes this lack of moral ethical foundation in his review of Allan Bloom's book, *The Closing of the American Mind*. Bennett says, "In years past. . .(our heritage was) rooted in three things—the Bible, the family and the. . .American political tradition centered on the Declaration of Independence."[97] Bennett quotes Bloom as stating that "the Bible was the common culture, one that united the simple and the sophisticated, rich and poor, young and old." [98]

That common culture and American tradition provided a background of moral and ethical guidelines and standards. Standards that most people, for the most part, could trust and respect. That culture of moral and ethical standards also provided a common bond leading to stability of individual, home, community, and country.

We are losing that. Morally and ethically, anything goes. What can you believe? Who can you trust? What background do we give young people on which to base and develop character, a code of ethics, and faith in humanity?

"The highest percentage of young people who are suicidal feel unconnected in any significant relationships,"[99] says Rich Van Pelt, pastor, author, teacher and speaker from Denver, Colorado. He says that while we are improving at suicide intervention, "the fundamental problems still exist."[100]

"We want our children to excel but expect them to do so without the necessary groundwork, without laying a secure foundation,"[101] says Lee Radziwill in an interview for McCall's magazine (Oct. 1988). She was comparing education and discipline between American and European schools, but I believe her statement about the lack of a secure foundation for proper education and self-discipline is all too true in the spiritual and moral aspect of character development as well.

In the rush to be free of sexual and moral confines, in the obsession with career, status, appearance, materialism, and instant gratification, we have replaced America's foundation of moral truths and values with a "me" philosophy which has created a social selfishness; the kind that can ruin individuals and nations.

Despite a rich plethora of knowledge, skills, and opportunity available for all, we have adopted a society characterized by noise, deep involvement with "nothing" relationships, obsession with the body beautiful, no-fault adultery, no-fault divorce, no-fault abuse, no-fault violence, no-fault slander, no-fault selfishness, no-fault sin, no-fault-sex, no-fault crime, and no-fault choices.

I believe we throw out the baby with the bath water when we throw out the Bible. And with it, we risk throwing out such valuables as a sense of honor, truth, self-respect, integrity, morality, and the strength of simple spiritual faith.

It's quite true that belief in God and traditional biblical values are accompanied by guidelines for behavior which demand observance of rules. However, those guidelines and restrictions provide security in knowing what is expected of oneself and others which is the basis for building trust. With traditional church values we paid respect to God, to others, and to oneself—in that order.

Nowadays, it is *self* first, *others* only if convenient for our own gain, and God not at all. We have lost the kind of security which instills trust. It's that uncertainty about basics, such as trust, which causes the anxiety leading to despair and hopelessness. Just as marriage is not stable without commitment, life is not stable without foundation.

"Some historians say that one of the major signs that a culture is on the brink of disaster is the disintegration of the family," claims Van Pelt. "The American family is falling apart all around us. It's no surprise that young people are feeling insecure. We need a spiritual awakening to move us back to a biblical, theological value base that sees the family as God's design to provide the security that young people need to navigate the turbulent waters of adolescence."[102] I think Van Pelt is talking about that inner security which stems from good character.

The sort of security which depends upon something outside yourself to make you feel good about yourself inside—such as possessions, achievements, status, flattery, ordering others about, or commanding attention—is both a lie and an illusion. Some people constantly seek feedback from others and their environment to get a sense of self-worth and identity. When the environment doesn't supply that, these people fall apart because they are nothing inside, only a void. Others, rather than analyzing themselves in order to develop insight, will opt to alter tactics—such as blaming someone or something else. None of these tactics build or replace strength of character. Rather, these tactics may project a false impression of self-assurance which is not actually tied to any sense of direction.

Nor is it enough to give lip service to honesty and integrity when attempting to impress a child or someone else, but then disregard those values when they don't serve some overwhelming self-directed purpose. One's lack of inner security is pretty obvious at those times.

Inner security comes from within and develops through the recognition and acceptance of one's abilities and limitations. *Inner strength* is based on a solid code of ethics and conscience from which one is willing to operate without dishonorable compromise. *Inner peace* stems from communion with and reverence for a supreme God. The sum of this security is refined and reflected by traits of good manners, integrity and sincerity, as well as respect, tolerance and esteem for others.

I believe this lack of spiritual foundation and inner strength has generated a fear in the human heart of life itself which contributes greatly to decisions of self-destruction by suicide.

Fear is, perhaps, the most powerfully energizing force within us when used in a positive way, but I believe fear (compounded by guilt and shame) is also the basic motivating factor behind most destructive feelings and actions. Fear causes us to lie, distort or withhold the truth, to be aggressive or evasive, to attack or run away. Fear is behind denial, deception, jealousy, greed, condemnation, stealing, murder, rape. Some people, when they feel threatened, intimidate others. Fear of disapproval motivates us to achieve or fail. It's fear of something that makes us feel angry, anxious, guilty, defensive, shy, secretive, or to put on an act, to cover up or to be the clown. We reject some people through fear and accept others through fear.

We fear the guilt of being found out, the shame of not measuring up. We are afraid of not being accepted, of not being wanted—of not being. There is the fear of being alone or lonely, and fear of pain. Some of us live because we fear dying and some of us die because we fear living. Fear can be passively or aggressively at work within us; a demon on our back or a whisper in our ear.

How do we conquer destructive fear? Some will say the family must instill inner security from early childhood through affirmation, approval and parental modeling. Some will say that life experiences will develop inner peace and security. (I believe that to be true primarily for people who are the thinkers—the insightful—the analytical observers.) But whether we grow from the family support system or personal experience or both, we must still have a base of strength to counteract all those fears.

"The answer to individual fear is a living glorified Lord; the answer to any collective fear is a corporate faith in a living God," says a prominent religious leader. While that has meaning for me, I realize that Judeo-Christian principles are not the answer acknowledged by all. Someone from another background or another philosophy may look to a different base on which to build his or her set of principles. But whatever our differences in belief, if we are to confront and conquer the specter of fear that destroys the joy of life—and the will to live—we must have that ethical and morally truthful spiritual center as a unifying force.

Krista

It was an unusual spring.
Things bloomed early,
and were very pretty.
But they didn't last long
. . .and Krista died.

When there are five, you don't have a favorite.
But each is.
For some, maybe all, of the others,
the words tell why each is favorite.

It was never that way with Kris.
I always knew.
But I don't think I told her
that she was the most precious,
because, like many things that are precious,
she was so fragile.
Too fragile to survive an early spring.

To California with Alison.
To Florida with Paula.
Homesick for Luekenbach, where she'd never been.
Behind the wheel of a Peterbuilt.
Back to her childhood.
Looking for a spot where a fragile bloom could survive.

She marched to a drummer we didn't even hear.
And now she's gone.
A precious moment in our lives.
A precious memory.
Somewhere. . .down her road,
We'll meet again.
Until then, we haven't parted.

Jerry Babel, May 22, 1980
Father of Krista (age 16)
Read at her funeral
Aurora, Illinois

Endnotes

1. Francine Klagsbrun, *Too Young to Die,* Boston: Houghton Mifflin Company, 1976, p. 105.
2. U.S. Department of Health and Human Services, *Alcohol, Drug Abuse, and Mental Health Newsletter,* Nov., 1984.
3. Eleanora "Betsy" Ross, from paper *Survivorship Following Suicide,* presented at the Sixteenth Annual Meeting of the American Association of Suicidology in Dallas, TX, April 21-24, 1983, p. 13.
4. John Bradshaw, *Bradshaw On: The Family,* Deerfield Beach, FL, Health Communications, Inc., 1988, p. 221.
5. U.S. Department of Health and Human Services.
6. From a paper by Gordon Winch and Karen Letofskty of Toronto in 1981; quoted by Adina Wrobleski, *Afterwords* (newsletter), Minneapolis, MN, April, 1985.
7. Wrobleski.
8. *Diagnostic and Statistical Manual of Mental Disorders, Third Edition.* The American Psychiatric Association, Division of Public Affairs, Washington, D.C., 1980, pp. 236-238.
9. Thomas P. Scarano based on an article by Mardi J. Horowitz, reprinted from the book *Human Stress Cognition and Information Processing Approaches* by Hamilton & Warburton, NY, Wiley and Sons, 1979.
10. Albert C. Cain, "Survivors of Suicide: Current Findings and Future Directions", from *Proceedings: Sixth International Conference for Suicide Prevention,* Robert E. Litman, Ed., Ann Arbor, MI, Edwards Brothers, 1972, p. 194-196.
11. Ann Kaiser Stearns, *Living Through Personal Crisis,* Chicago, The Thomas Moore Press, 1984, p. 82.
12. Cain, p. 195.
13. Cain, p. 195-196.
14. Cain, p. 195.
15. Dean Schuyler, "Counseling Suicide Survivors: Issues and Answers,"*Omega-Journal of Death and Dying,* Vol. 4, No. 4, 1973, p. 315.
16. Cain, p. 194.
17. Schuyler, p. 315.
18. Sue Dustow, "Suicide Causes Grief Chain Reaction,"*Canadian Funeral News,* Calgary, Alberta, Canada, Mar., 1988, p.36.
19. Morton M. Hunt, "Tears", *Guideposts,* Carmel, NY, October, 1985.
20. William Backus and Marie Chapian,*Telling Yourself the Truth,* Minneapolis, MN, Bethany House Publ., 1985.
21. *Diagnostic and Statistical Manual of Mental Disorders,* p. 214.
22. Abraham Schmitt, *The Art of Listening With Love,* Waco, TX: Word Incorporated, 1977.
23. Virginia Graham, "I Choose Life!" from *Life After Harry,* in *Modern Maturity,* Lakewood, CA,: American Association of Retired Persons, April-May, 1988, p.32.
24. Albert Cain and Irene Fast, "Children's Disturbed Reactions to Parent Suicide," *Survivors of Suicide* by Albert Cain, Springfield, IL: Charles C. Thomas, 1972, p. 93-120.

25. John H. Hewett, *After Suicide,* Philadelphia: Westminster Press, 1980, p. 68.
26. Glen Davidson, *Death. . .What Do You Say to a Child?* Springfield, IL: OGR Service Corp., 1979, p. 10-11.
27. Davidson, p.10-11.
28. Hewett, p.79-80.
29. Hewett, p. 69.
30. *NIV Study Bible,* Judges 9:54 (Abimelech), Judges 16:30 (Samson), 1 Samuel 31:4 (Saul), 2 Samuel 17:23 (Ahithophel), 1 Kings 16:18 (Zimri), Matthew 27:5 (Judas), Acts 16:27 (Paul's jailor).
31. Walther Zimmerli, *Old Testament Theology in Outline,* John Knotts Press, Atlanta, GA, 1979, p. 134.
32. Eleanora "Betsy" Ross, (presentation) "The Funeral Director and Suicide Survivors," North Dakota Funeral Directors Annual Conference, Bismarck, ND, 1984.
33. *Survivorship After Suicide* (videotape) edited by Eleanora "Betsy" Ross, produced by Ray of Hope, inc., 1983.
34. Iris Bolton, *My Son . . . My Son . . . A Guide to Healing After Death, Loss or Suicide,* Atlanta, GA: Bolton Press, 1983, p. 5-6.
35. Bruce H. Conley, Lfd., "The Funeral As 'First Aid' for the Suicide Survivor," from a paper presented at the 15th Annual Meeting of the American Association of Suicidology, NY, 1982. p.1.
36. Conley, p.3-6.
37. Wanda Johnson, *The Care of the Suicide Survivor: A Model for Funeral Home Personnel,* Dayton, OH: Suicide Prevention Center, Inc., 1982, p.5.
38. Johnson, p. 3-6.
39. Ed Vining, "The Funeral Director as a Caregiver," *The Forum Newsletter,* Association for Death Education and Counseling, Santa Cruz, CA: Vol. 7, No. 7, Oct., 1984.
40. Karen Letofsky in article by Sue Dustow, p. 36.
41. Dustow, p. 36.
42. William T. Anderson, (quote from letter, Oct., 1987) Exec. Sec/Tres., McLean Co., IL. Coroners Association, Springfield, IL, 1987.
43. Anderson.
44. Thomas Marsh, "The Coroner: A Working Relationship with EMT's," *Emergency,* Carlsbad, CA: HARE Publications, July, 1982, p. 22-25.
45. Boyd G. Stephens, M.D., "Forensic Medicine and the First Responder," Van Nuys, CA, *Emergency Medical Services,* Vol. 16, No. 7., August, 1987, p. 31.
46. *Coroner's Handbook on the Function and Operations of the Office of the Coroner.* Illinois Dept. of Public Health, Springfield, IL, January, 1980.
47. *Coroner's Handbook.*
48. Marsh, p. 22-25.
49. Johnson.
50. A. Alvarez, *The Savage God: A Study of Suicide,* NY: Bantam, 1971, p. 91-92.
51. Alvarez, p. 74.
52. Alvarez, p. 127.
53. Alvarez, p. 51.
54. Alvarez, p. 52.
55. Joseph Richman, *Family Therapy for Suicidal People,* New York: Springer Publ. Co., 1986, p. 189.
56. Richman, p. 167.

57. Richman, p. 167.
58. Richman, p. 167.
59. Richman, p. 168.
60. Richman, p. 168.
61. Richman, p. 168.
62. Richman, p. 164-166.
63. Bradshaw, p. 70.
64. Bradshaw, p. 72.
65. Richman, p. 145.
66. Richman, p. 146.
67. Richman, p. 167.
68. Richman, p. 129.
69. Richman, p. 129.
70. Richman, p. 130.
71. Richman, p. 129.
72. Richman, p. 133.
73. Richman, p. 131.
74. Richman, p. 165.
75. Richman, p. 189.
76. Richman, p. 189.
77. Bradshaw, p. 48.
78. Bradshaw, p. 42.
79. Bradshaw, p. 42-47.
80. Bradshaw, p. 53.
81. Bradshaw, p. 62.
82. Bradshaw, p. 164.
83. Bradshaw, p. 233.
84. Richman, p. 135.
85. Bradshaw, p. 197.
86. Richman, p. 172.
87. Richman, p. 148.
88. Richman, p. 129.
89. Bradshaw, p. 127.
90. Bradshaw, p. 1.
91. Bradshaw, p. ix (preface).
92. James J. Lynch, *The Broken Heart*, NY: Basic Books, 1977, p. 178-179.
93. Bradshaw, p. 115.
94. Bradshaw, p. 115.
95. Bradshaw, p. 115.
96. Bradshaw, p. 119.
97. Ralph Kinney Bennett, *An Editorial Review of the Closing of the American Mind* by Alan Bloom, Simon & Schuster, NY: (Reader's Digest) Oct., 1987, p. 83.
98. Bennett, p. 83.
99. Rich Van Pelt, "Don't Let Them Die," *Decision* magazine, Billy Graham Evangelistic Assoc., Minneapolis, MN: January, 1988, p. 23.
100. Van Pelt, p. 23.
101. Lee Radziwill, "What We Can Learn From European Women," *McCall's* magazine, NY Oct., 1988, p. 180.
102. Van Pelt, p. 23.

References

Alvarez, A. *The Savage God: A Study of Suicide.* New York: A Bantam Book, 1971.

Anderson, William. Exec. Secretary/Treasurer, Illinois Coroner's Assocation. McLean County, Bloomington, IL.

Augsburger, David. *Caring Enough to Confront.* Scottdale, PA: Herald Press, 1973.

Augsburger, David. *Caring Enough to Forgive.* Scottdale, PA: Herald Press, 1981.

Backus, William and Marie Chapian. *Telling Yourself the Truth.* Minneapolis, MN: Bethany House Publ., 1985.

Beattie, Melody. *Beyond Codependency.* NY: Harper & Row, 1989.

Beattie, Melody. *Codependent No More: How to Stop Controlling Others and Start Caring for Yourself.* NY: Harper & Row, 1988.

Berne, Eric. *Games People Play.* NY: Random House, Inc., 1964.

Bolton, Iris. *My Son . . . My Son. . . .: A Guide to Healing After Death, Loss or Suicide.* Atlanta, GA: Bolton Press, 1983.

Bradshaw, John. *Bradshaw On: The Family.* Deerfield Beach, FL: Health Communications, Inc., 1988.

Cain, Albert C. *Survivors of Suicide.* Springfield, IL: Charles C. Thomas Publ. Co., 1972.

Cain, Albert C. "Survivors of Suicide: Current Findings and Future Directions," from *Proceedings: 6th International Conference for Suicide Prevention,* ed. Robert E. Litman. Ann Arbor, MI: Edwards Brothers, 1972.

Coleman, William. *Understanding Suicide.* Elgin, IL: David C. Cook Publ. Co., 1974.

Conley, Bruce, Lfd. "The Funeral As 'First Aid' for the Suicide Survivor," from a paper presented at *the 15th Annual Meeting of the AmericanAssociation of Suicidology.* NY: 1982.

Coroner's Handbook on the Function and Operations of the Office of the Coroner. Springfield, IL: Illinois Department of Public Health, 1980.

Davidson, Glen. *Death... What Do You Say to a Child?* Springfield, IL: OGR Service Corporation, 1979.

Diagnostic and Statistical Manual of Mental Disorders, Third Edition. Washington, D.C.: The American Psychiatric Association. Division of Public Affairs, 1981.

Doyle, Polly. *Grief Counseling and Sudden Death.* Springfield, IL: Charles C. Thomas Publ. Co., 1980.

Dustow, Sue. "Suicide Causes Grief Chain Reaction." *Canadian Funeral News.* Calgary, Alberta, Canada: March 1988.

Evans, Glen. *The Family Circle Guide to Self Help.* NY: Ballantine, 1979.

Faulkner, William. *Collected Stories.* NY: Random House, 1977.

Graham, Virginia. "I Choose Life!" from *Life After Harry* by Virginia Graham. Lakewood, CA: *Modern Maturity,* AARP, April-May, 1988.

Grollman, Earl. *Suicide: Prevention, Intervention and Postvention.* Boston: Beacon Press, 1972.

Haycox, Ernest. *Sundown Jim.* NY: Coronet Communications, 1937, 1966.

Hewett, John H. *After Suicide.* Philadelphia: Westminster Press, 1980.

Hunt, Morton M. *Tears.* Carmel, NY: Guideposts, 1985.

Johnson, Wanda. *The Care of the Suicide Survivor: A Model for Funeral Home Personnel.* Dayton, OH: Suicide Prevention Center, 1982.

Kiev, Ari. *The Courage to Live.* NY: Thomas Crowell Publ., 1979.

Klagsbrun, Francine. *Too Young to Die.* Boston, MA: Houghton Mifflin Co., 1976.

Krementz, Jill. *How It Feels When a Parent Dies*. New York: Alfred A. Knopf, 1981.

Kuenning, Delores. *Helping People Through Grief*. Minneapolis, MN: Bethany House Publ., 1986.

"Let Go of Your Depression." *Cooperative Extension Service*. Ames, IA: Iowa State University, May 1984.

Lewis, C.S. *A Grief Observed*. NY: Avon Books, 1957.

Lukas, Christopher and Henry M. Seiden. *Silent Grief: Living in the Wake of Suicide*. NY: Charles, Scribner & Sons, 1987.

Lynch, James J. *The Broken Heart*. NY: Basic Books, Inc., 1977.

Marsh, Thomas. *The Coroner: A Working Relationship with EMT's*. Emergency, 1982.

Marshall, Catherine. *To Live Again*. NY: Avon Books, 1957.

New International Version Study Bible. Kenneth Barker, General Editor. Grand Rapids, MI: Zondervan Bible Publishers, 1985.

Peck, M. Scott, *People of the Lie*. NY: Simon & Schuster, Inc., 1983.

Proust, Marcel. *Remembrance of Things Past*. NY: Random House, 1934.

Radziwill, Lee. "What We Can Learn From European Women," *McCall's* magazine, NY: WWT Partnership, Oct., 1989.

Ray of Hope files and support group meetings. Iowa City, IA, 1978-1989.

Richman, Joseph. *Family Therapy for Suicidal People*. NY: Springer Publ. Co., 1984.

Ross, Elisabeth K. *On Death and Dying*. New York: Macmillan Publ. Co., 1969.

Saint Augustine. *The City of God*. London: Oxford University Press, 1963.

Seamands, David A. *Healing of Memories*. Wheaton, IL: Victor Books, 1985.

Schmitt, Abraham. *The Art of Listening With Love*. Nashville: Abingdon, 1982.

Schuyler, Dean. "Counseling Suicide Survivors: Issues and Answers" *Omega*. Vol. 4, No. 4, Amityville, NY: Baywood Publ., Inc., 1973.

Shneidman, Edwin, and Norman Farberow. *Clues to Suicide*. NY: McGraw Hill, 1957.

Stapleton, Ruth Carter. *The Gift of Inner Healing*. Waco, TX: Word Incorporated, 1976.

Stearns, Ann Kaiser. *Living through Personal Crisis*. Chicago, IL: Thomas Moore Press, 1984.

Stephens, Boyd G. *Forensic Medicine and the First Responder*, Van Nuys, CA: Emergency Medical Services, 1987.

Stone, Howard. *Suicide and Grief*. Philadelphia: Fortress Press, 1972.

Survivorship After Suicide (video), Iowa City, IA: Ray of Hope, inc., 1983.

Tillich, Paul. *The Courage to Be*. New Haven, CT: Yale University Press, 1952.

U.S. Department of Health and Human Services. *Alcohol, Drug Abuse and Mental Health Newsletter*. 1984.

Vail, Elaine. *A Personal Guide to Living with Loss*. NY: John Wiley & Sons, 1982.

Van Pelt, Rich. "Don't Let Them Die." Minneapolis, MN: *Decision* magazine, 1988.

Vining, Ed. "The Funeral Director As A Caregiver," *Forum Newsletter*, Vol. 7, No. 7, Santa Cruz, CA: Association for Death Education and Counseling, October 1984.

Wrobleski, Adina. "The Suicide Survivor's Grief Group." *Afterwords*, (Newsletter), Minneapolis, MN: 1982.

Part IV
Appendices

Survivor's Bill of Rights

I have the right to be free of guilt.

I have the right not to feel responsible for the suicide death.

I have the right to express my feelings and emotions, even if they do not seem acceptable, as long as they do not interfere with the rights of others.

I have the right to have my questions answered honestly by authorities and family members.

I have the right not to be deceived because others feel they can spare me further grief.

I have the right to maintain a sense of hopefulness.

I have the right to peace and dignity.

I have the right to positive feelings about one I lost through suicide, regardless of the events prior to or at the time of the untimely death.

I have the right to retain my individuality and not be judged because of the suicide death.

I have the right to seek counseling and support groups to enable me to explore my feelings honestly to further the acceptance process.

I have the right to reach acceptance.

I have the right to a new beginning.

I have the right to be.

JoAnn Mecca
Center for Inner Growth and Wholeness
P.O. Box 9185, Wethersfield, CT 06109

Postvention/Grief Resource Guide

Articles

Augenbraun, Bernice & Neuringer, Charles. "Helping Survivors with the Impact of Suicide." *Survivors of Suicide* by Albert Cain. Charles C. Thomas, Springfield, IL. (1971).

"Post-Suicide Grief Work in Family Therapy." *Journal of Marriage and Family Counseling* (1977).

Richman, Joseph. "Family and Environmental Aspects of Suicide." *Suicide and Bereavement*. MISS Information Corp. (1977).

Ross, Eleanora. "Suicide and the Stages of Grief." *Death Education:* Vol. 2, No. 4, (Winter 1979).

Schuyler, Dean. "Counseling Suicide Survivors: Issues and Answers." *Omega* Vol. 4, No. 4 (1973).

Shneidman, Edwin S. "Postvention: The Care of the Bereaved." *Suicide and Life-Threatening Behavior:* Vol. 2, No. 4 (Winter 1981).

Solomon, Mark. "The Bereaved and the Stigma of Suicide." *Omega:* Vol. 13, No. 4 (1982).

Bibliographies

Death Education: An Annotated Resource Guide. Vols. I & 2. Hannelore Wass, Hemisphere Publ. Corp.: Suite-1110, 79 Madison Ave., New York, NY 10016. (212) 725-1999

Suicide Bibliographic Recommendations. Central Office, AAS, 2429 S. Ash St., Denver, CO 80222. (303) 692-0985

Survivors of Suicide Bibliography. John McIntosh, 2707 Huntington Place, Mishawaka, IN 46544. (219) 258-0207

Widowed Persons' Service Bibliography. American Association of Retired Persons, 1909 K St., N.W., Washington, DC 20049. (202) 872-4707

Books

About Mourning: Support and Guidance for the Bereaved by Savine G. Weizman & Phyllis Kamm. Human Sciences Press: New York.

After Suicide by John H. Hewett. The Westminster Press: Philadelphia.

After Suicide: A Ray of Hope by Eleanora "Betsy" Ross. Lynn Publications: Iowa City, IA.

The Algebra of Suicide by Irving Berent, M.D. Human Sciences Press: NY.

Between Life and Death by Robert Kastenbaum, Ph.D. Springer Publishing Co.: NY.

Beyond Codependency: And Getting Better All The Time by Melody Beattie. Harper & Row: NY.

The Broken Heart: The Medical Consequences of Loneliness by James J. Lynch. Basic Books: NY.

Caring Enough to Confront by David Augsburger. Herald Press: Scottdale, PA.

Caring Enough to Forgive by David Augsburger. Herald Press: Scottdale, PA.

Children Who Don't Want to Live: Understanding and Treating the Suicidal Child by Israel Orback. Jossey-Bass Inc., Publishers,: San Francisco.

Clues to Suicide by Edwin S. Shneidman & Norman L. Farberow. McGraw-Hill Book Co.: NY.

Codependent No More: How to Stop Controlling Others and Start Caring for Yourself by Melody Beattie. Harper & Row: NY.

Comforting Those Who Grieve: A Guide for Helping Others by Doug Manning. Harper & Row: San Francisco.

Coping—A Survival Manual for Women Alone by Martha Yates. Prentice-Hall: Englewood Cliffs, NJ.

Coping with Separation and Loss As a Young Adult by Louis E. LeGrand. Charles C. Thomas Publ.: Springfield, IL.

The Courage to Live by Ari Kiev. Thomas Crowell Publ.: NY.

Creativity in Death Education and Counseling by Charles Carr, Judith Stillion & Mary C. Ribar. Association for Death Education and Counseling: Lakewood, OH.

Crisis Intervention and Suicide Prevention (Working with Children and Adolescents) by Gary A. & Letha I. Crow. Charles C. Thomas Publ.: Springfield, IL.

Dealing Creatively with Death: A Manual of Death Education and Simple Burial by Ernest Morgan. Celo Press: Burnsville, NC.

Dear Momma, Please Don't Die by Marilee Horton. Thomas Nelson Publ.: Nashville, TN.

Don't Take My Grief Away from Me: What To Do When You Lose a Loved One by Doug Manning. Harper & Row: NY.

The Encyclopedia of Suicide: the First Comprehensive A to Z Reference of Suicidology by Glen Evans and Norman Farberow. Facts on File, Inc.: 460 Park Avenue South, NY.

The Family Circle Guide to Self-Help by Glen Evans. Ballantine Books, Random House: NY.

Family Therapy for Suicidal People by Joseph Richman. Springer Publ. Co.: NY.

From a Healing Heart by Susan White-Bowden. Image Publ.,: Baltimore, MD.

Getting Through the Night: Finding Your Way After the Loss of a Loved One by Eugenia Oates. Ballantine Books: NY.

The Gift of Hope: How We Survive Our Tragedies by Robert Veninga. Little, Brown & Co.: Boston.

The Gift Of Inner Healing by Ruth Carter Stapleton. Word Books: Waco TX.

God's Foreknowledge and Man's Free Will by Richard Rice. Bethany House Publ.: Minneapolis, MN.

Grief Counseling and Grief Therapy: A Handbook for the Mental Health Practitioner by F. William Worden, Ph.D. Springer Publ. Co.: NY.

Grief and How to Live with It by Sarah Morris. Grosset & Dunlap: NY.

Grief Counseling and Sudden Death by Polly Doyle. Charles C. Thomas Publ.: Springfield, IL.

Grief Is Not Forever by Jeri Krumroy. Brethren Press: Elgin, IL.

A Grief Observed by C.S. Lewis. The Seabury Press: NY.

Group Counseling: A Developmental Approach by George M. Gazda. Allyn & Bacon: Boston.

Healing of Memories by David A Seamands. Victor Books: Wheaton, IL.

Helping a Child Understand Death by Linda Jane Vogel. Fortress Press: Philadelphia.

Helping Children Cope with Separation and Loss by Claudia Jewett. Harvard Common Press: Cambridge, MA.

Helping People Through Grief by Delores Kuenning. Bethany House Publ.: Minneapolis, MN.

How Can I Help? by Ram Dass & Paul Gorman. Alfred A. Knopf: NY.

How Do We Tell the Children? A Parents' Guide to Helping Children Understand and Cope When Someone Dies by Dan Schaefer & Christine Lyons. Daniel J. Schaefer Consulting Co.: Brooklyn, NY.

How It Feels When a Parent Dies by Jill Krementz. Alfred A. Knopf: NY.

How to Win Over Depression by Tim LaHaye. Zondervan Publ. House: Grand Rapids, MI.

In the Center of the Night: Journey Through a Bereavement by Jayne Blankenship. PaperJacks: NY.

Jewish Reflections on Death by Jack Reimer, Ed. Schocken Books: NY.

The Jewish Way in Death and Mourning by Maurice Lamm. Jonathan David Publ.: NY.

Leaning Into the Wind—The Wilderness of Widowhood: Journal of a Woman Whose Husband Committed Suicide by Betty Bryant. Fortress Press: Philadelphia.

Learning to Say Goodbye; When a Parent Dies by Eda Leshan. Macmillan Co.: NY.

Left Alive: After a Suicide Death in the Family by Linda Rosenfeld and Marilynne Prupas. Charles C. Thomas Publ.: Springfield, IL.

Legacy of Love: A Survivor's Financial Guide by Charles W. Sill. Webster Publ. Co.: 2108 S. Crystal Lake Dr., Lakeland, FL.

Letting Go with Love by Nancy O'Connor. La Mariposa Press: Apache Junction, AZ.

Loneliness: The World's Number One Killer by Ralph Wilkerson. Melodyland Publishers: Anaheim, CA.

The Many Faces of Grief by Edgar N. Jackson. Abingdon Press:
Nashville, TN.

The Many Faces of Suicide by Norman Farberow. McGraw Hill: NY.

The Meaning of Human Suffering by Flavian Dougherty, C.P. Human
Sciences Press, Inc.: NY.

A Minister Speaks about Funerals by Doug Manning. In-Sight Books:
Hereford, TX.

May I Hate God? by Pierre Wolff. Paulist Press: NY.

Moral Justification of Suicide by Jerry Jacobs. Charles C. Thomas Publ.:
Springfield, IL.

My Son, My Son by Iris Bolton. Bolton Press: Atlanta, GA.

On Becoming a Counselor: A Basic Guide for Non-Professional Counselors
by Eugene Kennedy. The Seabury Press: NY.

On Death and Dying by Elisabeth Kubler-Ross. Macmillan Co.: NY.

Pastoral Care and Counseling in Grief and Separation by Wayne E. Oates.
Fortress Press: Philadelphia.

A Personal Guide to Living with Loss by Elaine Vail. John Wiley & Sons:
NY.

River of Tears (a journal written about his wife after her death) by
Charles W. Clark. Carlton Press, Inc.: NY.

The Savage God: A Study of Suicide by A. Alvarez. A Bantam Book: NY.

Self-Help Organizations and Professional Practice by Thomas J. Powell.
NASW Publications & Sales: Silver Spring, MD.

Silent Grief: Living in the Wake of Suicide by Christopher Lukas and
Henry M. Seiden. Charles Scribner's Sons: NY.

Starting Over: For Young Widows and Widowers by Adele Rice Nudel.
Dodd Mead: NY.

Suicide by Norman Linzer, Ph.D. Human Sciences Press, Inc.: NY.

Suicide after Sixty: The Final Alternative by Marv Miller. Springer Publ.
Co.: NY.

Suicide: A Killer Is Stalking the Land by David Wilkerson. Fleming H.
Revell Co.: Old Tappan, NJ.

Suicide and Grief by Howard Stone. Fortress Press: Philadelphia.

Suicide and Its Aftermath by Edward Dunne, John McIntosh and Karen
Dunne-Maxin. W.W. Norton and Co.: NY.

Suicide Clusters by Loren Coleman. Faber & Faber: Winchester, MA.

Suicide: Prevention, Intervention, and Postvention by Earl A. Grollman.
Beacon Press: Boston.

*The Suicide Syndrome: Origins, Manifestations and Alleviation of Human
Self-Destructiveness* by Larry Morton Gernsbacher. Human Sciences
Press, Inc.: NY.

Suicide: Why? 85 Questions and Answers About Suicide by Adina
Wrobleski. Afterwords: Minneapolis, MN.

Sun Shower (her husband's suicide) by Karen Kenyon. Richard Marek
Publ.: NY.

Survival Handbook for Widows (And for Relatives and Friends Who Want to Understand) by Ruth Loewenshon. New Century: Piscataway, NY.

Survivors: After a Suicide What Can We Do? by Bill Steel and Mary Leonhardi. Ann Arbor Publishers: Naples, FL.

Survivors of Suicide by Albert C. Cain. Charles C. Thomas Publ.: Springfield, IL.

Telling Yourself the Truth by William Backus and Marie Chapian, Bethany House Publishers: Minneapolis, MN.

To Live Again by Catherine Marshall. Avon Books: NY.

Understanding Mourning by Glen Davidson. Augsburg Publ. House: Minneapolis, MN.

Understanding Suicide by William R. Coleman. David C. Cook Publ. Co.: Elgin, IL.

Unlocking the Secrets of Your Childhood Memories by Dr. Kevin Leman and Randy Carlson. Thomas Nelson Publisher: Nashville.

What Shall We Tell The Kids? by Bennett Olshaker. Dell Publ. Co.: NY.

What You Should Know about Suicide by Bill Blackburn. Word Inc.: Waco, TX.

When You're Angry with God by Pat McCloskey. Paulist Press: Mahay, NY.

The Widower by Jane Burgers & Willard Kohn. Beacon Press: Boston.

The Widow's Guide to Life by Ida Fisher & Bryon Lane. Prentice-Hall: Englewood Cliffs, NJ.

Widow to Widow by Phyllis R. Silverman. Springer Publ. Co.: NY.

When Going to Pieces Holds You Together by William A. Miller. Augsburg Publ. House: Minneapolis, MN.

When Someone Asks for Help: A Practical Guide for Counseling by Everett Worthington, Jr. Intervarsity Press: Downers Grove, IL.

Why Knock Rock? by Dan & Steve Peters with Cher Merrill. Bethany House Publ.: Minneapolis, MN.

Why We Hurt and Who Can Heal by John C. Cooper. Word Inc.: Waco, TX.

Why Women Kill Themselves. Suicide Prevention Group, P.A.: Millburn, NJ.

You and Your Grief by Edgar N. Jackson. Hawthorn Books: NY.

Your Particular Grief by Wayne E. Oates. Westminster Press: Philadelphia.

Booklets and Pamphlets
(Write or call for price list.)

After Suicide: A Unique Grief Process. E. "Betsy" Ross. Ray of Hope,
   P.O. Box 2323, Iowa City, IA 52244.   (319) 337-9890
Answers to a Child's Questions about Death. Peter Stillman. Guideline
   Publications, P.O. Box 245, Stamford, NY 12167.   (607) 652-4571
The Care of the Suicide Survivor: A Guide for Professionals. Suicide Prevention
   Center, Inc., P.O. Box 1393, Dayton, OH 45401.   (513) 223-9096
Death...What Do You Say to a Child? Glen W. Davidson. OGR Service
   Corp., P.O. Box 3586, Springfield, IL 62708.
Facts, Feelings and Beyond. Mrs. Trudy Friedman, c/o Widow to Widow
   Program of the YM-YWHA and NHS of Montreal, 5500 Westbury
   Ave., Montreal, Quebec, Canada H3W 2W8.   (514) 737-6551
Grief, What It Is And What We Can Do About It. E.P. Vining,
   404 W. Downer Pl., Aurora, IL 60506.
Healing a Father's Grief. William H. Schatz. Medic Publ. Co., P.O. Box 89,
   Redmond, WA 98073-0089.   (206) 881-2883
Healing Grief. Amy Hillyard Jensen. Medic Publ. Co. As above.
Mourning After Suicide. Lois Bloom. The Pilgrim Press, 132 West 31 St.,
   New York, NY 10001.
On Being Alone. American Association of Retired Persons, Widowed Per-
   sons' Service, P.O. Box 199, Long Beach, CA 90801.   (202) 356-5219
Sibling Grief. Medic Publ. Co., P.O. Box 89, Redmond, WA 98073-0089.
Suicide: A Pastor's Ministry Reference. Contains: "Suicide: Hearing the
   Call for Help." "Suicide: Someone I Love Has Died." Shepherd Staff
   Publications, Division of Logor Art Productions, Inc., 6160 Carmen
   Ave. East, Inver Grove Heights, MN 55015.
Suicide and the Church. Rev.Wasena F. Wright, Jr., Annandale United
   Methodist Church, 6935 Columbia Pike, Annandale, VA 22003.
   When the Seagulls Don't Come. Rev. Wasena F. Wright, Jr. As above.
Suicide of a Child: For Parents Whose Child Has Committed Suicide. Joy &
   Marvin Johnson, & Adina Wrobleski. Centering Corp.,
   P.O. Box 3367, Omaha, NE 68103   (402) 553-1200
Suicide: Your Child Has Died. Adina Wrobleski, 5124 Grove St.,
   Minneapolis, MN 55436-2481.   (612) 929-6448
   Suicide: The Danger Signals. Adina Wrobleski. As above.
   Suicide: Questions and Answers. Adina Wrobleski. As above.
When Reason Fails. Bruce Conley. Human Services Press, P.O. Box 2423,
   Springfield, IL 62705.   (217) 528-1756
   Handling the Holidays. Bruce Conley. As above.
   Understanding Bereavement by Suicide. Bruce Conley. As above.
   A Pamphlet for Friends. Bruce Conley. As above.
Why Women Kill Themselves. Suicide Prevention Group, P.A.,
   P.O. Box 863, Millburn, NJ 07041.

Camps

Camp Amanda (weekend camp for children coping with a family death. Also offers support group meetings and a monthly fun night for children). JoAnn Zimmerman, Director, 4217 University Ave., Des Moines, IA 50311 .   (515) 279-5444

Catalogs and Distributors

American Association of Suicidology. Educational Cassette Program. Chesapeake Audio/Video Communications, 6330 Howard Lane, Elkridge, MD 21227.   (301) 796-0040

Centering Corporation. P.O. Box 3367, Omaha, NE 68103.   (402) 553-1200

Compassion Book Service. 216 Via Monte, Walnut Creek, CA 94598.
                                                           (415) 933-0830

Human Services News. Human Services Press, P.O. Box 2423, Springfield, IL 62705.   (217) 528-1756

Human Sciences Press, Inc. 72 5th Ave., New York, NY 10011-8804.
                                                           (212) 243-6000

Medic Publishing Co. P.O. Box 89, Redmond, WA 98073-0089.
                                                           (206) 881-2883

Norton Professional Books. c/o National Book Co., Keystone Industrial Park, Scranton, PA 18512-9888.   1-800-233-4830

Resources—Grief/Suicide. John Miller. Office of Evangelization-Catechesis, 777 Valley Rd., Clifton, NY 07013.   (201) 777-8818

Springer Publishing Co. 536 Broadway, New York, NY 10012.
                                                           (212) 431-4370

SIEC: Suicide Information and Education Centre. Suite 201, 723 - 14th St., N.W., Calgary, Alberta, Canada T2N 2A4.
                                                           (403) 283-3031

Suicide Education Institute of Boston. 437 Newtonville Avenue, Newton, MA 02160   (617) 332-1673

Suicide Prevention Center, Inc. P.O. Box 1393, Dayton, OH 45406-5877.
                                                           (513) 223-9096

The Information Center. (Marv Miller) 1438 Sun Valley Rd., Solana Beach, CA 92075.

Directories

Death and Dying, A to Z. Croner Publications, 211-05 Jamaica Ave., Queens Village, NY 11428.   (718) 464-0866

Directory of National Self-Help/Mutual Aid Resources. AHA Services, Inc., P.O. Box 99376, Chicago, IL 60693.   1-800-AHA-2626

Directory of Survivor of Suicide Support Groups: United States and Canada. American Association of Suicidology, 2459 S. Ash St., Denver, CO 80222.   (303) 692-0985

Hot Lines

National Suicide Hot Line Number.   1-800-621-4000
National Suicide Help Center. Box 34, Rochester, MN 55903
                        Helpline 1-800-638-4357
For a list of hot line numbers and centers, contact: USA, Pouch A,
    Harrisburg, PA 17025.   (717) 232-3501

Journals

Death Studies. Hemisphere Publ. Corp., 79 Madison Ave., Suite 1110,
    New York, NY 10016.
Omega-Journal of Death and Dying. Baywood, Box D,
    Farmingdale, NY 11735.
*Suicide and Life-Threatening Behavior: The Official Publication of the
    American Association of Suicidology.* Human Sciences Press,
    72 Fifth Ave, New York, NY 10011.
Suicide Research Digest. Center for Suicide Research & Prevention: Rush-
    Presbyterian-St. Luke's Medical Center, Chicago, IL 60612.
Thanatos. P.O. Box 6009, Tallahassee, FL 32314.

Manuals

Adolescence and Depression. Dorothy Kinsey. National Institute for
    Mental Health: 5600 Fishers Lane, Rockville, MN 20857.
                                   (301) 468-2600
Bereavement Support Groups: Leadership Manual. Alice S. Demi. Grief
    Education Institute: P.O. Box 623, Englewood, CO 80151.
                                   (303) 177-9234
Children and Suicide: Training Manual. Suicide Prevention Center, Inc.,
    P.O. Box 1393, Dayton, OH 45406-5877.   (513) 223-9096
*Grief Counseling for Survivors of Suicide and Sudden Death Victims: A
    Training Manual of Concepts and Materials.* Polly Doyle. Charles C.
    Thomas Publ.: 301-327 East Lawrence Ave., Springfield, IL 62708.
*The Living Alternative Handbook: A Model for Guiding Adolescents in
    Coping with Depression and Suicide.* Polly Joan. Suicide Prevention
    & Crisis Service of Tompkins County: P.O. Box 313,
    Ithaca, NY 14850.   (607) 272-1616

Newsletters

Afterwords (A Letter About Suicide and Suicide Grief). Adina Wrobleski,
5124 Grove St., Minneapolis, MN 55436-2481.   (612) 929-6448
The Forum Newsletter. Association for Death Education and Counseling:
(ADEC) 638 Prospect Ave, Hartford, CT 06105.   (203) 233-5617
The Network News (the runaway suicide prevention newsletter). Human
Services Development Institute, University of Southern Maine,
96 Falmouth St., Portland, ME 04103.
Newslink. American Association of Suicidology, 2459 S. Ash St.,
Denver, CO 80222.   (303) 692-0985
Suicide Prevention Link. Wisconsin Chapter on Youth Suicide Prevention,
Box 478, Marinette, WI 54143-0478.   (715) 735-9549
Survivors. Center for Human Services, 3929 Rocky River Dr.,
Cleveland, OH. 44111   (216) 264-5409 or (216) 362-0000
Sharing & Healing. c/o Al & Linda Vigil, 3586 Trenton Ave.,
San Diego, CA 92117.
S.O.S., Coming Together is a Beginning. Suicide Prevention Center,
P.O. Box 1393, Dayton, OH 45401.   (513) 223-9096
Surviving Suicide. American Association of Suicidology, 2459 S. Ash,
Denver, CO 80222.   (303) 692-0985

Organizations

American Association of Retired Persons. Widowed Persons' Service.
1909 K St. N.W., Washington, DC 20049.   (202) 356-5219
American Association of Suicidology (AAS).
2459 S. Ash St., Denver, CO 80222.   (303) 692-0985
Association for Death Education and Counseling.
2211 Arthur Ave., Lakewood, OH 44107.   (216) 228-0334
Center for Inner Growth and Wholeness. JoAnn Mecca.
P.O. Box 9185, Wethersfield, CT 06109.   (203) 563-3035
Compassionate Friends (for parents who have lost a child) chapters.
P.O. Box 1347, Oak Brook, IL 60521.   (312) 323-5010
The Foundation of Thanatology.
630 W 168th St., New York, NY 10032.   (212) 928-2066
Grief Education Institute.
P.O. Box 623, Englewood, CO 80151.   (303) 777-9234
The International Federation of Widows' and Widowers' Organisations.
Cremerstraat 3, 6665 CZ Driel, The Netherlands.
Julie Penrose Center. La Rita Archibald (Heartbeat chapters).
1661 Mesa Ave., Colorado Springs, CO 80906-2998.   (303) 632-2451
National Center for Death Education.
656 Beacon St., Boston, MA 02215.   (617) 536-2460
National Mental Health Association.
1021 Prince St., Alexandria, VA 22314-1932.   (703) 684-7722

Ray of Hope , inc. (chapters).

    P.O. Box 2323, Iowa City, IA 52244.   (319) 337-9890

The Samaritan's Safe Place (chapters).

    802 Boylston St., Boston, MA 02199.   (617) 536-2460

Seasons: Suicide Bereavement (chapters).

    6805 Fairfax Rd., Apt. 123, Bethesda, MD 20814.   (301) 951-3665

The Suicide Education Institute of Boston.

    437 Newtonville Ave., Newton, ME 02160.   (617) 332-5165

Theos Foundation, Inc. (chapters).

    306 Penn Hills Mall, Pittsburgh, PA 15235.   (412) 243-4299

Youth Suicide National Center. 1825 Eye St. N.W., Suite 400,

    Washington, DC 20006.   (202) 429-2016

Videos and Films

A Family in Grief. The Ameche Story. Research Press, Box 3177, Dept. 84,

    Champaign, IL 61821.   (217) 352-3273

Children Only Die When We Forget Them. Pat Schwiebert, R.N.

    Compassionate Friends, P.O. Box 12553, Portland, OR 97212.

                                        (503) 284-7426

Death...What do you Say to a Child? (filmstrip with booklet). Glen W.

    Davidson. OGR Service Corporation, P.O. Box 3586

    Springfield, IL 62708.   (217) 544-7428

On the Edge. (a film about teenage suicide). The Young Alberta

    Filmmakers, Suite 1602, 8830-85th St., Edmonton, Alberta, Canada

    T6C 3C3.   (403) 469-0922 or 466-4259

SOS, Runaway and Teen Suicides: Coded Cries for Help. Human

    Services Development Institute: Center for Research and Advanced

    Study, University of Southern Maine, Portland, ME 04103.

Survivors. Bill Steel and Mary Leonhardi, Ann Arbor Publishers, P.O.

    Box 7249, Naples, FL 33941.

Survivors: After A Suicide What Can We Do? Suicide Prevention Group,

    P.A., P.O. Box 863, Millburn, NY 07041.

Survivorship After Suicide . Ray of Hope, Inc., P.O. Box 2323,

    Iowa City, IA 52244.   (319) 337-9890

Teenage Suicide: An Approach to Prevention. Perennial Education, 930

    Pitner Ave., Evanston, IL 60202.   (800) 323-9084

The Ultimate Rejection. James Craig. Wright State University,

    Dayton, OH. Order through Suicide Prevention Center, Inc.,

    P.O. Box 1393, Dayton, OH 45406-5877   (513) 223-9096

About Ray of Hope

Ray of Hope, inc., is a non-profit, self-help organization which provides service, education and consultation in the areas of suicide postvention, loss and grief. We hold workshops for survivors and interested groups, help establish Ray of Hope chapters and/or independent support groups and offer private counseling.

Support group meetings are open to survivors (family, friends or helpers), who are grieving over a loss by suicide. Meetings are held in a relaxed accepting atmosphere and provide the opportunity to share with others who have had similar experiences.

Emphasis is placed on anonymity and privacy. Professionals from education, medicine, counseling, etc. serve occasionally as speakers or discussion leaders. We do not provide medical or psychiatric treatment or material assistance. We are not a therapy group for suicidal persons. We are not a religious organization, nor allied with any sect or denomination. However, members may share their religious and spiritual views.

Individual counseling and support group organization consultation by telephone is provided by prearrangement and prepayment. Phone (319) 337-9890.

Our aims are to:

1.   View suicide as a social, health and spiritual problem that can be treated.

2.   Help provide comfort and group support for the bereaved individuals, their families and friends.

3.   Bring together the bereaved with other survivors and helpers so that through sharing of experiences and growth they may gain insights into behavior patterns and interpersonal relationships.

We believe that sharing what we have learned with someone else in need completes our own healing. By turning the grief process into a growth experience, we can find meaning in a senseless tragedy and hope for our future.

Funding: Ray of Hope is a non-profit organization. Tax deductible contributions are gratefully accepted and used to cover publication, distribution and program cost. Send donations to: Ray of Hope, P.O. Box 2323, Iowa City, Iowa 52244. Thank you.

About the Author

Eleanora "Betsy" Ross lives in Iowa and is the founder and Executive Director of Ray of Hope, inc. and is a speaker, consultant, workshop presenter, counselor and writer in the areas of loss, grief and after-suicide bereavement. She holds a B.G.S. in religion, journalism, and psychology and an M. A. in counseling.

Other publications include the videotape *Survivorship After Suicide*, the booklet *After Suicide: A Unique Grief Process*, a manual *After Suicide*, and other articles and pamphlets.

She has appeared on the *Today Show, Phil Donahue Show, Hour Magazine*, and local TV and radio programs and has been featured in numerous publications including the *New York Times, the Chicago Tribune, Death Education,* and *Who's Who in American Women.*

Ms. Ross is a member of the American Association of Suicidology, the Association for Death Education and Counseling, American Association for Retired Persons, and Omicron Delta Kappa.

She has received awards from the Gannett Foundation, PEO Continuing Education, the Kaltenborn Foundation, the Ella Lyman Cabot Trust, the Business and Professional Women's Education Award, the Soroptimist Intl. McCall Life-Pattern Award, the University of Iowa Honor Scholarships, the University of Iowa Foundation for Continuing Education for Women, the University of Iowa Special Support Services Certificate of Honor, and others.

ORDERING INFORMATION FOR PUBLICATIONS

After Suicide: A Unique Grief Process by Eleanora "Betsy" Ross explains in lay terms the dynamics and complexities of after-suicide bereavement. Sections include "How to Help Yourself"; "How to Help Others"; "The Art of Listening"; "What About God"; "What to Tell Children"; and more.

After Suicide: A Ray of Hope by Eleanora "Betsy" Ross is an expanded and revised version of *After Suicide: A Unique Grief Process*. In addition to information in the booklet, it includes recommenda- tions for recovery and healing, both for grieving persons and for professional care givers. Additional sections include, "Widowed by Suicide"; "Voices of Survivors"; "Survivor's Bill of Rights"; suggestions for the funeral, organizing a support group, a "Survivor Resource Guide," a letter of comfort to survivors, the author's personal story, and more. Foreword by Joseph Richman, Ph.D.

Survivorship after Suicide is a 50-minute educational videotape which defines and demonstrates the unique after-suicide bereavement characteristics of survivors. Useful for counselors, educators, students, mental health and medical professionals, clergy, funeral directors, parents, and survivors-- anyone whose life or profession has been touched by suicide. Excellent for classroom use. Includes study guide. See order form.

Please Send:

copies of booklet *After Suicide: A Unique Grief Process*. $5.95. $

copies of book *After Suicide: A Ray of Hope*. $16.95. $
20% discount for 2—5 books, for 6 or more books, see below.
Add $3.00 shipping and handling for first book; 50¢ for each additional book.

videotape *Survivorship after Suicide*. $75.00 $
Shipping and handling included.

information on the videotape.

Shipping and Handling for Booklets: 1 booklet, $1.75; 2—5 booklets, $2.50; 6—9 booklets, $3.50, 10—15 booklets, $4.00. Over 15, call for discount and arrangements.

Total amount for books, booklets, videotape: $

Shipping and Handling: $

Total Amount Enclosed: $

Name _____ Date: _____

Address: _____

City: _____ State: _____ Zip _____

Send order to Lynn Publications, c/o Ray of Hope, P.O. Box 2323, Iowa City, Iowa 52244 (319) 337-9890. Prepaid orders only. No refunds. Discounts by arrangement. U.S. funds only. Prices subject to change without notice.